Australian Chamber Music with Piano

Australian Chamber Music with Piano

Larry Sitsky

E PRESS

Published by ANU E Press
The Australian National University
Canberra ACT 0200, Australia
Email: anuepress@anu.edu.au
This title is also available online at: http://epress.anu.edu.au/

National Library of Australia Cataloguing-in-Publication entry

Author: Sitsky, Larry, 1934-

Title: Australian chamber music with piano / Larry Sitsky.

ISBN: 9781921862403 (pbk.) 9781921862410 (ebook)

Notes: Includes bibliographical references.

Subjects: Chamber music--Australia--History and criticism.

Dewey Number: 785.700924

All rights reserved. No part of this publication may be reproduced, stored in a retrieval system or transmitted in any form or by any means, electronic, mechanical, photocopying or otherwise, without the prior permission of the publisher.

Cover design and layout by ANU E Press

Printed by Griffin Press

This edition © 2011 ANU E Press

Contents

Acknowledgments vii
Preface ix

Part 1: The First Generation
1. Composers of Their Time: Early modernists and
   neo-classicists. 3
2. Composers Looking Back: Late romantics and the
   nineteenth-century legacy. 21
3. Phyllis Campbell (1891–1974) 45
   Fiona Fraser

Part 2: The Second Generation
4. Post–1945 Modernism Arrives in Australia. 55
5. Retrospective Composers. 101
6. Pluralism 123
7. Sitsky's Chamber Music. 137
   Edward Neeman

Part 3: The Third Generation
8. The Next Wave of Modernism. 161
9. Maximalism 183
10. Pluralism 187

Part 4: The Fourth Generation
11. The Fourth Generation 225

Concluding Remarks 251
Appendix 255

Acknowledgments

Many thanks are due to the following.

To the Australian Research Council, without whose financial assistance this book and all the published scores stemming from the research would have been impossible.

To The Australian National University for backing the project and for providing rooms and facilities for all the work to be carried out.

To the School of Music for all its tolerance of my demands. Special thanks to our Head of School, Professor Adrian Walter.

To Marguerite Boland, research assistant extraordinaire, currently a PhD candidate in composition with me at the ANU.

To Dr Jenny Gall, who assisted in many areas and provided initiative, support and creative ideas.

To Jono Stephens, for his high-level computer skills and expertise in proofing and music layout.

To Fiona Fraser, also a current PhD candidate, who joined the project towards its end, and has been absolutely invaluable in typesetting the music examples and formatting the finished book generally. Fiona also very generously contributed the entry on Phyllis Campbell—a composer related to her PhD topic.

To various libraries and institutions including the National Library of Australia, the many State libraries, the Australian Music Centre, and the University of Newcastle Cultural Collections.

To Edward (Teddy) Neeman, exceptional pianist, for contributing the chapter on my music in the midst of performing commitments. I thank him especially for his patience, diligence and thoroughness.

Preface

Some years ago, when my book *Australian Piano Music of the Twentieth Century* was first published, there were still certain perceptions in place concerning our 'art music', especially the music coming from the earlier part of the century, which was often badly preserved, researched, or even understood. It seemed axiomatic to many earlier musicologists that Australia—being a long way from the centres of European music and thought—lagged painfully behind in information and particularly in the unfolding of the exciting avant-garde of Europe and the United States. Quite naturally, with the advent of the computer age, such claims became patently absurd. It was clear that whatever Australian music was or was becoming, it was not due to a time lag, but rather to a direction dictated by the current identity of the Australian psyche.

The myth of the tyranny of distance was, however, still somehow tacitly understood to represent a general truth. *Australian Piano Music of the Twentieth Century* did, however, demonstrate that our leading-edge composers, even early in the century, were well informed and aware of what was taking place elsewhere. It might have taken a little longer, but the information was there, and was certainly absorbed.

True, we had our share of conservative, stodgy and unadventurous souls, eager to please—but doesn't every culture?

Running parallel with the writing of the above book was a publication project of Australian 'heritage' music, with me as general editor. To date, this venture has produced approximately 70 scores by major Australian composers, including early modernist works unknown to the majority of Australian musicians and music lovers. As far as I am concerned, the rediscovery and publishing of worthwhile Australian music are the most valuable parts of this research. My books are merely a personal commentary on some of the works. I certainly call it as I see it, but beyond that, I do not claim any superior understanding of the vast field.

All this was possible thanks to support from the Australian Research Council (ARC). Just a week before writing this, I completed a recording of Hooper Brewster-Jones's *Bird Impressions*—a significant series of some 73 pieces for solo piano, using his personally notated calls of birds as thematic material. Brewster-Jones captured calls of Australian birds in and around his hometown of Adelaide and on the property of his friend the painter Hans Heysen. All these works had lain in the Barr-Smith Library in Adelaide for a long time; they were composed in the early 1920s—an idea that came to Brewster-Jones 30 years before Messiaen issued his bird-inspired works. Brewster-Jones's manuscript was a mere scrawl, just barely decipherable. The point was that he put together these works—which would have been considered experimental in Adelaide at that time, and have startling moments even now—purely for himself. There was no fine copy ever made, so nobody ever performed the pieces. The ARC grant allowed me to pay a research assistant to spend some months typesetting the works, which were then published by the excellent Keys Press in Perth, and have now been recorded for the first time in complete form. They will now become part of the *Anthology of Australian Music* issued by The Australian National University, overseen by the School of Music, and going back to the heady days of the bicentennial celebrations. Such projects—a researcher's dream—are possible only with financial support. We can change the erroneous perspective of our own history, and cancel the image of pretty, post-colonial, cheaply nationalistic as peculiar to our musical culture.

I have taken the liberty of using first names when writing about some composers; this is not name-dropping on my part, but simply a quiet declaration of the fact that I knew those composers on a first-name basis and we were friends and colleagues. No disrespect is intended. Neither does a more formal mode of address mean anything other than my knowledge of that particular composer was professional, not personal.

Limitations were, of necessity, imposed on the material to be surveyed. First of all, a decision was made to look at only those chamber music scores that had a piano part. This seemed a logical and comfortable transition from the previous book, which dealt with solo piano music only. Then, we decided to include vocal repertoire: this immediately opened a Pandora's box, since the amount of parlour-music songs with piano accompaniment was impossibly huge. As well, many choral works with piano simply used the keyboard as a doubling instrument. A selection process was then imposed that favoured including songs or song cycles that were somewhat akin to German Lieder—that is, the content was almost always serious, the use of words had literary merit, and the piano part was not merely a vamping accompaniment, but was integral to the music argument. Moreover, as in the previous book, here, we were searching for adventurous pieces with an often-demanding keyboard part. In general—again repeating the aesthetic pose of the previous volume—we were looking for a modernist thread in Australian chamber music. I am happy to shoulder the blame for a stance that was, in the end, unashamedly idealistic, perhaps romantically so. To me, this type of elitism implies a high level of craftsmanship as well as an intent generally linked to presentation in the concert hall; it includes a personality generally more concerned with inward exploration than with outward ostentation. Not every composer in this book fulfils such criteria; some have been included because of their high profile in the community, and not perhaps due to their artistic achievements. We, like most countries, have our share of composers—whether from early in the twentieth century or much more recently—who unashamedly write to please at all costs, are politically correct and repeat themselves endlessly. There is room for them, of course, but as Mr Pickwick so eloquently put it, 'not in *my* cab'.

Composers are, despite all of the above, pragmatic folk, so it is not surprising that the chamber combinations most utilised were ones that mirrored the availability of instruments, personal connections or music composed for particular events and commissions.

A similar, but slightly less onerous, quandary manifested itself when we began to search for works for piano duet, or for two or more pianos: there was, not unexpectedly, a huge volume of pedagogic works for piano duet, continuing the traditions of composers such as Diabelli, sometimes with one part for the 'teacher' and another part for the 'pupil'. Most of these works had to be omitted to save us from becoming submerged. Once again, it is not a case of feeling superior to such material.

The Australian Music Centre has now an active and informative web site (an important one of many—see the Database for further information) that provides biographical material on composers as well as much other supplementary information. Given this current state of easily available online information, we decided that it was no longer necessary to provide raw factual data that are easily accessible elsewhere. This was not the case only some few years ago. It was endlessly fascinating to revisit composers written about in the piano book some years ago, and to note artistic continuance, an aesthetic shift or composers dropping out of the field altogether. It was a little like catching up with family members after some years.

I like the precept that a picture is worth a thousand words. In a book on music, surely a representative music example says things about a composer that would take many paragraphs of laborious prose to convey. As a practical musician, I find such examples leap out of the page at me, and the sound of even a short fragment is like tasting a wine. I have, therefore, liberally sprinkled the text with music examples in the hope that the 'tasting' will inspire readers to go and find the complete work.

I should add here that the entry on my own chamber music, written by Teddy Neeman, was not in any way influenced or supervised by myself. Marguerite Boland liaised with Teddy over the entry, and I insisted on knowing nothing about the contents of the entry. Indeed, as I write this Preface, I still have no idea what is in this part of the book. Teddy, as an ex-student and a brilliant musician, is uniquely qualified to the task.

Part 1: The First Generation

1. Composers of Their Time: Early modernists and neo-classicists

Roy Agnew (1891–1944)

Roy Agnew was a composer for the piano; all of his output is directed towards it. There was either no opportunity or no interest in writing chamber music. He did, however, compose about 20 songs and published roughly half of them. There is also a set of two *Songs Without Words* for voice and clarinet. The totality of the songs is now available through the Keys Press, so it is worth listing all of them for the record in the hope that some attention can be drawn to them; it is music by one of our finest composers.

1. 'Beloved Stoop Down thro' the Clinging Dark' (Zora Cross Smith)
2. 'O Moonlight Deep and Tender' (James Russell Lowell)
3. 'Dirge' (Percy Bysshe Shelley)
4. 'Sorrow' (Alfred Lord Tennyson)
5. 'Infant Joy' (William Blake)
6. 'Dusk' (Rita Williams)
7. 'Hie Away, Hie Away' (Walter Scott)
8. 'June Twilight' (John Masefield)
9. 'A Widow Bird Sate Mourning' (Percy Bysshe Shelley)
10. 'The World's Wanderers' (Percy Bysshe Shelley)
11. 'Beauty' (John Masefield)
12. 'The Flowers of Sleep' (Victor Daley)
13. 'Cradle Song' (Sarojini Naidu)
14. 'Cradle Song' (Louis Essen)
15. 'I Don't Like Beetles' (Rose Fyleman)
16. 'She Comes Not When Noon is on the Roses' (Herbert Trench)
17. 'To a Sleeping Child' (William Blake)
18. 'To Morrow' (Percy Bysshe Shelley)
19. 'Invocation' (John Masefield)
20. 'Tears' (Wang Seng-Su)
21. 'To a Dead Violet' (Rita Williams).

Songs 6 and 21 are identical, but appeared under different titles. This was discovered only after the songs were published, Number 21 having been painstakingly transcribed from a recording with Agnew at the piano.

Agnew also prepared a voice/piano version of his *The Breaking of the Drought* (Harley Matthews), originally for voice and orchestra. This is perfectly performable as a work for voice and piano.

As is to be expected, the piano parts of these songs are exceedingly well crafted, as are the melodic lines. Agnew has a real feeling for the words he is setting, and the whole output of songs is of a uniform high standard, to be treasured as an Australian body of work. Compared with what was being produced all around him in this genre, the Agnew songs stand shoulders above the efforts of others and are highly recommended for recital and recording.

Margaret Sutherland (1897–1984)

Margaret Sutherland is indisputably one of our most important composers from the earlier part of the century. I say this because in this book, there will not be as much space allocated to her as to her contemporaries such as Dorian le Gallienne and Raymond Hanson. The reason is not in any way judgmental on my part. The fact is that there is now an excellent book on this composer available, whereas the other two still await their definitive tomes to appear. David Symons' book *The Music of Margaret Sutherland* was published by Currency Press, Sydney, in 1997. This is an excellent book, not just for its biographical information, but as well for its profound insights into the music itself. David has copiously illustrated his book with generously sampled and numerous music examples, assuming, quite correctly, that a snapshot of even a few bars of a work will say more about it than any amount of dry musicological discourse. It is for this reason alone that my entry on Sutherland will be brief, and I refer interested readers to Symons' monograph—available in an inexpensive paperback format.

What is clear after reading this book is that there are some significant gaps in our extant holdings of manuscripts (and associated information) by Sutherland. Some of these would perhaps shed some light especially on the way the early music seems to spring to life fully formed, as it were. My teacher Winifred Burston gave me her copy of the Sutherland *Violin Sonata*, with some notes and alterations written upon it by both the composer and Winifred herself. Sutherland must have met Winifred during one of her trips to Sydney, and perhaps she oversaw a performance of the work given by Burston and Henri Verbrugghen (the other possible violinist at the time might have been Cyril Monk, who, like Burston, was a foundation member of the NSW State Conservatorium of Music).

I knew Margaret Sutherland quite well in the late part of her life. She was a close friend of Maie Casey, whose husband was Governor-General of Australia for a period, which coincided with the early years of the Canberra School of Music (now the ANU School of Music). Maie Casey arranged musicales at Government House and often invited Margaret to be the guest at the house. I had also met Margaret in Hobart earlier during our operatic premieres (her *The Young Kabarli* and my *Fall of the House of Usher*). She was interested in what the then younger generation was producing, and also made very clear her likes and dislikes, as well as her total disdain of fashion and the intellectual poverty of the idea of an 'Australian music', which did not interest her in the least. She reminded me of Winifred Burston in many ways: in her fearlessness and the passion of her beliefs.

Despite personal difficulties and illnesses, Margaret produced an impressive body of works. It is necessary to understand that some parts of this output at least were either educationally motivated works for students or a form of 'family' chamber music—a concept to which she was certainly drawn, and which at times perhaps gave her music an impression of being lightweight and a descendant of the English pastoral style. It is true that in her middle life at least, there is some superficial relationship to that style. With Sutherland, however, even if she consciously wanted to write something in that vein, there is always a tinge of acid or sadness in the resultant sound, reflecting her own troubled and turbulent life. Any real recognition came very late to her. By then, her eyesight was really bad, and she had gradually withdrawn from playing in public, partly due to her physical state, but partly because her heart was never really in it. The keyboard was most important to her, she discovered much by just sitting at it, and even her instrumental music has the ghost of the piano hovering over it. The composers she admired most were pianists: Bartók, Stravinsky, many of the French school such as Milhaud and, of course, Bax. Hindemith no doubt attracted her with his concepts of *Gebrauchmusik* and wider tonality. So her relationship with the piano was a fluctuating one, and one that led her more and more to being a composer and less a performer.

Similarly, she had a troubled connection with academia. Her beliefs were at odds with the often-rigid methods of teaching music at tertiary levels in her time. But later in life, she often spoke to me quite bitterly about the neglect she had suffered at the hands of the tertiary establishment in Melbourne, which probably found her too much of a handful and therefore elected to ignore her. Resultantly, a whole generation of students was denied the privilege of hearing her thoughts on music and composition.

If one wants to get to know her vocal music, the most important of the settings are those of words by John Shaw Nielsen and Judith Wright, as well as the earlier William Blake. Of the instrumental sonatas, there is the astonishingly precocious sonata for violin and piano, as well as the sonata for saxophone (or cello) and piano, the evocative sonata for clarinet (or viola) and piano, and some works for two pianos.

Margaret Sutherland certainly found a fluid technique early in her life, and her beginnings are to be located in the late romanticism and opulent harmonies of her mentor, Bax (and possibly a glance at other composers such as Scriabin). But then, she discovered the world of the neo-classicist and was drawn towards it. This gave rise to some highly polished and economical music and to the introduction of an important rhythmic, driving component to her music. It also allowed her to write more quickly and perhaps the negative side of her love affair with neo-classicism was the odd lapse into a comfortable and sometimes predictably mannered style of writing. But it also gave her the means to control—very finely—elements of irony, sarcasm and biting harmony. All this was rarely exuberant; rather, more often, it was nudging the tragic, but never in a breast-beating, self-pitying way; more in an accepting manner. Her final works seem to me to have found a middle path between the rhapsodic early language and the more logical middle-period music. She was never one for systems of any kind, and had to arrive at her own view of what was considered avant-garde late in her life. That she continued to search was admirable. That her eyesight prevented a full exploration of her newly found language was, like so much in her life, very sad.

Peggy Glanville-Hicks (1912–90)

The circle of composers and writers that Peggy Glanville-Hicks circulated in was essentially marked by a neo-classical ethos—the strong anti-romantic reaction that gripped the Western music world between the two World Wars and continued until approximately mid-century. In her work, there seems to be a consistent striving for the artist as an objective creator. The sound of the Les Six group is also ever-present in Peggy's composition. So, if you pick up the score of her little *Sonatina for Treble Recorder or Flute & Piano* (1941), you cannot possibly escape this observation. Given this kind of aesthetic, it is a consequence that personal traits tend to be eroded, and aspects of craft come to the fore, especially given that even in matters of form, the past is invoked as a role model by the composer. Fortunately, the composer was not a dogmatic follower of the ideas of others, although she was no doubt influenced. In the air, during this same period, various forms of interest in Orientalism began to manifest themselves, so, in her *13 Ways of Looking at a Blackbird* (1951), set to text by Wallace Stevens, Glanville-Hicks composes a cycle of 13 very short songs, creating a Zen-like attitude to music and to the world around her. This is perhaps not so novel now, but it was different in 1951; Peggy, in masterly fashion, sets the mood of each song by an opening deft touch from the piano. Here are the openings of songs 1 and 6:

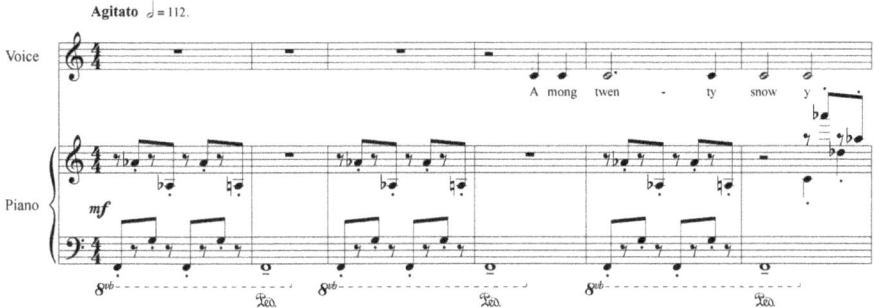

Example 1.1 P. Glanville-Hicks, *13 Ways of Looking at a Blackbird*, I, bars 1–6

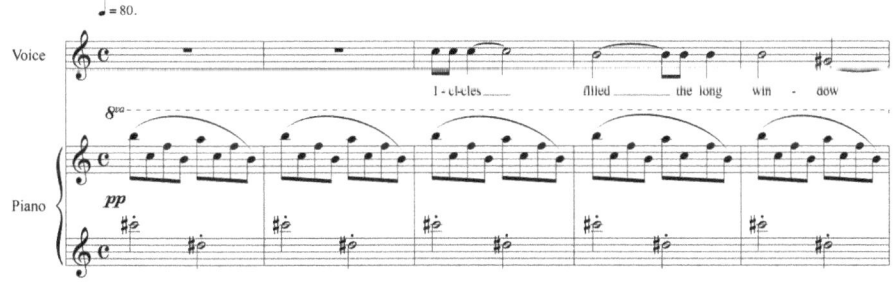

Example 1.2 P. Glanville-Hicks, *13 Ways of Looking at a Blackbird*, 6, bars 1–5

The vocal lines are often static, sung in parlando style, mostly moving by step in a modal fashion. When leaps do happen, however, they are very telling; play through the melody of song 4, and this will become immediately apparent. The harmonies used in these and other songs favour the perfect fourth and perfect fifth, so that implications of major and minor are not normally present, and the sound remains transparent. Depending on what is happening in the hands and voice, there are ever-present flirtings with bitonality. The other songs that I know are not as aphoristic as the blackbird songs, but Peggy is never verbose. I should mention at least some of the other songs. A set of *Five Songs* (1952) to text by A. E. Housman has the following titles: 1) 'Mimic Heaven'; 2) 'He Would Not Stay'; 3) 'Stars'; 4) 'Unlucky Love'; and 5) 'Homespun Collars'. Louise Dyer of the renowned Éditions de l'Oiseau-Lyre, issued—in beautifully engraved layout—the following, separately: *Rest* (1938), words by George (A. E.) Russell; *Be Still You Little Leaves* (1938), words by Mary Webb; *Come Sleep* (1938), poem by John Fletcher (1579); and *Frolic* (1938), poem by George (A. E.) Russell. These are all medium-length songs and can be performed separately. Personally, I do not think she ever excelled the fine etching of the blackbird songs.

The *Sonata for Piano and Percussion* (1951) caused a bit of a stir when it was first heard, but it is a little too well behaved for contemporary ears. By 1951, the Bartók work for two pianos and percussion was an established masterpiece, part of the new canon, and Peggy's piece simply is not in that class. To be fair, I do not think she tried to outdo the Hungarian master. There is only one piano here, and the percussion is restricted in size, number and effect. The Glanville-Hicks sonata is a more modest, more lyrical outpouring, with the piano playing strongly melodic modal lines of moderate difficulty. The dimensions of the work are closer to a sonatina model, and perhaps it is only in the central slow movement that the sombre parallel seventh chords, accompanied by metallic percussion, still have a personal voice.

Example 1.3 P. Glanville-Hicks, *Sonata for Piano and Percussion*, mvt 2, bars 1–5

The last movement has some genuinely playful interactions of duple and triple metre. These days, the difficulty is programming such a work. It might fit well into a solo piano concert, as a welcome diversion. Within the context of a contemporary percussion concert—and certainly in the presence of the Bartók sonata—it comes off decidedly second best. In this respect, the *Concertino da Camera* (1946), for flute, clarinet, bassoon and pianoforte, with its combination of Milhaud and Stravinsky, is easier to cope with, and still sounds fresh and valid. By the pressures of the time she lived in, we lost the presence of Peggy Glanville-Hicks in this country for most of her life. She could have had an invigorating effect on music here. Her achievements, however, especially in the world of opera, might not have been possible in the Australia of that time. It is hard enough now!

Raymond Hanson (1913–76)

Most of Raymond Hanson's songs have, until very recent times, remained in manuscript and therefore are largely unknown. It might even be a surprise to many musicians, who associate Hanson with larger-scale works for orchestra and instruments. The scholar Graham Hardie has issued a catalogue of Hanson's works, and further details can be found there of these songs and other compositions; a biography is forthcoming from the same pen. It should also be noted here that Karl Hansen, listed below, was actually Ray's eldest brother, Ken. He used the name Hansen as a pen name. Apparently the family name was originally Hanssen but was altered at the time of World War I to Hanson.

The songs for voice and piano that we examined are

Op. 3: *I Dreamt that She Sat by My Head* (Rabidranath Tagore)

Op. 4: *Three Songs* (Karl Hansen)[1]
1. 'In Fairyland'
2. 'Shades of Night'
3. 'The Wide World'.

Op. 6: *Fallen Veils* (Dante Gabriel Rossetti)

Op. 7: *Two Songs* (Dame Mary Gilmore)
1. 'Night'
2. 'The Pilgrim'.

Op. 13: *War* (Karl Hansen)

Op. 14: *This is My Delight* (Rabidranath Tagore)

Op. 16: *Three Songs* (Marian Memory)
1. 'The Cliff'
2. 'Mirage'
3. 'Spindrift'.

Landing Barge—Off Shore (Campbell Howard) (1960)

The Cyclone (John Manifold) (1960).

What is clear in these songs is that, right from the early Op. 3 song, there is evidence of a mind attracted towards a certain class of literature that lends itself

---

[1] The *Three Songs Op. 4* were originally written for baritone, and have been published separately in that form by the Keys Press, as have all the other songs listed above, in three volumes.

to musical setting; the piano writing is unsurprisingly very accomplished, but more—it is apt to the setting, and tends to set the mood almost at once. The changes of mood in the words are always mirrored in a modulation or some other device in the writing for the piano. In the first of the Op. 4 songs, the right hand has an independent existence in flowing quavers, whilst the left hand more closely parallels the vocal line. The second and third songs are more restless and chromatic—a tendency noticeable right through his vocal output. By Op. 6, the modulations have become increasingly sophisticated. The setting of these well-known verses of Rossetti begins with a long, throbbing syncopated pedal on C; then, in preparation for the line 'You have been mine before', a wonderfully evocative transition happens in the music.

Example 1.4 R. Hanson, *Fallen Veils*, bars 16–20

The drop from C to B is one of many examples of unexpected modulations in the Hanson songs. He manages to achieve this even when there is a continuous running figuration, as in the first song of Op. 7, where there is an instant setting of the mood, as there is with the second song—a more dramatic piece.

The powerful song *War!* needs only a bar to get going.

Example 1.5 R. Hanson, *War!*, bars 1–5

The Op. 14 song achieves a kind of ecstasy by staying with the opening figure and weaving harmonic alteration. Having just played through the le Gallienne songs before doing the same with the Hanson songs, I found the difference between these two highly gifted composers was obvious. Le Gallienne was less of a pianist, and the settings are more block chords, with their own connotations; Hanson writes for the piano as a concert pianist, and these piano parts make the distinction amply clear.

By the time of Op. 16, the vocal writing has moved closer to operatic in style, with powerful low octaves supporting the strident line of the voice. In the second song of this opus, a trick of expectation is carried out. After the sounding of a kind of bugle call five times between the notes E going up to A, the ear confidently expects A to be the tonality, but instead, this is what occurs (remember that the song title is *Mirage*):

Example 1.6 R. Hanson, *Mirage*, bars 3–7

The third song of the set is in Hanson's mature chromatic language. The last two songs from 1960 are definitive arrival points in Hanson's treatment of the lieder genre. I use the German word quite deliberately, for there is nothing parlourish about the Hanson songs, nor do they seem to have much affinity with the more self-conscious English equivalents. Instead here we have a composer writing in a rugged, individualistic manner, more in the American tradition, and certainly with an understanding of the European heritage. So, the opening of *Landing Barge—Off Shore* is a case in point.

Example 1.7 R. Hanson, *Landing Barge—Off Shore*, bars 1–6

The last song is a torrent of fast quaver triplets in parallel motion, including some difficult leaps and breakaways into contrary motion near the end. The mood, again, is immediate.

Example 1.8 R. Hanson, *The Cyclone*, bars 1–5

So much for the songs. There is not much purely instrumental music. There is a strange little *Romance*, for tuba and piano, in which Hanson solves the built-in problem of writing for tuba and piano by managing the distribution of the tessitura of the solo instrument very carefully and skillfully. His *Idyll*, for violin and pianoforte, is assigned Op. 2; the manuscript originally had the pen name 'Scorpio' on the cover—evidently the work had been submitted for a competition. I recall 'Sagittarius' being used for one of the solo piano works for the same reason. The composer has written '6 minutes 15 seconds' as the duration of the work, possibly for a broadcast. The *Idyll* in D minor is in a fairly straightforward ABA form, in which the outside section features a rocking bass in crotchet octaves, which slowly modulate, whilst the middle section is dependent on running figures in both instruments. Finally, there is the Op. 10 *Sonata for Flute and Pianoforte*. It opens with chords borrowed from jazz, which Ray loved.

Example 1.9 R. Hanson, *Sonata for Flute and Pianoforte*, bars 1–7

In fact, the opening figure is subject to variation not unrelated to jazz improvisation. The sonata itself is in the traditional three movements, but Ray is not averse to making connections between the movements by cross-referencing motivic material. As far as I know, this charming early work has not been published, and should be on someone's schedule to be done, as it would be a fine example from our past for flute—an instrument not much written for until more recent times.

Dulcie Holland (1913–2000)

It is indisputable that Dulcie Holland was a miniaturist: her whole voluminous output proclaims it. So much of it was aimed at the educational market and she became so adept at meeting this market that she was able to churn out these miniatures—pedagogic pieces at all levels—by the dozen. It was probably inevitable that to some extent this affected her more extended works; that writing on a certain level and scale for others she was able only to a limited extent to pull herself out of a compositional habit. Not that there was anything intrinsically wrong with composing all those pieces for children. Apart from the fact that she earned her living within the educational market, she might very well have preferred to produce this kind of work, as there did not seem to be any strenuous attempts to do anything else compositionally. She was certainly not a Dr Jekyll and Mr Hyde character as a composer. The language she spoke in her miniatures was consistent, and hardly altered over the many years of her long life. But small changes did occur. If you play through her *Cradle Song*, for violin and piano (1947), and then jump to the *Rondel*, for cello and piano (1985), there is some extension of the language, a longer delay in the resolution of 'dissonance', a braver inclination to hold the dissonance, perhaps even a reluctance to fill up empty spaces with endless arpeggios. The melodic lines have not altered much, and the strings keep sounding like Vaughan Williams of *The Lark Ascending* variety. I do not wish to repeat my opinions already expressed in *Australian Piano Music*; readers who are interested are directed there, wherein I have illustrated the text with many characteristic music examples, including some divergences from her habitual style.

When I learnt and recorded Dulcie's sonata for the piano, I was surprised by the amount of grit in it, which was unexpected; my friend the composer Nigel Butterley had alerted me to the piano sonata, which he regarded highly. Perhaps Dulcie, imagining herself at the keyboard rather than a student, was inspired to write uncharacteristic things. To some extent, this applies to her instrumental sonatas with piano as well. The sonata for violin and piano was composed in 1937, and the normal three-movement format takes the composer only 15 minutes to arrive at the end, which of course averages at five minutes, which is only a fraction longer than a miniature piece for the same combination would take. Holland, therefore, does not allow herself to dwell overly long on the development sections, and follows the stricter dictates of the classical formal plan of a sonata movement. More than half a century later, in 1993, Dulcie wrote her sonata for cello and piano. As in the miniatures, there was much that was the same, but some parameters had moved. Probably the main motif of the cello sonata is an octave leap, which is unusual enough; furthermore, the writing is austere and there is far less arpeggio filling in the fabric of the work. If anything, it is more compressed than the earlier string sonata. Jumping back again, her piano trio from 1944—apart from some bar-length changes in the opening and some less usual intervals in the thematic core of the piece—contained little else that was unexpected.

I returned to more of Dulcie Holland's output after writing all of the above, feeling that perhaps I had been somewhat harsh. For the record, the new pieces I looked at were: *Autumn Sarabande* (1976), for violin and piano; a song, *Sky Roses* (John Wheeler), from 1958; *Sad Serenade*, for flute and piano; *On Safari* (1976), for violin and piano; *Lullay, My Tiny Child* (1974), for recorder and piano; *Follow Me* (1957), for violin, viola and piano; *Sonatina for Two Soprano Recorders and Piano* (1964); *Summer Afternoon* (1995), for viola and piano; *Elegy* (1964), for flute and piano; and *Ballad* (1954), for clarinet and piano. The selection had a good coverage of dates, instruments and scope. Some works were still unpublished. Certainly, the teaching material did not disclose anything new. The piece for violin and viola was actually meant to introduce children to the idea of canonic imitation, and serves this purpose quite wittily. The sonatina with two recorders won the first prize in a competition sponsored by the Recorder Society of New South Wales in 1962. Two works, however, stood out: the *Elegy* for flute and piano was another prize-winning work, this time for the Warringah Summer Arts Festival of 1964; and the *Ballad* was composed for the famous Australian clarinetist Clive Amadio. Both of these medium-length pieces pushed Dulcie's musical language a little further than usual. The flute work, dedicated to John Barber (a name I was not familiar with), was plainly aimed at a professional level, as was the work for Clive Amadio. This must have meant to Dulcie that she at least visualised herself at the piano, and this image of a concert rather than a teaching scenario must have had some impact on the outcome of the music.

Dorian le Gallienne (1915–63)

Dorian le Gallienne—almost 100 years after his birth—is slowly but inevitably being recognised as an important and seminal figure in Australian music. He died young, but left behind, if not a huge body of work, certainly a significant one. As a teacher and critic, he was influential, and fought the good fight for the cause of Australian music and music by Australian composers. At a time when music was important only if written abroad, he espoused the cause of local training, performance and encouragement of the Australian composer. Much of what was achieved later owed much to him and to other pioneers. His output, for the purposes of this book, falls into the two classes of vocal music and instrumental sonatas.

The songs with piano fall into a number of categories. There are the Shakespeare songs

Farewell! Thou Art too Dear for My Possessing, Sonnet No. 89 (published 1954)
Fear No More the Heat of the Sun, from *Cymbeline*, Act IV (1943)
No Longer Mourn for Me, Sonnet No. 71 (1946)
How Oft, When Thou, My Music, Sonnet No. 128 (1946).

Then the songs on Australian texts

Moonlight (Hugh McCrae, 1948)
The Cactus of the Moon (Nancy Keesing, 1956).

Song cycles

Four Nursery Rhymes (1945)

Three Songs (1957)
1. 'The Ghost' (Omi Okura, translated by C. A. Walsh)
2. 'Winter' (J. C. Hobson)
3. 'Cranes' (T. W. Earp).

Four Divine Poems of John Donne (published 1950)
1. 'A Hymne to God the Father'
2. 'Death be not Proud'
3. 'At the Round Earth's Imagin'd Corners'
4. 'Batter My Heart, Three Person'd God'.

Songs for stage productions
1. *Solveig's Cradle Song* (transcribed from the full score by the composer; Ibsen, *Peer Gynt*)
2. *Solveig's Song* (Ibsen, *Peer Gynt*).

For detailed information about the history of some of his songs, I refer the reader to the excellent publication by the University of Melbourne Centre for Studies in Australian Music (1999) devoted to le Gallienne's then unpublished songs. Here we are more concerned with a compositional overview. The Shakespeare settings were generally treated chordally, the mood created by the movement of unrelated triads, giving these songs an archaic flavour. Le Gallienne favoured a monolithic treatment of text generally; there is little active counterpoint in his settings. But as time went on, the movement of the left and right hands strayed into what was then dissonant territory, often by unexpected stepwise progression. The austere musical language drifts towards bitonality in some of the later songs. Here as an example is the opening of *Moonlight*.

Example 1.10 D. le Gallienne, *Moonlight*, bars 1–5

Or, the introduction to *The Ghost*.

Example 1.11 D. le Gallienne, *The Ghost*, bars 1–5

Winter arrives at dissonance by simple tone and semitone movement.

Example 1.12 D. le Gallienne, *Winter*, bars 26–7

If the incidental music and the nursery-rhyme settings are the least important of le Gallienne's vocal settings then, surely, the most important must be the settings from John Donne. Here the language is highly charged, dramatic and passionate. The songs need to be performed as a cycle to achieve maximum effect. The first song contains a rare excursion into counterpoint.

Example 1.13 D. le Gallienne, 'A Hymne to God the Father', from *Four Divine Poems* of John Donne, bars 19–22

A wonderful moment occurs on the word 'shine' towards the end of the same song.

Example 1.14 D. le Gallienne, 'A Hymne to God the Father', from *Four Divine Poems* of John Donne, bars 46–9

The relentless march is the keystone of the musical language in the third song, whilst the last begins and consistently uses chords built up in fourths.

Example 1.15 D. le Gallienne, 'Batter My Heart, Three Person'd God', from *Four Divine Poems* of John Donne, bars 1–5

The two instrumental sonatas with piano are for flute (1943) and violin (1945). They are both blood brothers to the sonata for solo piano (1951). The flute sonata is the more lyrical and gentle of the two. It uses a sonata–allegro form for the first movement, and is tinged with the gentleness of the English pastoral style, perhaps resembling Vaughan Williams at times, though it does move into far less tonal worlds on occasion. There are four movements, and in the last, le Gallienne writes in 7/8.

Example 1.16 D. le Gallienne, *Sonata for Flute and Piano*, mvt IV, bars 1–5

This idea is inverted later in the movement.

Example 1.17 D. le Gallienne, *Sonata for Flute and Piano*, mvt IV, bars 103–6

The violin sonata is closer in technique, mood and scope to the piano sonata. Its passionate outbursts lead into an almost Shostakovich-like sound.

1. Composers of Their Time: Early modernists and neo-classicists

Example 1.18 D. le Gallienne, *Sonata for Violin and Piano*, mvt IV, p. 5, bars 42–4

Or this very bleak point:

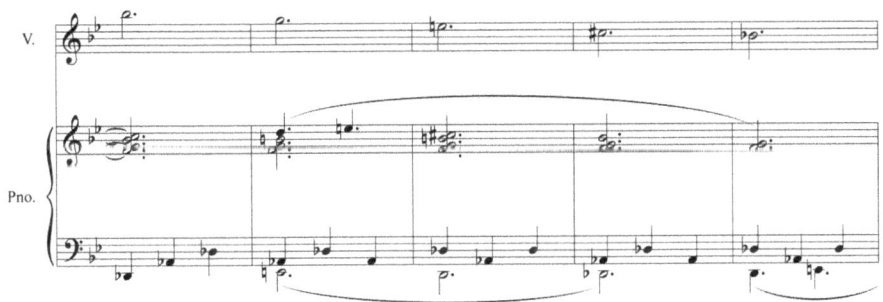

Example 1.19 D. le Gallienne, *Sonata for Violin and Piano*, mvt IV, p. 17, bars 192–6

There is a *Legend* for two pianos, as well as a four-hand sonatina. These are characteristically sparse, and were published for the first time only recently by the Keys Press under my general editorship. It is difficult to know whether they were intended eventually for orchestral treatment or not. Performance indications are few and far between, and the lines moving contrapuntally in octaves seem to constantly suggest an orchestral guise.

2. Composers Looking Back: Late romantics and the nineteenth-century legacy

Alfred Hill (1870–1960)

If one reads *A Distant Music: The life & times of Alfred Hill 1870–1960*, by John Mansfield Thomson, one comes away with a sad realisation. The book certainly tells the story of the man and paints a likeable portrait of someone who was energetic and idealistic, and who produced vast quantities of music. But what of the music itself? Almost nothing is said about it. The fact is that, although everyone seems to acknowledge Alfred Hill as an important figure in Australia's early music, there is little of it heard and little has been written about it. It certainly would be a daunting task when one looks at the output. Even for the modest scope of this book, there would be at least 73 songs with piano to consider, a massive amount of chamber music, ranging from trifles to full-length sonatas, as well as trios with piano. After playing through a sizeable fraction of this totality, my head was spinning—not from the joy of discovery or the exhilaration of rediscovery, but rather from the awful realisation that, however much one dresses it up and extols it, the music is the same from beginning to end. Hill never shifted from his late-romantic stance; it is as though the major portion of the twentieth century that he witnessed had never happened. That is difficult to understand, as he was at least part entrepreneur, part educationalist, part arts administrator, very much a man of the theatre, a busy string player and conductor—and time certainly does not stand still in any of these fields. Perhaps part of the problem was artistic burnout; many pieces were recast, and sometimes quite surprising reincarnations happened—such as a string quartet becoming a symphony or a piano concerto becoming a solo piano piece. Some years ago, at a conference devoted to an early period of Australian music, there was an orchestral concert; it just happened that a work by Hill was followed by a composition of James Penberthy. It was obvious to everyone there that a major step had occurred in Australian music, amply demonstrated before us: what was comfortable, soft, post-colonialism with a dash of amateurism had suddenly moved into an international and professional arena. Maybe Hill—a dominant figure on our musical landscape for many years—had simply been left behind. I remember him from his last decade, as he was a presence in Sydney on the scene even then, and feel somewhat guilty writing this way, for there was no pretension to the man, certainly not a trace of arrogance—he was what he was, with no apology, but there was nothing self-righteous about his musical stance.

I began my playing marathon—just by chance—with his little *Humoreske*, for violin and piano, dedicated to Cyril Monk, who was a colourful character from Sydney's early days. The piece is copyrighted 1911 and illustrates my point very well. Two World Wars did not dislodge this world. The piece is well written, eminently playable, rhythmically staid, harmonically predictable, formally text bookish. It is genteel, Kapellmeister music, in the ternary form, which Hill continually utilised.

Hill was not a pianist, and although he knew what was available, it never stretches the possibilities. Even in the trios and the sonatas, the piano part is mainly supportive, with some dialogue occurring. In some of the songs, one does come across a quasi-operatic outburst now and then, just to remind us that Hill did compose a number of operas. But the overall piano parts are variants of rolled chords with an echo thrown in.

The songs fall into a number of categories. Most are parlour songs, expressing comfortable bourgeois emotions without going overboard—that would never do. There is a dreadful class of patriotic songs full of marching rhythms, hymn-like accompaniments, dotted figures and jingoistic sentiments. I used to collect these because the covers were by far the best part of the total production. Some have a faded charm to them, such as *An Old Remembered Song* (1952), written in memory of Dame Clara Butt. Some are almost pure music hall; a good example would be *A Brigand Am I*, extolling the virtue of being a brigand, but in a nice way, of course.

The vocal music that now seems the most valuable and probably the most interesting are Hill's excursions into ethnic song. He was interested in Maori music, as well as Australian Aboriginal music and music from New Guinea. The various songs drawing on these cultures are a mixture of Europeanised and ethnically more authentic types, just as sometimes he used legends or words *from* these cultures but provided the musical setting from his own world. For example, in *Maori War-Song*, he translates the original into English, but sets both languages; the song says 'arranged by Alfred Hill', so there are classes of mixtures, with the proportions varying. *Poor Fella Me* is a moving example of a successful synthesis between the music of the white man and that of the black man. We must remember that Hill's interest in ethnomusicology went back a long way, and did break new ground in Australia as well as demonstrating a compositional possibility to future composers. The collections are fairly readily available and the publications often contain background material and legends pertinent to the song setting.

The instrumental music contains a mass of pedagogic matter illustrating form and technique to student players; Hill even composed miniature chamber works demonstrating classical methods of construction. There was a market for such material; I have my doubts about it as music. This is not *Mikrokosmos* in the making. I am afraid that the 'serious' sonatas—and there is even one for cornet (an instrument Hill used to play)—fall into the same trap of working to a well-worn formula. But my personal opinion is really of no import. What I am trying to propound here is a serious study, including a detailed catalogue of Alfred Hill's output. No doubt some gems will be found; more fundamentally, it is a veiled part of our history, and we need to know about it in some detailed and scholarly way, even if there is some doubt about the ultimate value of much of the music. Hill died only 50 years ago, and already seems a distant and forgotten figure.

Frederick Septimus Kelly (1881–1916)

The music of Frederick Septimus Kelly has turned out to be somewhat of an embarrassment in musical circles. When the composer's output was rediscovered in the National Library of Australia, as well as some written material such as a diary, there was a bit of a buzz, especially as it was revealed that Kelly had attended some important performances of early twentieth-century pioneer composers, and knew important figures in the world of music such as Tovey and Grainger. Regrettably, hearing music by Debussy and others seems to have had singularly no influence on Kelly's own ultra-conservative style and outlook, even though in his writings he seems to admit the importance of the new music to which he was exposed. I have played through a number of manuscript works, of which the most substantial is a *Serenade for Flute and Piano*. This is Kelly's own arrangement of a work originally for flute, harp, horn and string orchestra. The title page seems to be a preparation for publication by Schott, and is given as 'Op. 7'. As soon as one begins to play, one realises that nothing very exciting is going to occur. The work is in five movements

I. 'Prelude'

II. 'Idyl'

III. 'Menuet'

IV. 'Air and Variations'

V. 'Jig'.

The first movement is textured very lightly and lives in a Mendelssohnian atmosphere. The second movement has some quite lovely moments, especially in the middle section, where the flute arabesques could have come out of a Chopin nocturne. The variations movement is very strict and classical, essentially elaborating the simple tune in a melodic manner, in the style of a minor early nineteenth-century salon composer. The jig does not even try to develop counterpoint, which one would have expected. Overall, there was nothing in the score that would have made an early nineteenth-century composer blush! There were two violin sonatas in D minor—one complete and one breaking off in the middle of the first movement. The completed sonata has an adagio introduction before it launches itself into the usual three-movement format. The manuscripts are not easy to read, and the works would have to be published before a performance could take place. The model for the violin sonatas seems to be Beethoven more than anyone else, although ghosts of other composers do surface. There is also a piano trio in B-flat major, with a throbbing triplet accompaniment, for which the model is possibly Schubert, with a trio in the same key. The trio has two movements—perhaps, like Schubert and his symphony, Kelly did not live to complete this trio either. I also glimpsed a string trio from 1911, which turns out to be complete, and easier to read, in four movements. I mention it only since it manifested itself amid the Kelly material. There were no special surprises in it either. I must say, again, that though this very early Australian pianist/composer would have been an attractive founder of our music, especially given his sporting prowess at Olympic level, this was not to be. He comes across as a well-meaning amateur when one views the scores dispassionately.

Adolphe Beutler (1882–1927)

Beutler was a composer whom we came across very late in the production of the piano music book. His works are retrospective in style, but nevertheless form an interesting part of Sydney's musical history. Beutler was part of Normal Lindsay's 'revitalisation' movement. They very vocally opposed the encroachment of modernism, which they perceived as being detrimental to social order. Rather, they idealised the great romantic composers such as Beethoven and Brahms, seeking to create an Australian expression of romanticism, which they optimistically believed would enable the 'new world' to lead the 'old world' to a cultural renaissance.

Although we are aware of several relevant works by Beutler, including a *Sonata in C Major* and a *Sonata in D Major* for piano and violin and a *Septett in G Major* for two violins, viola, cello, double bass, flute and piano as well as a number of songs, we were not able to access a sufficient sample of this work to give an adequate analysis of the material.

2. Composers Looking Back: Late romantics and the nineteenth-century legacy

Mirrie Hill (1892–1986)

Mirrie Hill, like her husband, Alfred Hill, still awaits thorough investigation and study. She probably suffered by being in her husband's shadow, which is ironic in a way, as most of the compositional fraternity think she was a far better composer than her husband. But she had to subjugate herself, the times being what they were, and word had it that she had to compose using the kitchen table (after clearing it and washing up, no doubt), whilst Alfred's study table was sacrosanct and could not be disturbed. Alfred no doubt helped her in the early days after their marriage in 1921. They were both on the staff of the NSW State Conservatorium of Music, so Mirrie would at least have had exposure to a wider world of music. She taught both piano and theory at the conservatorium. Most of her chamber music output consists of miniatures, both instrumental and vocal. Her piano writing is richer and more diverse than Alfred's, and she departs from using the keyboard as a mere harmonic accompaniment.

For example, if one plays through her *Bourée*, for flute and piano, there is immediately a sense of the neo-classic, with the keyboard participating in the active counterpoint. It might not have the cheeky insouciance of Prokofiev, but is not too far away from it. The *Sarabande* for the same combination possesses a stately charm. The miniatures that are more obviously of a romantic cast live in a world that has a richer palette than Alfred's ever did; a typical instance is *Come Summer*, for clarinet and piano, in which there exists not just a play of equal partners, but a glimpse into the world of the soloist in the form of a cadenza for the clarinet. *In a Moonlit Garden*, for violin and piano, is closer to a pedagogic piece, and is designated on the cover as of 'moderate difficulty'. *The Dancing Fawn*, for flute and piano, though light in mood, nevertheless has a sense of the exotic such as one might find in the music of the Russian exoticists such as Rimsky-Korsakov.

Example 2.1 M. Hill, *The Dancing Fawn*, bars 9–12

The *Four Songs for Medium Voice* gives us a glimpse into her vocal writing. The cycle consists of: 1) 'Sweet Wind that Blows' (Oscar Leighton); 2) 'Flowers Above' (Richard Howe); 3) 'My Star' (Robert Browning); and 4) 'Rest' (Anon.). The songs are delicate and understated.

A piece named *Abinu Malkenu. Ashkenazic Ancient Melody. Our Father, Our King* exists in a number of versions. I played through the one for violin and piano. It is a powerful two-movement work, drawing on Mirrie Hill's Jewish ancestry. The prayer is well known, and the modelling here would have been Max Bruch and possibly Ernest Bloch, though it does not quite have Bloch's high emotional temperature. Nevertheless, it does come from the same world.

Example 2.2 M. Hill, *Abinu Malkenu*, bars 1–4

Hill is not reticent about quite grinding semitones when the music has worked up and needs release.

Example 2.3 M. Hill, *Abinu Malkenu*, bars 28–31

The two movements proceed without a break. *Abinu Malkenu* is a strong contribution to the violin repertoire of Australian music. We know that Mirrie Hill was very involved in Alfred Hill's ethnomusicological pursuits and aided him in those, as well as composing a number of works herself using Maori and

Australian Aboriginal themes. Some listings of her output mention two student works: a piano trio and a piano quartet, both from 1914. We do not know whether they are extant.

Arthur Benjamin (1893–1960)

The highly respected Arthur Benjamin spent most of his time away from Australia; like so many of his generation, for him, there was not enough *work* back home. His story is another still waiting to be told in full, with special reference to his musical techniques and his distinguished output for the operatic stage and for film. His attachment to working with folk songs is well known, and although most of this interest seems to have been directed towards the Caribbean, there is also his *Five Negro Spirituals* (1929), for violin and piano. The original spiritual melodies are preserved, and the words are given after each setting. They are

1. 'I'm A-Travellin' to the Grave'
2. 'March On'
3. 'Gwine to Ride Up in the Chariot'
4. 'I'll Hear the Trumpet Sound'
5. 'Rise Mourners'.

It appears that the famous violist William Primrose was somehow involved in the publication project (perhaps editing the violin part), for my copy of this score, after the title, has 'Arranged by Arthur Benjamin' followed by 'Transcribed for Violin by William Primrose'. These settings used to be heard in solo recitals but have now dropped out of favour. Benjamin's other folk-song activities include instrumental and vocal versions of folk material. The *Negro Spirituals* were set in a straightforward manner, but some of the settings include added colour as in, for instance, *From San Domingo* (1945), for violin and piano, dedicated to William Primrose.

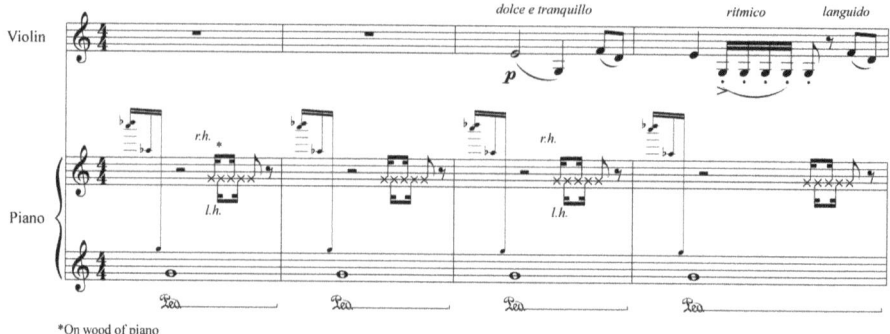

Example 2.4 A. Benjamin, *From San Domingo*, bars 1–4

This is a fairly full setting, with a rich, contrasting middle section. The piano parts in these settings are rarely simple. Here is the opening of *Linstead Market*, dedicated to the then famous singer Jennie Tourel:

Example 2.5 A. Benjamin, *Linstead Market*, bars 1–4

Sometimes Benjamin credits the folk singer who gave him the tune; the famous *Song of the Banana Carriers* carries above the title 'Taken down from the singing of Miss Louise Bennett'. This is the tune later immortalised by Harry Belafonte. Benjamin's original songs also tend towards a folk-like simplicity, although we did not collect all of them. But in *Three Songs* (1935), for voice and piano, we certainly found this to be the case (I. 'Shepherd's Holiday', II. 'Wind Song', III. 'Wind's Work'). His instrumental chamber music is the most substantial of the works for this book. *Le Tombeau de Ravel. Valse-Caprices* (1958) exists for either clarinet or viola and piano. The title has two associations. First, the name is an obvious reference to Ravel's own piano *Noble and Sentimental Waltzes* as well as the orchestral and piano versions of *La Valse*. As a pianist, Benjamin would have also known and probably played the Schubert–Liszt *Valse Caprices*, which, like the Ravel work, collects a series of short waltzes and combines them into a larger composition. Benjamin begins very softly and eerily, much like the orchestral Ravel piece.

Example 2.6 A. Benjamin, *Le Tombeau de Ravel*, bars 1–6

After this introduction, Benjamin gives us six separate waltzes, all running into each other, and rounds off the work with a finale containing reference to the opening material. Near the end, the piano thunders out a harmonically saturated version of one of the melodies—again imitating the Ravelian gesture.

Example 2.7 A. Benjamin, *Le Tombeau de Ravel*, Figure 25

Benjamin's largest contribution in the genre—once again dedicated to Primrose—is his *Sonata for Viola and Piano* (1947). Benjamin writes in the score: 'This work can be performed with orchestra as a Viola concerto. The title in a concert programme should be, in this case, "Concerto for Viola and Orchestra".' The composer does not call this score a rehearsal score, or a reduction from the orchestral score. It is quite possible that he composed the piece originally as a sonata and orchestrated it later, rather than the other way around. Even though the music is essentially the same, the piano part of this viola sonata is completely pianistic. The work is important in the world of the violist especially, since it is one of the pioneer attempts to give the instrument a standing comparable with its flashy partner, the violin. Indeed, Benjamin writes for it in a quite uninhibited manner.

Example 2.8 A. Benjamin, 'Elergy', from *Sonata for Viola and Pianoforte*, p. 8, second system

The movements all have subtitles: I) 'Elegy'; II) 'Waltz'; III) 'Toccata' (this last preceded by a short adagio introduction partially serving the function of a traditionally located slow movement; but of course, Benjamin in this work had already begun with a slow movement). The second movement, which opens with a piano solo announcing quick quaver figurations, is set out like the *Valse-Caprices*—that is, a series of five waltzes and a reprise. At one point the viola takes over the piano figurations, with the keyboard playing a counter-theme. Note the quasi-orchestral instruction in the piano part. Benjamin appears to be already thinking of the orchestral version.

Example 2.9 A. Benjamin, 'Waltz', from *Sonata for Viola and Pianoforte*, p. 14, second system

The 'Toccata' movement brings to mind dance music from the Caribbean. It is a relentless rush in semiquavers, with cross-rhythms and accents, leading to some difficult moments in the piano part.

Example 2.10 A. Benjamin, 'Toccata', from *Sonata for Viola and Pianoforte*, p. 29, second system

Two shorter works remain. The 1924 *Sonatina for Violin and Pianoforte* is almost of sonata proportions. It, too, seems to have a French feel to it, with a suave harmonic flow. The solo and piano parts are sometimes barred independently. The second movement, titled 'Scherzo—Di Stile Antico', is in the favoured 3/4 and has the sound of a fast waltz. Both instruments in this example are treated staccato and leggiero.

Example 2.11 A. Benjamin, 'Scherzo', from *Sonatina for Violin and Pianoforte*, p. 13, third system

The last movement is a brilliant 'Rondo'. We get some idea of Benjamin's pianism and the size of his stretch—noticeable in much of his piano writing.

Example 2.12 A. Benjamin, 'Rondo', from *Sonatina for Violin and Pianoforte*, p. 21, third system

The *Sonatina for Cello and Piano* (1939) is a much less taxing work. As noted by the composer, it was written for a thirteen-year-old player. The movements here carry subtitles as well: I) 'Preamble'; II) 'Minuet'; and III) 'March' (with a performance instruction 'allegro grottesco').

Linda Phillips (1899–2002)

This long-lived (Linda Phillips died at the age of one hundred and three) and prolific composer is another creator waiting for her story to be told. Her work falls into various categories, and we could examine only a small percentage of her output. A few things were published in her lifetime, and some were very popular; many remained in manuscript. The Keys Press has only recently issued for the first time in print what we consider to be some of the more important works. She was, at heart, a miniaturist and a songwriter, often setting her own words, since she was interested in writing poetry all her life.

Her shorter art songs are probably the least weighty of her output. Unless indicated, they are all for voice and piano. We looked at

A Ship, An Isle, A Sickle Moon (James Elroy Flecker)

Cherry Blossom (Kathleen Dalziel)

Tell Me, Thou Soul of Her I Love, sixteenth-century air (Old English), arranged for voice, piano and cello

Orchard Zephyr

Plum Tree (Kathleen Dalziel)

Cradle Song

What Secret Hath the Rose?.

These songs, though evocative, tend to also be somewhat sentimental and seem to belong more to the drawing room than the concert hall. Phillips was a natural melodist, so singers find her vocal music lies well. The instrumental backing is generally less important, and merely provides a harmonic backdrop—quite often merely arpeggios, sometimes with voice doubled, rarely with any sense of counterpoint.

Her songs devoted to the Australian bush have a more passionate voice. She seemed to regard the bush itself, as well as the characters populating it, with an almost mystical awe, so the settings, though meant to be simple, do take on a life of their own. Whether purely instrumental, such as *Bush Evening*, for violin and piano or vocal, there is a richness of feeling and harmony sometimes absent in her 'domestic' songs. She wrote the words for her *Bush Lyrics*, which comprises the following four songs

1. 'Wattle Tree'
2. 'Bird Call'
3. 'Bracken Brown'
4. 'Where the Coloured Parrot Flies'.

At the head of the second song, the composer writes: 'The treble figure in the accompaniment represents the actual notes of a bird call from the hills around Emerald, Victoria.' The fourth song was very popular and one heard it sung by many singers in concerts and competitions. There is a similar set named *Songs of the Outback*

1. 'The Settlers'
2. 'Rail Workers'
3. 'Droving Song'.

Phillips' many instrumental works are mostly for soloist with piano. Possibly the most ambitious of these is a *Rhapsody Sonata*, for violin and piano. This, together with *Two Moods*, for clarinet and piano, finally achieved publication with the Keys Press in 2009. The sonata is in one movement, and highlights Phillips' weaknesses as a composer in this genre: an over-reliance on sequences and a dependence on modulations and seventh chords to achieve colour, with little work on the formal aspects, or the interplay between the instruments. The solo instruments are treated above all like a voice with an accompaniment. There are plenty of shorter works, and we looked only at a *Serenade*, for violin and piano, which was more successful, and had a joyousness about it, with the piano imitating guitar plucking, coupled with a sense of dance that is present in the piece. This has also recently been published in our Heritage Series.

I would rate the various settings from James Joyce as the next important group of pieces in Phillips' output. We have published all 11 of Phillips' settings. It is unknown whether these were meant to be a cycle or not; nor do we have any idea as to the correct order, if they were meant to be sung as a group. So, since they all come from Joyce's collection of poems *Chamber Music*, we have published them in the order in which they appear in that collection. Singers will no doubt have different ideas about this. I think that now it is important to hear these settings as a group. The words are powerful, and seem to lift Phillips' music that extra notch. The songs are

1. 'Strings in the Earth and Air'
2. 'The Twilight Turns from Amethyst'
3. 'Golden Hair'
4. 'Apple Trees'
5. 'Who Goes Amid the Greenwood?'
6. 'Winds of May'
7. 'Bright Cap and Streamers'
8. 'Go Seek Her out all Courteously'
9. 'Arise, My Dove'
10. 'Monotone'
11. 'The Charioteers'.

Finally, we come to a section of Linda Phillips' output that I consider the most important and individual. Yet, they were precisely the ones that were never published (until now) and seem to have attracted no attention. I speak of her 'Jewish' pieces. She was not a fervently religious person, but did have an abiding interest in Jewish music, mostly sacred or traditional song. We do not know enough about her to definitively say something about her knowledge of Jewish music, but she certainly seems to have had memories of and access to it in some shape and form. Using Jewish melodies as a basis inspired her to attempt larger-scale pieces, and imbued the pieces with a passion and strength. *Exaltation, Chassidic Air and Dance* (1939), for oboe, violin, cello and piano, is the most impressive of the Jewish pieces. In all of these, she quotes authentic materials without subjecting them to change or development, using reinforcement and dynamics to build towards the big moments.

2. Composers Looking Back: Late romantics and the nineteenth-century legacy

Example 2.13 L. Phillips, *Exaltation*, bars 280–3

Near the end of the piece, the oboe is asked to imitate the sound of the shofar (ram's horn), which is sounded unaccompanied in the synagogue once a year during the celebrations attending the New Year. Phillips calls this, in the score, '[t]he clear sound of the shofar'.

Example 2.14 L. Phillips, *Exaltation*, bars 349–53

Other similar works include *Purim* (1935), for violin, cello and piano—a more joyous rather than solemn work, in keeping with the meaning of this particular festival. The sound here achieved has now become commonplace, in that it is related to *klezmer* music that seems to have arrived at international popularity. Comparisons with the music of Ernest Bloch are inevitable; but Phillips' compositions—unlike Bloch's very personal and often complex treatment of such materials—are more direct and straightforward. *Lamentations* (1935), for piano trio, has, as a feature, a string of solo cadenzas reminding one of the unaccompanied cantorial singing that is a common experience in the synagogue service. Interestingly, the recently published *Two Hebrew Songs: Ash trees (Oronim Yerukim)*, words by Elisheva Bichovsky, translated by Linda Phillips, and *The Golden Bird (Tayas z'havi)*, words by Hayyim Nahman Bialik, translated by Linda Phillips, display a curious trait: stylistically, they are closer to her normal songs than to her Jewish instrumental music. Here, both the Hebrew and the English are set to more or less the same melodic lines. There are more such pieces that are still awaiting publication: *Yigdal*, for violin and piano; *Trio (Festival)* (1939), for flute, cello and piano; and *Trio (Feast of Weeks)* (1934), for violin, cello and piano. I hope that there will be renewed interest in this composer, especially in this group of works, which occupies a unique place in early Australian music.

Alex Burnard (1900–71)

Burnard belongs to a generation of Australians who were, to some extent, eclipsed by the vicissitudes of trying to function as composers during World War II. Even if they had desired to go abroad, they were stuck in Australia. Burnard spent most of his professional working life teaching harmony and counterpoint at the NSW State Conservatorium of Music. In those days, it was the closest one could come to being taught composition. Burnard, who was the author of an excellent textbook on harmony, taught and composed in a language that was most familiar to him and from which he could quote copiously from memory: Peter Warlock (Philip Heseltine), Percy Grainger, Frederick Delius, as well as any number of Bach works. His songs, therefore, use Warlock more than anyone else as a role model, both in the use of the voice and in the writing of the accompaniment. Grainger's rather thick chordal settings of folk music were another source, and we often see Burnard's piano parts following the same path. He had large hands, and among his manuscripts there are 'simpler' versions of some of the piano parts, probably requested by pianists who could not cope with the demands he made in the realm of stretching chords.

Sadly, during Burnard's lifetime, Australian composers were hardly ever published, nor were they taken seriously in their native country. Burnard was a pupil of Ralph Vaughan Williams and a fine pianist—evidenced by the chords and textures found in his songs and instrumental works. Like so many of his generation, he looked to England as the mother country in more ways than one—not just for guidance but also for performance and publishing opportunities. The fact that his music never made it into print is no reflection of their innate musicality and sensibility; Burnard had a high sense of taste and style, and the very belated publication of some of his works will bring a new fount of repertoire for musicians everywhere, particularly those interested in the traditions of the English art song.

Although the Alex Burnard archive is kept in excellent order in Newcastle, much work needs to be done to issue a comprehensive catalogue and begin to analyse the music itself. I would like to list the songs that we gathered

The City Child (Tennyson) (1924), Op. 1, No. 1

Birdie and Baby (Tennyson) (1925), Op. 1, No. 2

Three Somerset Folk Songs (1926)
    'The Brisk Young Widow'
    'Early, Early'
    'Oh Sally My Dear' (No. 3 is missing at this juncture. The accompaniment is for violin, viola, cello and piano.), Op. 3.

Three Songs for Voice and Piano (1927–28), Op. 5 (words from Fellowes' *English Madrigal Verse*)
    'Poet's Plaint'
    'Philosophics'
    'I Know a Bank'.

Three Songs for Voice and Piano (1929), Op. 17
    'Ghosts'
    'Clown's Philosophy' (our copy is marked Op. 17b, dated 1934)
    'Weathers'.

Australian Song of Festival (1937), Op. 22

Four Australian Songs
    'Song of Brotherhood' (the manuscript says 'words and music by Andrew Aguecheek')
    'Australia Felix' (the manuscript says 'words and music by Toby Belch')
    'To Thee, Beloved Land' (the manuscript says 'words and music by Robin Goodfellow')
    'Rise, Australia' (the manuscript says 'words and music by Launcelot Gobbo'). [Burnard had a well-developed sense of humour, and these pompous words and settings brought out the worst of it. We do not yet know what prompted the composition of these songs.]

Three Songs of Farewell (1970), Op. 50
    'To Daffodils' (Robert Herrick)
    'Come Away, Death' (Shakespeare)
    'Fear No More the Heat o' the Sun' (Shakespeare).

This last song is marked 'R. V. W.'—obviously meant for Ralph Vaughan Williams.

Example 2.15 A. Burnard, 'Fear No More the Heat o' the Sun', from *Three Songs of Farewell*, op. 50, bars 1–7

The Heritage Series of the Keys Press has now brought into print *The Answer, for Soprano and Piano* (Maurice Maeterlinck, translated by John Wheeler), Op. 30.

Here is a good example of the harmonic richness of Burnard's song settings:

Example 2.16 A. Burnard, *The Answer*, Keys Press, p. 3, second stave

The Heritage Series also now includes *A Cycle of Six Songs for Baritone and Pianoforte* (John Wheeler)

1. 'The River'
2. 'Night Piece'
3. 'Berceuse'
4. 'There's Snow on the Mountain'
5. 'Magnolia'
6. 'Carol'.

The songs sometimes suggest canonic and other imitations—not really surprising given Burnard's training and teaching expertise.

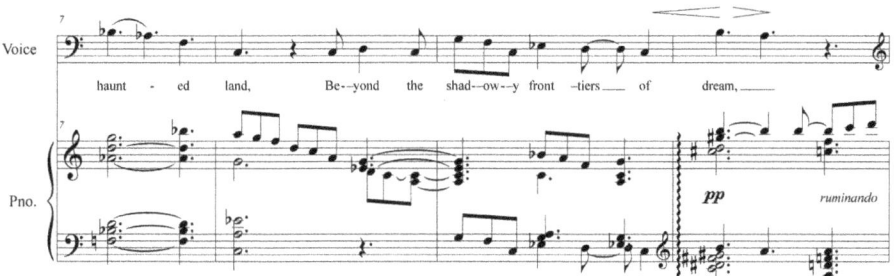

Example 2.17 A. Burnard, 'Berceuse', from *A Cycle of Six Songs*, bars 10–13

The few instrumental compositions that we studied include

Rhapsody for Pianoforte and Two Violoncelli (this was originally titled a sonata)

Suite for Piano and Violin (1940–41), Op. 25

1. 'Overture'
2. 'Reverie "Rapt in Thought I Wander"'
3. 'Village Merrymaking "On a Sunday Holiday"'
4. 'Corydon to His Cruel Phillida: His pipe plaineth of her flontings & inconstancy'
5. 'Walking Piece (Fantasy) Happy Through the Hills I wind along the Winding Byroad'.

In the Preface to his book *Harmony and Composition* (1950, Angus and Robertson, Sydney), Burnard makes clear an important point concerning the modern style:

For three reasons, I abandoned my original intention of including a section on modern harmony and methods: lack of space, the existence of several excellent books on the subject, and the fact that those who have the itch to compose are invariably keen enough to make the acquaintance of works likely to influence their writing. Such enthusiasts will find in this book continual urgings to prosecute their search. Similarly, those of a more sedate and philosophical bent who wish to write chorale-preludes will be helped best by the perusal of living models, and they will know where to seek for such models. I have stopped at the chorale itself.

Burnard himself was so imbued with folk song and with the folk song-based works in the music of the composers he admired most (named above) that his own compositions owe much to this love, and much sounds like quasi folk even when he perhaps had not consciously desired it. We found this to be the case in many bars of his vocal and instrumental music. But at his best—such as the songs that we selected for publication, and in some of the solo piano folk settings and chorale-preludes—Burnard is in the front rank of Australian composition.

Song Composers[1]

Ernest Wunderlich (1859–1945); Arundel Orchard (1867–1961); Una Bourne (1882–1974); Lindley Evans (1895–1982); Horace Perkins (1901–86); Esther Rofe (1904–2000); Percy Grainger (1882–1961)

Until the formation of orchestras and ensembles, the first generation of Australian composers was severely limited in their possibilities. The amount of music for solo piano was vast, closely followed by the composition and publication of songs. We have, of necessity, looked only at songs that had at least some claim to be related to the European art song, and thus have avoided the thousands of parlour songs meant for home consumption—often sentimental or plain soppy, often patriotic, if that was what sold well. Every household with any sense of being cultured boasted a piano, so songs had a ready market of performers and amateurs. Some composers produced only a handful of vocal compositions, so it was convenient to group them together in this section. The first generation also saw much traffic; some composers had limited opportunity at home, so pianist/composers such as Boyle, Hutchison and Grainger spent much of their professional life out of Australia; in due course they could be found listed in various reference books as American composers. We begin our short survey with a composer who came to Australia from Europe: Ernest Wunderlich. From him, we have a setting of a poem of Uhland translated into English verse by Catherine M. Bradley. *The Minstrel's Curse* (1936) is quite a long balladic narrative, and is set in a late-romantic, Wagnerian style, with a rich texture from the piano and continuous modulation. In one section you can even hear the minstrel playing his harp. The work is really a kind of concert aria rather than a short art song. In contrast, we next look at some songs from an English composer who spent some time in Australia. Arundel Orchard thus represents an English traditional approach to the voice, and his songs are simpler, more direct and more stable tonally. Good examples of his approach are contained

---

[1] Horace Keats (1895–1945) would also belong in this category; however, he has not been included here as his voluminous output is discussed extensively in his biography. See Keats, Brennan 1997, *A Poet's Composer: The biography of Horace Keats, 1895–1945*, Publications by Wirripang, Culburra Beach, NSW. Wirripang has also published his music. Further information is available at <http://www.australiancomposers.com.au/authors/horace-keats>

in his *Troubadour Songs*—twelfth-century texts translated by Jethro Bithell. These were published in England, but his *Two Songs* from the comic opera *The Emperor* (words by W. J. Curtis) come from John Sands (374 George Street, Sydney). On the title page, it says: 'These songs may be Sung in Public without Fee or License except at Theatres & Music Halls.' These are, naturally, lighter, as are *Two Elizabethan Lyrics* (1. 'Echo's Lament of Narcissus', from *Cynthia's Revels*, words by Ben Jonson; and 2. 'What Should I Say?', words by Sir Thomas Wyatt). These have not yet arrived at a notion of pastiche or some attempt to give an archaic atmosphere to the settings; they are simply quite mild romantic songs. The pianist and composer Una Bourne—who also spent much time out of Australia—contributes here *A Cloudless Night* (1925), which is rather poor melodically, but nevertheless was included by Dame Nellie Melba in her programs, or so it proclaims on the cover.

Lindley Evans was very well known in Australia as an accompanist; he accompanied Nellie Melba on some of her tours, as well as many other famous soloists; it is not surprising that he composed some songs himself. We found *The Tale of a Fairy* (words by A. T. E. Blanks) as well as *The North Has My Heart* (words by William Watson). The harmonies have now become more cloying, and augmented chords appear in the harmonic flow. The suave harmonies, ironically, also seem to have diminished the role of the piano to a background, merely supporting the voice—maybe that is how Evans viewed his role? And of course there is the ubiquitous *Australia, Happy Isle* (1937, words by Jessie M. G. Street), a two-part song that was heard everywhere, with a pompous, hymn-like accompaniment, somehow elevating it to an almost religious experience. It begins: 'O God of ours and all that we command, Who gave to us Australia happy isle.'

Horace Perkins' idiom has moved on somewhat and includes references to what was perceived as impressionism; this suggested being fashionable, maybe even daring, and it allowed a return to a more lush and full piano role, with longer pedal effects. Generally, the piano filled in the gaps between verses by echoing the last phrase sung, imitating it or unashamedly filling in the silence with various species of rolled chords. Perkins had a taste for high literature and his vocal settings include *The Prelude* (William Wordsworth). The title page has: 'The words are from THE PRELUDE (Childhood and Schooltime) showing "how Nature by extrinsic passion first peopled the mind with forms sublime or fair… in that tempestuous time".' The scenes from Wordsworth are: I) 'The River'; II) 'The Vale'; III) 'The Lake'; and IV) 'The Cottage'. The second, third and fourth songs require narration of some of Wordsworth's texts before the song commences. Perkins also set Charles Kingsley's *Young and Old*, Edgar Allan Poe's *Hymn* and Tennyson's *A Farewell*. The songs are all timed, suggesting that they were broadcast in the early days of the Australian Broadcasting Commission (now

Corporation; ABC), where Perkins worked for many years. Another composer who worked within the ABC was Clive Douglas, who was predominantly an orchestral composer; we found a tiny song by him called *The Road*, set to his own text, with a simple piano accompaniment in A minor.

Esther Rofe died a short time ago, almost reaching the age of one hundred. Most of her career seems to have been tied to the theatre, but we, to our shame, know very little about this composer, and, playing through her songs, I was painfully aware that I knew nothing about the context of these settings. Were they part of a theatre show? An extract? *Dinah's Song* (lyrics by Tom Rothfield) certainly has the atmosphere of a musical. But recently an Esther Rofe songbook was published, which suggests that there were songs written outside the theatrical context. Witness, for example, her very fine atmospheric settings from Walter de la Mare. These five songs (1936, 1940) comprise *Clavichord*, *The Horseman*, *As I Went to the Well-head*, *Wild are the Waves* and *Hi*, and are obviously designed as a cycle. The songbook also includes some other songs such as two settings from William Blake for mezzo-soprano and flute, *The Winds of Change* (words by Frieda Jonsson, Esther Rofe's pen-name); *Curtain* (1930s, words by Grant Uden); *Somebody Ask (A Spiritual for the 1990s)*, words and music by Esther Rofe composed in 1996–98; and *The Tired Man* (1935, revised 1994, words by Anna Wickham). Esther Rofe was obviously functioning as a composer till the very end. Her story is waiting to be written, and could well be fascinating.

I must admit that I could not face the task of wading through all of Percy Grainger's arrangements, transcriptions and rehashes of his various folk songs and quasi-folk songs. John Bird's excellent book lists all the works; most of the material was folk music from 'Nordic' countries, and the use of the piano in them is often of a secondary level—that is, an arrangement of an arrangement. Folk-song settings were never part of this book's plan anyway. I freely admit that I have a problem with assigning Grainger—fine pianist as he was—a patriarchal role in Australian music, for many and varied reasons. I think we have people whose personality—musical and personal—was far less flawed to assume such a mantle.

I need to end this survey of the song repertoire with reference to Horace Keats. I first came across his music when I was earning money as a student at the NSW State Conservatorium by being studio accompanist to that very fine baritone Harold Williams. This was in the 1950s, and all the singers sang Horace Keats; I played dozens of songs by him. Williams was very proud of having an orchestral setting of Keats' *La Belle Dame sans Merci* dedicated to him by the composer. A recent biography published by Wirripang, *A Poet's Composer*, gives a fine overview of Keats' work as a composer as well as showing how much Australian poetry he set to music. I recommend this to interested readers. Keats was a very important song composer in Australia.

Other Instrumental Works

Edgar Bainton (1880–1956); Frank Hutchens (1892–1965); Iris de Cairos-Rego (1894–1987); Clive Douglas (1903–77); Esther Rofe (1904–2000); Marjorie Hesse (1911–86); Charles Edgar Ford (1881–1961); Franz Holford (1909–94); Henry Krips (1912–87); Rees Morgan (dates unknown)

Just as we gathered an array of songs with piano, so here is a selection of instrumental works by various composers, drawing attention to forgotten repertoire in most cases, with quite a number of these works still unpublished and including one or two exciting 'discoveries'. Edgar Bainton's *Sonata for Cello and Piano* (1953) is in four movements. Bainton is not a composer who pushed boundaries, so the first movement is in sonata form, with a scherzo, lento and gigue allegro forming the rest of the piece. The solo part is, by today's standards, only modestly pushing the solo part, with the pianist adding most of the sweep to the totality of the work. The cello is never too high or too fast, and these days, this sonata would be a good student work. Frank Hutchens has a number of violin and piano pieces. One, *Always Afternoon*, is, in its manuscript form, entitled *A Summer Evening*, but the idea is a lazy, indolent atmosphere, which prevails in other Hutchens violin works (and many solo piano works). There is a published *Elegy*, but I am also aware of pieces such as *Fairy Ships*, *Fairy Tales*, *Vision*, *Legend* and *Syrinx*. Some of these works are arrangements of piano works, with the melodic line extracted to make a violin line. Hutchens also composed and arranged many works for two pianos because of his long-lasting partnership with Lindley Evans. Evans was not a prolific composer, although there is a waltz for two pianos, which was much performed by them and others. But Hutchens was quite industrious, and, as well as arranging music by Bach, Handel, Grieg, Mendelssohn, Couperin, Hummel and Chopin for two pianos, his compositions for this genre include *Christmas Bells*, *Seascape*, *Interlude Promenade*, *Phantom Dancer*, *Croon*, *Lullaby for Three Blind Mice*, *Toccata*, *Serenade*, *Vision*, *At the Bathing Pool*, *Ship Ahoy* and *Connie at the Con*. Most of these are still in manuscript. Both Hutchens and Evans were influenced by the two piano transcriptions of Maier and Pattison, who toured Australia and whose concerts the two attended whenever possible. I heard Hutchens and Evans a number of times, and remember their two piano sounds as mellifluous and suave, rather than brilliant.

Iris de Cairos-Rego wrote a piano trio in A minor. This seems to be an early work and was never published. Despite some attractive harmonic progressions, the writing is rhythmically stodgy and the instruments never seem to depart from a predominantly vertical way of thinking. Clive Douglas is represented here with a *Pastorale and Ritual Dance* from the symphonic suite *Namatjira*. Douglas was an ABC conductor, and wrote *Namatjira* when the fashion began to be 'Australian'. At the head of the score of this extract arranged for violinist Harry Hutchins, Douglas wrote:

In the land of the Aboriginal painter Albert Namatjira, the Red Centre of Australia, there occurs the most remarkable of the continent's phenomena, not duplicated in any other country. A land of vast distances and grim remorseless desolation of sandy desert and gibber plain, contains incredible mountain formations and geological wonders unique in the world. In this dramatic setting of fiery cinnabar mountain ranges, stone-age man still enacts the savage rites of his race.

Douglas was an expert orchestrator and here the piano has to do the bulk of the colouration; one misses the orchestra here and there. It is somewhat amusing that despite everything, Douglas still manages to be more adventurous than some of our more recent composers!

Esther Rofe wrote a *Lament* for alto flute and piano in 1924. This is really a 'song without words', with the flute carrying all the argument and the piano playing underneath in minim chords. There is also apparently a flute sonata from 1929, but only the scherzo from it was available. This is in standard ABA form, with the trio in andante tempo and the outer sections sprightly and colourful. If the rest of the sonata proves to be as attractive, it could add to the repertoire. On its own, the scherzo is a snippet of film music, and out of context.

We now have some very light and lightweight music from some composers. Marjorie Hesse wrote her *An Irish Croon* (1939) for the violinist Phyllis McDonald, who used to play light music on air for many years. This is a melodic and undemanding piece in every respect. Edgar Ford was a prolific composer from Perth, and here we looked at his *Echo and Narcissus* as well as *Thalia*, both apparently possible on either violin or clarinet. These are in simple ternary form and strike one as rather amateurish in execution. Franz Holford wrote a good deal of oboe/piano music and some clarinet/piano music too. I confess to being bored by it; my harmony professor, Alex Burnard, used to refer to such harmonic progressions as we find here as 'slops'. Need I say more? Holford was very active in the 1970s and had a strong connection with Albert & Son, who published all the music that we saw by Holford. There are at least four sonatas for oboe and piano; we played through Number 4, which was dedicated to Ian Wilson, a lovely lyrical player from the Sydney Symphony. Henry Krips's *Southern Intermezzo* (1956), for alto saxophone and piano, is really a rather schmaltzy cabaret piece whilst Rees Morgan's *Romance* for his friend the clarinetist Gabor Reeves is in a similar genre.

3. Phyllis Campbell (1891–1974)

Fiona Fraser

Phyllis Campbell is a very interesting composer whose music has only come to light since the first volume on piano music. Campbell was an active member of Sydney's Theosophical Society who was clearly influenced by their mystical ideas about music. Perhaps because of this, she had trouble obtaining recognition outside theosophical circles in her own lifetime.

Many theosophists were interested in the spiritual significance of sound vibrations and overtones, believing that, like the swirl of colours in an abstract painting, certain sound combinations could transport an audience to a corresponding cosmic plane of enlightenment. It is no accident that Scriabin's so-called 'mystic chord' has a close relationship to the harmonic series.[1]

American composers influenced by these ideas, such as Cowell and Ruhdyar, explored the capacity of the piano to produce resonant overtones by developing a unique style based on cluster chords, often including fists full, literally, of piano bass notes to create the maximum number of overtones.

Campbell experimented with these ideas in a series of solo piano works entitled *Nature Studies*, most of which were written between 1925 and 1928. While she does use the 'mystic chord', she does not extend to the 'ultra-modern' extremes of Cowells. She does, however, use other complex aggregate chords and chord clusters that she presumably invented while improvising at the piano. Her enharmonic spelling is not consistent with any tonal system and she frequently writes sharps against flats in a most atypical fashion, suggesting that she is focused on finding the 'right' sound at the keyboard rather than working within the harmonic language that would be relevant for a particular key. Most frequently, she chooses chords with added sixths, sevenths and ninths, so, in practice, Campbell's solo piano music is probably more reminiscent of Debussy than Scriabin. Unlike Debussy, however, she uses very little melodic material, building her piano works on the gradual transformation of sound brought about by small, but often surprising, harmonic shifts of a repeated ostinato pattern. This is demonstrated in the following example from one of her *Nature Studies*.

---

1 The 'mystic' chord uses the first six notes of the harmonic series excluding the fifth and repeated notes. The relationship between the 'mystic chord' and the harmonic series was discussed at length by Scriabin's contemporaries. See, for instance, Clutsam, G. H. 1913, 'The harmonies of Scriabine', *The Musical Times*, vol. 54, no. 1, pp. 156–8.

Australian Chamber Music with Piano

Example 3.1 P. Campbell, *A Tree*, bars 27–8

Given this technique, it was interesting to see what Campbell would do with the addition of a solo instrument.

Campbell herself was a violinist and viola player as well as a pianist, so it is no surprise that she wrote extensively for stringed instruments. Her oeuvre includes approximately 34 pieces for piano and violin and two for piano and viola. Many of these pieces are miniatures with names such as *Dreaming Earth, Song of the Rain* and *Day Closes*, which are similar in style to her *Nature Studies*. Typical of such pieces is an early piece in her output, *Unfolding Rose* (1926), in which, unusually, the violin is used as a bass instrument, while the piano plays in a higher register. Unusually for Campbell, the violin and piano actually play in counterpoint, although the left hand plays typical aggregate chords, which are basically triads with added notes.

Example 3.2 P. Campbell, *Unfolding Rose*, bars 4–8

Such counterpoint is unusual for Campbell. Her piano parts are more usually chordal or arpeggiated accompaniments. When examined closely, however, the violin 'melody' is essentially an arpeggiated version of the chords played by the left hand. This suggests that even in music for a solo instrument, the music is based on harmony rather than the horizontal interplay of different voices.

Campbell, like many of her contemporaries, made numerous folk-song arrangements and tried to introduce elements of 'Australiana' into her music. But even here, Campbell does not conform to the usual sentimental, facile treatment of such material. It is not clear whether she wrote these pieces for her own amusement or for an audience, but her peers would have been surprised to listen to a piece called *Lullaby to a Kookaburra* (early 1930s), which concludes in a way that would conventionally be considered dissonant.

Example 3.3 P. Campbell, *Lullaby to a Kookaburra*, final six bars

This example also demonstrates Campbell's fondness for fourths and fifths that are often favoured over conventional triads as common building blocks used in her melodies and her harmonic construction.

In addition to the miniatures there are some more extended works including five sonatas for violin and piano (one of which has sections missing), two lengthy sonatinas for piano and violin, two 'phantasies' for violin and piano and a 'phantasy' for viola and piano. The first, written in 1924, is her *Sonata in B minor*. Campbell uses the traditional classical/romantic model for writing a sonata with four movements

1. 'Allegretto' in conventional sonata form
2. 'Lento non Troppo'
3. 'Scherzando'
4. 'Molto Giocoso'.

While it predates the harmonic experiments in her *Nature Studies*, Campbell is clearly struggling with conventional harmony, although she still includes key signatures (which she later dispenses with). Nevertheless, the following example from the opening 'Scherzando' would no doubt have perturbed Alfred Hill, who was her composition teacher for a time. It starts with a quirky whole-tone theme before settling into a more orthodox harmonic structure and cadencing in G major at bar 18.

Example 3.4 P. Campbell, *Sonata in B Minor for Piano and Violin*, mvt 3, bars 9–15

Her more free-flowing 'Phantasies' are some of her most successful works. Unconstrained by traditional formulae, Campbell takes a much more rhapsodic approach, extending the material in a quasi-improvisatory fashion. Although it is unlikely that this work was ever performed in a formal concert in Campbell's lifetime, the added sixths, sevenths and ninths and abrupt chromatic shifts give a surprisingly modern sound to the music that would probably make it more appealing to contemporary audiences than the predictable music of some of her more famous contemporaries!

Example 3.5 P. Campbell, *Phantasy for Violin and Piano* (1930 version), bars 31–3

Her second *Phantasy* (1933), for violin and piano, is similar in style. It is a later piece and Campbell here seems very comfortable in her harmonic world, the writing simpler and more free-flowing, with both instrumentalists making sweeping runs up and down their instruments.

Example 3.6 P. Campbell, *Phantasy for Violin and Piano*, bars 36–9

The viola 'phantasy' was originally labelled a 'sonata', confirming that Campbell probably turned to writing 'phantasies' to free herself from following the conventional approach she obviously thought was expected when composing a sonata. It begins intriguingly with a theme based on the notes of Scriabin's 'mystic' chord, but is drafted only roughly in pencil in some places and the score becomes quite confused at the end with many crossings out and alterations suggesting that Campbell was not sure how to finish the piece. It is marked as being 'incomplete', but it might be possible to put together a performance edition by careful editing of the existing score.

The remaining three sonatas see Campbell returning to more conventional forms and a simplified if not altogether conventional harmonic language. The last sonata, dated 1932, is the most interesting as Campbell tries to extend the traditional sonata structure with the first two movements flowing into each other before any formal recapitulation of the main themes as would conventionally be done at the end of the first movement. Rather, the recapitulation is deferred until the end of the third and final movement. After a formal statement of the initial themes from the first movement, the work concludes with a coda marked 'tranquil', 'expressive' where the main subjects of the first movement are restated softly in the violin's upper register, creating a quasi-mystical effect. Here Campbell seems to be trying to combine the more free-flowing technique of her 'phantasies' with nineteenth-century thematic development techniques. In this work, Campbell demonstrates a growing comfort with larger-scale works, connecting the various movements thematically to create a unified whole.

The sonatinas (composed in 1931 and 1932) for violin and piano are substantial works also, being almost as long as the sonatas and 'phantasies' and not appreciably easier to play. The first sonatina starts conventionally enough in C major with triadic harmony. It is as if Campbell is making a real effort to conform to expected tonal norms, but by this stage, her vocabulary has changed, and she cannot help but break out into her usual complex chords, or her beloved fourths and tri-tones. In addition, the accompaniment is not easy to play, as this excerpt from the slow movement, with its parallel fourths, shows.

Example 3.7 P. Campbell, *Sonatina No. 1*, second mvt, bars 23–6

The second sonatina likewise begins more conventionally with the first subject in C major, although the chordal accompaniment contains the usual added notes. By the last movement, however, this work has taken on a distinctly exotic flavour with the solo part favouring pentatonic melodies and the accompaniment often using parallel fourths and fifths.

Example 3.7 P. Campbell, *Sonatina No. 2*, mvt 3, bars 66–9

Campbell's unique compositional style is even more apparent in her songs. With more than 100 such songs composed during her most creative period in the 1920s and 1930s (after which she sadly gave up composing), Campbell must be one of Australia's most prolific composers of art songs. While the titles of some of these songs suggest they might be of the more conventional parlour-song variety, as with the violin music, there are usually some surprises. For instance, the innocuously titled *The Bush* (1930) is nothing like a traditional folk or bush ballad. Rather, the opening is based on the whole-tone scale both in voice and in piano parts—something that would have been considered 'ultra-modern' in her time.

Example 3.8 P. Campbell, *The Bush*, bars 1–4

She set an eclectic range of poets including Edith Sitwell, William Yeats, Arthur Symons, William Sharp (under the pseudonym Fiona McLeod), Mary and Percy Shelley, Alice Meynell, Seumas O'Sullivan, George William (A. E.) Russell, James Cuthbertson (Scottish-Australian poet), Ernest Rhys, Maurice Baring and James Stephens, as well as German-language poems (Campbell went to school in Germany) by Joseph Eichendorff, Martin Greif, Theodor Körner, Goethe and Nietzsche. In addition, there are several sets of Chinese and Japanese poems, which are set in translation. Although Campbell was herself a poet and later published several volumes of poetry, there is no evidence of her setting her own poetry.

At times, the poetry inspires adventurous forays into atonality and dramatic chord clusters, as shown in the following excerpt from a setting of a Japanese poem, *The Dragon-Flies* (no date given but probably part of a series of Japanese poems set in 1928).

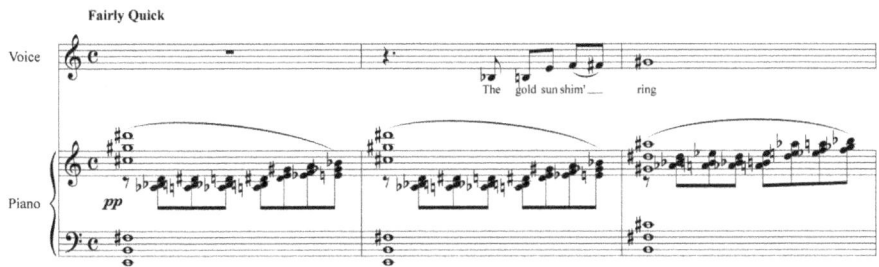

Example 3.9 P. Campbell, *The Dragon-Flies*, bars 1–3

Generally, Campbell's use of rhythm is quite conventional, and she uses standard time signatures, showing a preference for 3/4 and 6/8. She does, however, venture into 5/8 in her setting of another Japanese poem, *The Fallen Maple-Leaves* (1928), in which differing right-hand and left-hand chords give a bitonal effect.

Example 3.10 P. Campbell, *The Fallen Maple-Leaves*, bars 1–4

There are many such examples and it would be interesting to know whether she had singers prepared to perform such material. Certainly, it seems unlikely that she would write so many songs without possible singers in mind, yet such material would have seemed quite difficult for singers in her time who might not have had much experience with such modern compositional techniques. If the songs were performed it was probably at informal home gatherings as there is no reference to any public performance of her songs among her papers, although there is mention of a small number of performances of some solo piano works and at least one of the violin sonatas.

Campbell's unorthodox style and extensive output demonstrate that the 1920s and 1930s were far from being barren in terms of musical creativity. Believing in the spiritual nature of all things, she looked to her own environment for inspiration. In Campbell's case, this meant that she needed to invent a musical language appropriate to her environment, pre-empting a move by later Australian composers to seek inspiration outside the Western harmonic tradition to express their engagement with the Australian landscape. There is still more to discover about this interesting composer and the circles in which she moved and a treasure trove of works awaits performance and recording.

Part 2: The Second Generation

What is commonly labelled postwar modernism arrived fairly suddenly and quickly in Australia in the early 1960s. Its representative composers were born just before the outbreak of World War II, and, by the 1960s, they were at a time in their lives when such changes were ripe. The mix of composers included many who arrived in Australia as part of the huge wave of postwar immigration, and they brought with them the necessary materials and mind-set to overturn the hitherto dominant Anglocentric culture in our music institutions. The historic first Conference of Australian Composers, held in Hobart in 1963, was a clear demonstration of almost palpable open warfare between the first and second generations. New ideas from the avant-garde of Europe and America began to infiltrate our composers' thinking. For the first time in our history, composers became employable as teachers of composition in our tertiary institutions, instead of being smuggled in under the guise of teachers of harmony, counterpoint, history and aural training. Universities moved away from their traditionally dusty musicological roles and began a transition to centres of new musical thinking and live music making. The idea that one had to go abroad to complete one's education was now seriously questioned. The Australian Contemporary Music Ensemble appeared to be the prototype for many such ensembles in the years to follow. Australian music began to appear in the normal course of concerts, instead of being a frankly ghetto culture. For a while—regrettably short—the Australian Broadcasting Commission (now Corporation; ABC) was in the front rank of commissioning and performing bodies, actively encouraging the new Australian music. The meaning of the term 'Australian composer' had to be redefined and, for most, it was a move away from narrow nationalism and jingoism. The patriotic card was still being played, though, as it is still being played in the twenty-first century.

4. Post–1945 Modernism Arrives in Australia

Felix Werder (1922–)

Some years after writing *Australian Piano Music of the Twentieth Century*, I find myself in a quandary yet again, faced with the problem of writing about Felix Werder.

Available listings of his output include many early works, many written after the young composer came to Australia. These works now seem to be unavailable. A few years ago, I rang Felix and asked him about these works, which I wanted to look at, as a composer's first efforts often pinpoint key tendencies in their artistic stance. Felix said to me, with some passion, that all these early works had been burnt, because nobody showed any interest in them. I did not get to first base in the conversation, neither was I inclined to try again. It was certainly nothing personal: we had always got along over many years; it was just a very bitter and possibly disillusioned Felix who was speaking. I hope that what he said to me was not true and that these works are still extant, but I have no way of knowing.

Another problem facing anyone writing about Werder is the sheer volume of material produced. He once said to me that he saw himself as a hack composer such as Telemann (his words). I cannot say with any certitude that Telemann was a hack, neither do I see why Werder aligns himself with someone whom he might perceive as a hack (there is a work entitled *Tafelmusik* by both Telemann and Werder). Perhaps he thinks of his role as utilitarian rather than artistic? We obtained what we hope is a representative sample of his output; it would be impossible to claim to have seen everything, or even approach a complete survey.

Werder is a highly educated and trained musician; his writings and teachings, not to speak of his music criticisms, all show a very sharp mind, encyclopedic knowledge, and the ability to leap from one art form to another with elegant ease, brushing philosophy on the way. Just very occasionally, a personal, slightly sour or cynical note breaks through, betraying Werder's personal demons.

A further issue is Werder's own 'style'. I use the word with some hesitation, as I am certain that he would object to it. What he has said about his own music suggests that he is against any recognisable style; in fact, that what he is aiming for is 'discontinuity' (his word). One could retort that this in itself will produce a style of writing; Werder's compositions often sound like a stream of consciousness of sounds by someone who has heard and studied a lot of music. But there are no quotations to be found, or anything that 'sounds like…'. The closest one can get to defining the Werder score is to say that often what it betrays is its descent from the Second Viennese School minus the rigour. In recent years, some of his works have been published in Germany.

Probably the best thing I can do is to present some representative samples of Werder's approach. Mostly, the scores are unbarred and quasi-graphic in appearance—that is, the exact point of entry for an instrument is not given.

Example 4.1 F. Werder, *Aristophanes*

Do the actual notes themselves matter, if the vertical correspondence does not? One has to assume that they do, but now and then the composer either becomes impatient or declares that shapes and gestures are the thing, not the actual pitches, so wavy lines and wiggles of varying thickness make an appearance. Piano parts, especially when played directly on the strings, are often notated in this approximate fashion.

In his music-theatre works, his disjointed style is at times used with great effect to underline a particular movement; *Blake's Emanations*, for soprano and piano quartet, could be wryly amusing, if performed with assurance; I say this because the works require considerable rehearsal and virtuoso conducting.

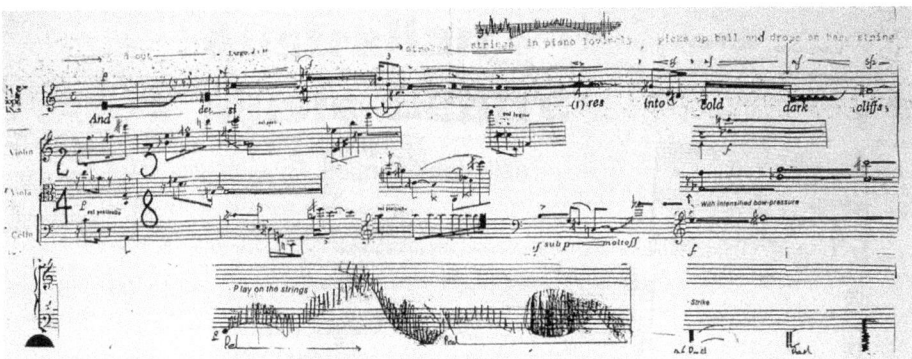

Example 4.2 F. Werder, *Emanations*

In the piano plus one instrument pieces, the pianist has to take on the role of director, unless the other player uses a full score, which then raises issues of a second page turner—not usual, although perfectly possible. For instance, *Conference*, for cello and piano, is sometimes barred, but this does not help the ensemble unless the cellist either sees the piano part or really remembers what the pianist is doing.

Example 4.3 F. Werder, *Conference*

The printed scores are a little easier to read than the composer's autograph, and will perhaps make performances more possible. I have *Encore*, for violin and piano, open in front of me as I write this, and can therefore attest to this fact. Typesetting Werder's scores cannot be easy, and might be expensive—yet another problem in our effort to gain a bird's-eye view of his output. Looking at a published score such as *Vier Lieder nach Gedichten von Walther von der Vogelweide*, it is also clear that singers of Werder's music would need to have near perfect pitch to cope with the demanding parts.

In summary, Werder's approach to composition does not seem to have altered over the years; but we need someone to devote time and energy to write about this composer and perhaps come to some understanding of what thought is lurking behind the printed score.

Australian Chamber Music with Piano

Don Banks (1923–80)

It is fitting, in writing about Don Banks, to commence with his *Commentary for Piano and 2 Channel Tape*. The reason is simply that the piece demonstrates not only Don's interest in the then cutting-edge technology (1971), but also his equally important propensity for problem solving, usually in the form of marrying genres and sound sources usually considered difficult. *Commentary* addresses itself to the problem of combining tape and piano in a musical and flexible way. This is achieved by having an operator on the tape machine starting and stopping the tape at strictly marked points. Moreover, when the piano and tape play together, often the tape part is barred with the piano part, so the pianist knows exactly how to fit against the tape. At other times, only starting and ending points are indicated in the piano part, and one has to listen for a particular effect or voice. I found, in preparing the piece for performance, that practising with the tape was not vastly different from rehearsing with another player, except that at least one member of the team was rather unyielding as far as rubato was concerned! The piano writing is flashy and virtuosic, and Don exploited the strengths of the pianist Paul Crossley, who gave the first performance. Among Crossley's specialities, apparently, were fast parallel chords, and Don drew my attention to a passage where this is exposed.

Example 4.4 D. Banks, *Commentary*, one bar after figure 7

Commentary is also distinguished by a lighter touch: the presence of two 'personages', one in each of the stereo speakers; it just happens that one of the voices is Don Banks himself. But, at any rate, a conversation takes place between the two speakers before the pianist finally begins to play. Some of the dialogue:

'Okay, let's get this show on the road'

'Is the audience quiet yet?'

'How can I tell? Sitting here all cramped and cooped up in this crazy box—how should I know what the audience is doing?'

'Tell me, is the pianist any good?'

'He's fine—it's the piano that's the trouble.'

'Yes. I know what you mean, it's such an outmoded instrument. Frequency response is only 27.5 to 4186 c.p.s., whereas WE can cope with 20 to 20,000—providing they've hired decent speakers.'

'Cycles, shmykles! What I want to know is the pianist ready yet.'

'I can only see his legs from down here.'

'God, I hope it's not going to be one of those pieces where he keeps jumping up and reaching inside the piano. I mean, like, it's so passé these days.'

'Shhhhhh.'

'Shhhhhh?'

'Shhhhhh…'

The last 'Shhhh…' is transformed electronically into a white-noise sound, and the pianist begins. That is how Banks sets the tone of the work. Compared with many other attempts to combine piano and tape from the era, this is an especially elegant solution to the problem, with a deft touch of humour to boot.

Don produced a few duos: *Three Episodes for Flute and Piano* (1964); *Prologue, Night Piece and Blues for Two* (clarinet and piano, 1968); and *Three Studies for Violoncello and Pianoforte* (1954) with common characteristics. I might have written elsewhere that most of Don's music has a hidden jazz beat in the background, from his early days as a jazz pianist in Melbourne. I have even tried certain passages from various works with a jazz drummer, especially when there are offbeat accents and other rhythmic subtleties. I found it quite amazing and revealing to hear the passage with the drumming added. Of course, I am certainly not suggesting any such thing be done in public, but it confirmed to my ears how influential and pervasive the early jazz playing proved to be in his future output as a composer.

Don had to be totally pragmatic to survive, and he earned his living writing for film and meeting strict deadlines whilst he lived in the United Kingdom; this super-professional attitude spilled over into his 'serious' music and was constantly exhibited in his high level of craft as well as his meticulous knowledge of the instruments he was writing for. Almost inevitably, he wrote for people and ensembles that he knew personally, so works were composed with particular people in mind, who probably gave the first performance of the new work. Don's writing tended to be quite linear and very refined; it was not in his nature to bludgeon an audience into submission. The style is generally lyrical and full of feeling. He did not tend to systemise durations, allowing his natural instincts to prevail in that realm. Pitch, however, was a different matter. The Banks archive at the National Library of Australia contains many pencil sketches and workings of various works—one can study the scores and see the composer at work with pitch rows and matrices, and even deduce why certain pitch successions were rejected and others approved. Don found his own way with an essentially fluid, 12-tone technique that was rarely Germanic, and, thanks to the tutelage of Matyas Seiber (and probably Luigi Dallapiccola), contained elements of jazz and popular music despite a very high level of craftsmanship.

Here is a very typical example of the writing—perhaps, to some, paradoxically combining a jazz feel with a serially controlled pitch succession. Similar passages can easily be found in the other works listed above.

Example 4.5 D. Banks, *Three Studies for Violoncello and Piano*, bars 25–7

The clarinet/piano work is, by its title and nature, intentionally closer to jazz. Don must have found the juggling act between film music and 'art' music exhausting, and must have thought that when he was presented an opportunity to return to Australia (first, as a Visiting Fellow at The Australian National University and then as a lecturer at the School of Music) life would become simpler. As it happened, that was not quite what happened, as he found himself heavily involved in various aspects of institutional administration. The flow of music began to slow and then virtually came to a halt before his premature death.

A special place in his output must be given to the *Sonata for Violin and Piano (In one movement)*, dedicated to his teacher Seiber and written soon after leaving Australia (1954). Don used to refer to it as his 'Opus 1', as he must have felt that it was the first piece in which he found a personal voice. Seiber certainly taught him thematic control, and Don clung to this aesthetic for the rest of his life. The work is concentrated and takes only 13 minutes in performance, but much happens in that short time. The seeds that were planted in his early *Piano Sonatina* here come to some fruition for the first time.

Example 4.6 D. Banks, *Sonata for Violin and Piano*, bars 171–3

Of roughly the same length is the lovely *Horn Trio*, written for his friend the great Australian horn player Barry Tuckwell. Unlike the *Violin Sonata*, this trio is in three elegant movements: 1) 'Lento' introduction leading into the allegro moderato movement, and including a cadenza for the horn; 2) 'Adagio Espressivo', containing a cadenza for the horn with the violin; and 3) 'Moderato Scherzando', an exciting movement in compound time with all sorts of syncopated interplays between the instruments. The piano's role here is very close to the rhythm section of a jazz ensemble, with many bars of repeated quavers.

Don Banks is an important composer in Australian history: with his friends and fellow students Keith Humble and James Penberthy, he represented the immediate postwar generation of composers who brought a new sense of professionalism and internationalism to this country.

Tristram Cary (1925–2008)

Tristram Cary always seemed to embody the total professional. He is best known for his pioneering work in electronic music, but some people are surprised to learn of his activities in the general areas of music. I had this realisation years ago when there was a CD being produced by the Australian Youth Orchestra, with settings by many Australian composers of Christmas carols. Upon receiving the CD, I saw Tristram's name among the list of composers and went to that track—and then was suitably impressed and somewhat astonished to hear a full symphonic rendering of a carol, obviously written by an assured and dab hand. Since then I have learnt, of course, that Tristram had made a living working in the world of BBC productions and films, so that his personal interest in producing the very first prototypes of electronic musical instruments were funded by less esoteric compositions.

Australian Chamber Music with Piano

So, I now have in front of me his *Songs for Maid Marion*, written for a radio play in 1959 and revised for publication in 1998. The set of six songs is charming and pastiche-like, in an eighteenth-century style, with a mixture of original folk songs and popular tunes as well as some of Tristram's own melodies. As the original songs were accompanied by guitar, the piano writing is hardly adventurous, and the composer says this himself in the preface; he even draws attention to one of the songs in which he deliberately gives the guitar some florid passage work, originally in the key of E major, which lay under the guitarist's hands very well, especially as the guitarist was Julian Bream.

Earth Hold Songs, Five settings for soprano and piano of poems by Jennifer Rankin is in another world altogether. Composed in 1993, these were written only a few years after the University of Queensland Press issued Jennifer Rankin's collected poems in 1990. *Earth Hold* in the original comprises 27 poems, from which five were chosen by Cary to create this song cycle. The idiom is highly chromatic, and the vocal lines interweave with the piano; quite often the right hand of the piano part continues a line begun by the soprano and running out of its range. The piano constantly comments and colours the vocal part and the words. The titles of the poems selected give a flavour of what the songs are about: 1) 'I Had a Room'; 2) 'Black Cockatoo'; 3) 'Earth Hold'; 4) 'Earth Wind'; and 5) 'Sand'. There is an attractive improvisatory feel to the songs, as though they are springing to life as they are being performed. Repeated note patterns at various speeds are a feature of the writing and give thematic cohesion to the settings. It is only the second song that has a lighter feel to it—a bouncy, almost folkdance atmosphere in 2/4, and quite short. The other songs are more expansive and deal with the elements of the Earth, of being Earth-bound as a human being as against being able to fly, like the cockatoo. Sometimes the composer cannot resist the suggestion of the words, as in the opening of the fourth song.

Example 4.7 T. Cary, 'Earth Wind', from *Earth Hold Songs*, bars 1–4

Tristram died shortly before I commenced writing this book. Looking back on his long life, I cannot help wondering if Australia in general and Adelaide in particular used the resource of his wide experience wisely, whether he was sidelined to some extent. My colleague and friend the composer Jim Cotter did a series of interviews with Tristram shortly before the composer's death. It is to be hoped that these interviews will in due course become available for further insight into this man's work.

Edwin Carr (1926–2003)

Edwin Carr is more properly a New Zealand composer, although he did spend some time working in Australia. We came across two works of his in our research: *Five Wolfskehl Songs, For baritone and piano*; and *Two Dances for Viola and Piano*. The works are probably from the time he was in Australia (1960s–1970s). Both are in a rather dry Germanic style one associates with 12-tone music, although I did not analyse the music enough to confirm/deny this statement. The viola pieces require considerable agility, whilst the baritone songs are serious and expressive. The settings are in German.

Keith Humble (1927–95)

In contrast with Richard Meale, who seemed to have a problem finding a style that served him and allowed him to evolve, Keith Humble stood at the other end of the spectrum: he found his style very early in his life and spent his entire compositional career refining and expanding an essentially 12-tone language. Keith was especially fascinated with tone rows or segments of rows, which had a limited number of permutations, following his own complex rules. The Humble archive is now safely lodged within the National Library of Australia, so we can study the evolution of composers such as Keith Humble in some comfort. Allan Walker, pianist, composer and expert theoretician, currently working with me here at The Australian National University as a PhD candidate, has broken the 'code' of Humble's technique(s) and will publish the results in his forthcoming dissertation. It is quite clear that Keith—patiently writing column after column of permutations of given cells—was greatly influenced by composers such as Webern and Wolpe, trying to limit his raw material into clearly comprehensible aural geometry, rather than work with a system that evaded clarity of hearing. The result of Walker's work will clearly demonstrate the increasing focus of the Humble technique over the years, initially stemming from a Schoenbergian model and gradually moving into an almost ascetic world of Zen-like contemplation.

Keith's music has a crystalline transparency, and although the inner workings cannot be aurally deciphered, the music is clearly the product of a very sharp and curious mind, and in the midst of what might sound free-flowing and improvisatory, there is strict logic. Keith himself played in a curiously remote manner, with little pedal and a kind of objectivity that one hears mostly from composers playing their own material. Although most commentators align Humble (correctly) with the Second Viennese School—and this was certainly the focus of much of his performing and compositional life, with Webern occupying a special place in Keith's aesthetic—there were other influences. Over the years, Keith would nag me about my first book, which was on Busoni, and at first I thought that his interest in Busoni had to do with the Liszt connection (another composer Keith admired), but gradually it became clear that the interest was not so much pianistic as compositional. It was compositional because Keith hoped that I would throw some light on Busoni's thought processes in his more visionary works. I hope he was not disappointed when the book finally emerged. Lurking behind his curiosity, however, was an interest in Busoni's (and Webern's) pupil Stefan Wolpe. He was keen to uncover the origins of Wolpe's way of manipulating sounds. I remembered all this upon opening the very first Humble score that we collected, his *Five Pieces in Two Partsfor Violincello and Piano* (1982). Even the title sounds like a Wolpe piece, and much of the transformational technique—applying itself to more than just pitch, and involving tempo discontinuity as well as concentration on particular intervals—is to be found in Wolpe's mature music. Interested readers will have to wait for Allan Walker's writing on Humble to become available; I would not dream of attempting to say anything analytical here, as Allan has a much deeper understanding of Keith's technique than I could ever aspire to.

I do need, however, to give some representative examples of the Humble score. In the cello/piano work named above, the second piece begins with a characteristically pointillist gesture.

Example 4.8 K. Humble, *Five Pieces in Two Parts for Violincello and Piano*, no. 2, bars 1–5

Both Keith and his fellow student in Melbourne Don Banks had a jazz beginning, and it is fascinating, so many years later, to see the opening of the *Sonata for Flute and Piano* (1991) with the tempo direction 'Fast–Swinging'. It really is as though there is a jazz drummer present in a phantom way, and there is an invisible drum kit moving the piece along. He uses 'swinging' again in the *Trombone Sonata* written a year later.

Example 4.9 K. Humble, *Trombone Sonata*, bars 1–4

The *Trombone Sonata* is still in manuscript, although it seems complete, and has been used to play from; there are some crossed-out bars, but it is all there, though not a fine copy. The work was written for the Australian trombone virtuoso Simone de Haan, and Allan Walker tells me that Simone's name is musically encoded in the main motif of the sonata.

The *Sonata for Flute and Piano*, like so much Humble, is in short movements. It should be noted that even when the movements are longer, as in the trombone/piano work, there are often internal subdivisions. Another characteristic of Keith's style, however, is the constant counterpoint at play.

Example 4.10 K. Humble, *Sonata for Flute and Piano*, first mvt, bars 46–9

Layering is quite common, sometimes quite dense, and often sparse.

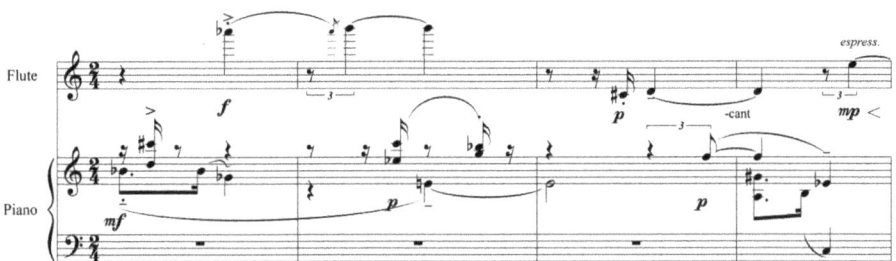

Example 4.11 K. Humble, *Sonata for Flute and Piano*, mvt 2, bars 51–4

In the past few years, Humble's music has begun to appear in print—a good sign that its quality is finally being recognised. There is, however, still much important material in manuscript, including a very early *Sonata in C Minor for Violin & Piano*, composed in Paris in 1951. It is in three movements: the first in a rhapsodic sonata form, the second a set of variations, and the third a quite short rondo-like movement. I had expected a virtuoso piece from the young pianist-composer, but despite its late-romantic language and key signatures, the geometry of mature Humble is already there, and the piano part is in fact surprisingly restrained and linear rather than chordal throughout. The subdivision into shorter sections is also already present. Truly, the child is the father of the man! Some 10 years on (1967), there are the Webernesque *Five Short Pieces for Violin & Piano*. These are still in manuscript but hopefully will be typeset sometime soon. They are tiny pieces of one page each, or less.

Finally, in the instrumental field, we looked at *Trio No. 2* (for violin, clarinet and piano; 1980, revised 1989) and *Trio No. 3* (for flute, percussion and piano, 1985). The second of these works is freer than the first, there are more barless, gesticulatory and colouristic devices, and the piano is generally now a part of the percussion ensemble, joining the vibraphone and marimba in a highly textured work. In the earlier of the two trios, there is a moment when the composer is almost shouting 'look at this, look! This is where all my music comes from!' The clarity of the scoring as well as the play with the intervals in the following example highlights Humble's raw materials.

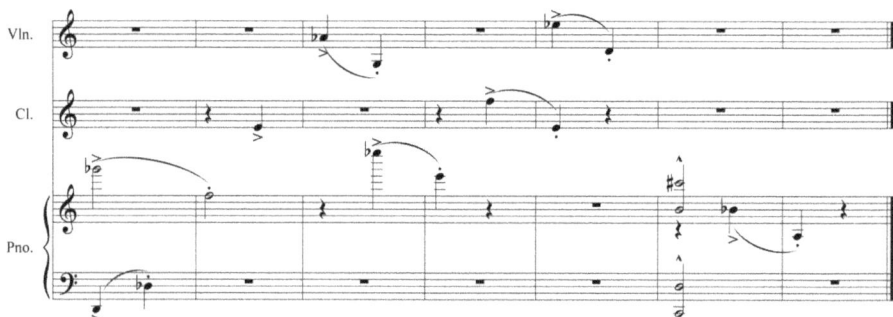

Example 4.12 K. Humble, *Trio No. 2*, mvt 1, bars 147–53

There are some settings for voice and piano as well. In *A Book of Songs of Love & Death*, Humble chose to fragment and separate the vocal and piano parts by putting them, literally, into boxes, thus cleverly avoiding metrical sense altogether.

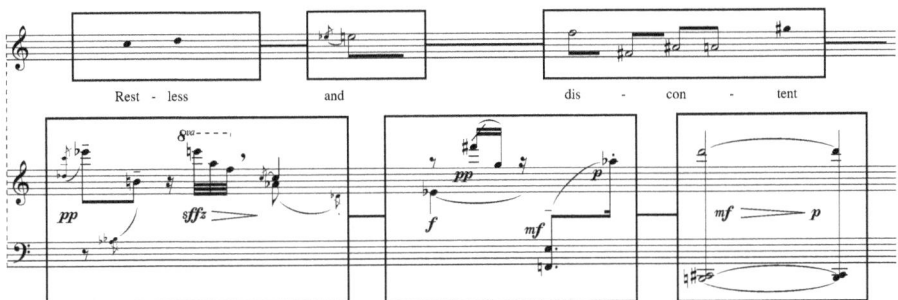

Example 4.13 K. Humble, *A Book of Songs of Love & Death*, opening

The *Songs of Depression*—settings from the Chinese in Arthur Waley's well-known translation—are, like the first cycle, aphoristic in nature. There are eight songs in this Zen-like cycle, and, unlike the earlier-mentioned cycle, these are more conventionally notated; they are also earlier (1955), made while the composer was still in France. From 1970, when the composer was in La Jolla, California, there are three equally short settings: *Trois Poemes d'Amour*.

Keith was fluent in French, and in these three songs he went back to writing for voice/piano in a very free graphic notation, once again avoiding an inference of beat. The piano writing demands considerable agility.

Humble is in the front rank of Australian music of the twentieth century, and each passing year is consolidating his stature.

Peter Tahourdin (1928–2009)

Peter Tahourdin is yet another member of the second generation who passed away recently. I was saddened by his sudden death, as those of us who knew it had always held his music in high esteem. His name implies a French connection, and it seems to me that his music also was marked by a Gallic refinement. The main focus of his work appears to be in large forms, and here, in the chamber music realm, as in the work for solo piano, we find that the output was not huge.

There are two works for violin and piano: *Dialogue* (1971) and *Sonata for Violin and Piano* (2008), which would make the second one of his last compositions. *Dialogue*, in one movement, is a tightly knit piece, with well-defined motifs that are easily grasped and remembered. Although the work moves through a variety of tempi, the thematic unity holds it all together, and there is a clear sense of reprise towards the end. Much of the composition sounds like a slightly demented Prokofiev, with its tendency to spiky figurations and sharp interjections.

Example 4.14 P. Tahourdin, *Dialogue*, bars 14–19

There is a most effective passage in the middle of the piece, when the violin becomes the bass part, and the piano has a soft undercurrent as well as counterpoint—all higher than the violin.

Many years later, the sonata takes up a similar way of treating the two instruments. The sonata is somewhere between a sonata and a sonatina, as the three movements take only 14 minutes to play. More importantly, the texture and mood are light in approach, playing with an elusive tonality, and sometimes coming close to openly stating it, like the very lyrical opening of the second movement, almost in D major. This same middle movement, however, builds and gains in intensity; it is the most substantial part of the sonata, and the short scalar passage in the beginning becomes a long and dramatic sweep of scales in both instruments by the end. The third movement, though, is back to a short and angular language close to *Dialogue* from 30-odd years earlier, although there is a short, slow interlude in the middle.

There are a number of vocal works. *Ern Malley Sequence*, for tenor and piano (2007), uses texts from that wonderful, audacious literary hoax that rocked Australian poetry in mid-century. A funny but relevant thought came into my head when I opened the score: how does one gain permission to set such a text, supposedly by a fictitious author, later revealed to be the work of a group of writers? Who owns the copyright? Did Tahourdin bother with obtaining permission? It is a tantalising question, but on to the music. The cycle is substantial, in that 11 poems, or verses from poems, have been chosen. Since the work is a curiosity, the reader might be interested to know which Ern Malley poems were selected

1. 'Sweet William'
2. 'Durer: Innsbruck, 1495'
3. 'Sonnets for the Novachord (i)'
4. 'Sonnets for the Novachord (ii)'
5. 'Boult to Marina'
6. 'Night Piece'

7. 'Sybilline' (verse 2)

8. 'Perspective Lovesong'

9. 'Young Prince of Tyre' (verse 3)

10. 'Colloquy with John Keats' (verse 1)

11. 'Envoi' (from *Palinode and Petit Testament*).

There is no sense of send-up in Tahourdin's setting of these words; quite the contrary, he treats it very seriously, and, in a sense, this opens the original debate of whether the whole Ern Malley material has literary merit. The piano plays an integral role in the unfolding of the vocal line, and there are strong thematic links between the songs.

There are two more song cycles. *Songs of Love and Fortune* (1992) contains five settings from *Carmina Burana* (absolutely no common ground with Orff!) for baritone and piano. *Chanson Intimes* (1996) has seven settings from Brunin, this time for tenor and piano, and is in French; the *Carmina* settings are in English, although the titles are given in the original Latin. The two collections have much in common in their treatment of text and piano. Tahourdin generally breaks up the text into short fragments, so there is little instance of a long, unfolding melodic line—rather a constant interplay with the piano, sharing motifs, with space between phrases and sentences. The piano part of the Brunin settings is more elaborate, but tends to be single lines unfolding in the hands, whereas the *Carmina* settings occasionally move into chordal accompaniment. There is even a passage with octaves in the piano—a rare occurrence in Tahourdin's music.

Example 4.15 P. Tahourdin, *Songs of Love and Fortune*, bars 15–19

Harold Allen (1930–83)

It is a great pleasure to write a few words here about Harold Allen, a name probably forgotten even among scholars of Australian music. There is a composition prize at the School of Music of the ANU in his name, arranged some years ago, by his son. We found a work written in 1974, and lodged two years later in the National Library of Australia. It is his *Sonata for Clarinet in B-flat and Piano*, in two movements. The composer gives the duration of the work as 12 minutes. The work is in three movements—a 'Poco Allegro', a 'Lento', with a 'Vivace' to conclude—thus following a standard format. Like his handful of known piano pieces, the clarinet sonata is in a kind of Webernian language. It is not strictly 12 tone, although there are 12-tone conglomerates to be found everywhere; but the economy of Webern and the sparse intervallic gestures of the Austrian master are also ever present. A melodic cell favoured by the clarinet of D, E-flat, F and B makes up a kind of theme, and there is a palindromic gesture right at the start of the sonata paying fairly explicit homage to Webern.

Example 4.16 H. Allen, *Sonata for Clarinet in B-flat and Piano*, mvt 1, bars 4–7

The second movement tends to feature dry, repeated and widespread tessitura.

Example 4.17 H. Allen, *Sonata for Clarinet in B-flat and Piano*, mvt 2, letter G, bars 75–80

The last movement begins with a binary-form segment, much like Webern's piano variations in the second movement; the opening featuring the clarinet 'theme' with the piano part is still very sparse indeed. What follows after this is again akin to the Webern variations, third movement, with short, segmented episodes in a more rhapsodic vein, before the opening vivace returns, and the sonata ends in a flamboyant gesture. The clarinet part in the score is very sensibly written at sounding pitch.

The work needs publishing. It is a great pleasure to make a genuine discovery of a worthwhile piece in the course of research, and I commend the work to clarinetists searching for repertoire.

Lawrence Whiffin (1930–)

Lawrence Whiffin (Laurie to his friends) is a composer who unfailingly provides the delightful and unexpected on perusal of his scores. His cycle of 10 short songs *Mots d'heures: gousses, rames*, for soprano and piano, is no exception. The original collection of these short poems (known as *The d'Antin Manuscript*) apparently goes back to Gothic times, but the exact date is problematic. The text is quirky, and even the titles suggest what the composer describes as 'cryptogrammatically ambiguous prose of a Nostredamus'

1. 'Un petit d'un petit'
2. 'Eau la quille ne cole'
3. 'Eh! Dites-le, dites-le'
4. 'Oh, les mots d'heureux bardes'
5. 'Des rois é lus dolmen'
6. 'Et qui rit des curés d'Oc?'
7. 'Jacques s'appré te'
8. 'Pisterre, pisterre'
9. 'Terre, vasé, Korus'
10. 'Lit-elle messe, moffette'.

The settings are appropriately humorous and light, veering somewhere between Satie and Milhaud brought up to date. The composer is obviously enjoying himself setting these strange texts, and he has set the first 10 of the total of 40 extant. The settings constantly hint at or are explicitly tonal, but there is always a twist or a barb somewhere—from the folksy opening to the lurching drunkenness of the second, to the third and fourth mixed together, with some rhythmic recitation. The sixth song leaps all over the piano.

Example 4.18 L. Whiffin, 'Et qui rit des curés d'Oc?', from *Mots d'heures*, bars 1–3

The piano writing can be busy.

Example 4.19 L. Whiffin, 'Et qui rit des curés d'Oc?', from *Mots d'heures*, bars 13–14

The vocal writing is elegant and light. After the tenth song is concluded, the score has: 'TIENS, DE OH! PARDOINE!' Is this meant to be spoken out loud, or is it merely an annotation by the composer?

The other work that we looked at could not be more different. The title page reads '*Red Letter Days, cycles 6a, poetry of Max Richards*'. The settings are for baritone, with flute, oboe, trombone, percussion and electric piano (synthesiser). The keyboard is only an ensemble member here. The text is often vocal sounds rather than actual words. The conductor and other players often have to declaim parts of the text. The baritone often spits out vowels and consonants, as well as singing, rhythmically reciting and doing *Sprechstimme*. In one extraordinary passage, the trombonist joins the singer, using the instrument like a megaphone, while the synthesiser sounds glissandi on a *ondes martenot* setting.

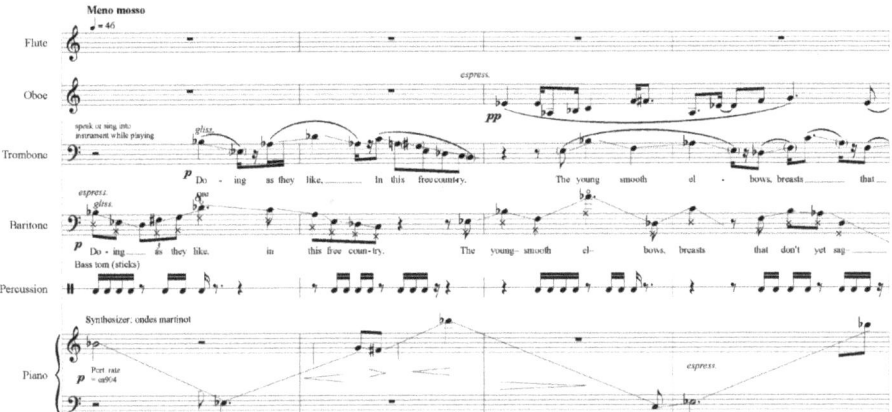

Example 4.20 L. Whiffin, *Red Letter Days*, bars 59–62

This is not only deadly serious, but grim stuff, depicting a harsh urban landscape and everyday realities of life. *Red Letter Days* is not the sort of music that is going to be done often, nor is it to be taken lightly or easily, but it certainly makes a strong statement and should be heard and recorded.

David Lumsdaine (1931–)

A few years ago, David Lumsdaine announced that he was not going to compose any more. He has stuck to his guns in this matter, so we might regard what he has produced to date as definitive and complete.

As David approached the point at which he decided to stop composing, the music—at least judging by what is in front of me in the chamber domain—became more and more mellow. For example, in *A Little Cantata; Tracey Chadwell, in Memoriam* (1996) Lumsdaine, setting his own words, invokes many images from nature, and even names some birds and insects. This parallels his growing and eventually consuming interest in constructing sonic landscapes out of raw material recorded in nature. This short work, for treble recorder, soprano and piano, contains many such insect/bird calls, in response to David's own words.

If we go back roughly 10 years, to 1985, we arrive at *Bagatelles*, for flute/piccolo, clarinet, piano, violin, viola and cello. We find, in the composer's own introduction:

The somewhat surreal landscape of Bagatelles is an exotic litter of fragments of familiar-sounding musical objects in an overgrown garden. Vines, ramblers and tree roots resumed concrete and marble…a mosaic in which no matter what path we take, like Alice in the Garden of Live Flowers, we continually find ourselves approaching that same door by which we went out (in?)?

It seems as though the fascination goes back some little while. The *Bagatelles* vary the combinations constantly: 'Whichever way you hear it, the musical texture is made up of different combinations of solos, duos, trios and quartets. Only for a moment in the middle, and again at the end, does the sextet come together in a tutti.' The composer here makes a somewhat enigmatic statement: 'Oddly enough, those fragments still recognisable come from music whose subject matter is other music. Who heard them first? In what garden? Who is hearing them now?' I do not fully understand what Lumsdaine is saying here, except for the reference to quasi bird calls, which appear here and there.

There are, however, two separate references in this introduction and in the music itself that lead directly to other preoccupations of the composer. The reference to the labyrinth in Alice's garden brings to mind the composer's interest in aleatory structures. We have three such works here. *Kangaroo Hunt* (1972), which was for a while quite well known in Australia, is scored for piano and percussion. The piece consists of nine separate building blocks, with quite complex suggestions as to how the blocks might be used to construct a piece. Considerable freedom is built into the score, and the performers are given a real compositional role as to the final shape.

Easter Fresco (1966, revised 1971), for soprano and ensemble, requires a conductor. The structure is fixed, but much of the score allows instruments to go their own way, at least for the duration of a passage, so that vertical control is at least partially relinquished.

Example 4.21 D. Lumsdaine, *Easter Fresco*, p. 2, system 1

The text used is from the New Testament; even here, there is a garden reference, when Mary mistakes the resurrected Jesus for the gardener!

Caliban Impromptu (1972) adds tape and amplification to the normal piano trio. Into the texture is woven a large slab of the *Schubert Op. 90 No. 1 Impromptu*, unidentified by the composer. The score I have is a facsimile and not easy to read, but David refers to the piano's 'bird-song' in the course of the proceedings. There are quite free sections of ad-lib playing, and it seems as though much of the material is ultimately derived from the Schubert quotation. Here again, the actual sequence of events is controlled, although there are many variables on the way. Is Schubert identified with Caliban? Since the Schubert quotation is only fragmentary at the beginning, and given in full only at the end, this is a kind of variations in reverse, where the raw material is stated at the conclusion.

Many of the techniques described above come together in a major work: *Mandala 3* (1974–78), for flute, clarinet, viola, cello and piano. The movements are

1. 'Transcription of Chorus' from *St Matthew Passion, No. 78*

2. 'Sonata'

3. 'Ruhe sanfte, sanfte ruh', piano solo with reflections.

The structure is quite clear from the above. The first movement is a lovely transcription of the chorus from Bach, with the piano playing rich left-hand octaves, in a Busonian approach to the transcription. Part of the original Bach returns in the last movement, near the end, but without the piano. The second movement calls for the addition of a bell, and is played largely without the piano. The bell probably represents the aspect of meditation tied to a mandala image. The material is clearly derived from the Bach fragment; the piano enters twice with tiny quotations from the Bach original. Finally, in the last movement, the piano comes into its own, as this is essentially an extended and difficult solo, with some soft interpolations from the rest of the ensemble, mostly from the original Bach, or close to it. These dozen or so sections, sometimes with bell, merely offer soft comment to the piano solo. There is a solo piano piece with the same title as the third movement, issued separately by the composer. *Mandala 3* is clearly a very significant piece in the chamber music output of this country. It needs a virtuoso pianist to successfully project the powerful message of this composition.

Hellgart Mahler (1931–)

I need to say a few words here about Hellgart Mahler. We found just two works of hers to peruse: *Isochasm: Trio for violin, cello and piano* and *Skyscapes for Five Players*. The second is really a piece for massed percussion, and the piano just happens to be one of the instruments. The piece itself is colourful and very carefully thought out, just outside the scope of this book. The trio, though, is another matter. Like so much of Mahler's music, here the textures are consistently changing; she generally avoids time changes, and, like Xenakis, manages to write her quite complex music in ordinary time signatures. All of the instruments, however, need to be flexible rhythmically, as well as coping with various extended techniques. The music is restless and not easy to coordinate; the tempo changes are less of a problem. Mahler knows her instruments thoroughly, and the trio, like many of her other pieces, needs to be published and disseminated. Mahler presents a curious case in Australian music. She has made little attempt to gain the limelight and has lived quietly in Tasmania for many years. Some piano pieces made it into print, and have had some circulation, but she is the author of much music, including some large-scale music, and her work is unknown even to her colleagues, let alone the general public. She is another Australian composer who needs to be studied carefully and documented, before the material vanishes, as it has a habit of doing in our country. The piano part of the trio requires some playing directly on the strings, but everything is notated fully and with great attention to detail. But the verdict on Mahler's music cannot be honestly made without some exposure and investigation. All I am saying here is that it seems to me that the effort to do this would be worth it.

Malcolm Williamson (1931–2003)

The second-generation composers from my earlier book are gradually passing away. Malcolm Williamson is yet another who died recently. As I wrote earlier, Malcolm was a complex character with a host of personal demons to contend with on just about every level. I expressed the hope that his story would soon be told and a book on his life and work has recently emerged; I have not had time to read it as yet, although I did contribute to it. Williamson's contribution to chamber music with piano was, as one would expect, extensive. A highly literate and well-read man, he wrote songs as well as operas.

Celebration of Divine Love, for high voice and piano, is noteworthy because here Malcolm uses words by an Australian poet. He always defended his Australian identity and claimed, perfectly correctly, that one could be an Australian composer without resorting to the obvious such as didgeridoos and the like.

James McAuley, whose words are set in this work, would no doubt agree, as he was himself magisterially aloof from such nonsense. The work in question extends over some 26 pages and is therefore a concert aria, with a most important piano part. At first, the partners announce themselves separately: there is a virtuosic piano introduction, followed by quite a long unaccompanied passage, before the two finally get together. At that point, some of Malcolm's favourite devices emerge. Cross-rhythms are a favourite technique.

Example 4.22 M. Williamson, *Celebration of Divine Love*, bars 31–4, 'Andante', p. 3, bars 1–4

Williamson allows his music to drive this idea for a significant part of the aria. The same fragment shows him building harmony using fourths, which appeals to his pianistic, as well as compositional, aesthetic. Bitonality, arrived at by the use of simple juxtaposition of pianistic triadic chords, is another trademark.

Example 4.23 M. Williamson, *Celebration of Divine Love*, 'Lento', p. 13, bars 3–6

This is a powerful work, the result of two major creative figures, both with somewhat tortured and convoluted attitudes to religion and dogma.

Malcolm also felt at home with miniatures, and in *From a Child's Garden*, after Robert Louis Stevenson, he sets 12 of these charming verses in a quasi-tonal way. By this I mean that, although the songs have key signatures, and the vocal line is mostly tonal, there is a certain deliberate blurring of tonality, due mostly to the piano part shifting away from the established tonality, via bitonality, or groups of minor and major seconds. Amusingly, the ninth song, 'From a Railway Carriage', is in 7/8—so the carriage lurches somewhat!

'Hasselbacher's Scena', from the opera *Our Man in Havana*, after the famous novel by Graham Greene, is Williamson's reduction for piano and voice from the orchestral score. Although a highly dramatic and effective point in the opera, the moment is not done justice by the piano reduction, and the piano 'rumbles'—though necessary for the reduction—lend a somewhat melodramatic colouring to this scene.

The *North Country Songs* are very much part of the English tradition of serious art composers arranging folk songs. Williamson would certainly have been aware of this from his mentor Eugene Goossens, as well as the already established tradition at the Conservatorium of Music in Sydney of such settings by composers such as Burnard and others stemming from the English school. These four short settings make an effective recital group, although the piano part is not routine 'accompaniment' by any means.

The *Piano Trio* (in memory of Sir Arthur Bliss) is a work in three movements: slow, fast, slow. The last movement is explicitly marked 'Lament'. Much of the trio has key signatures assigned; but given Williamson's natural propensity for tonal instability leading to chromaticism, the key signatures often result in many accidental signs and naturals, which would otherwise be unnecessary. Still, obviously Malcolm felt that passages had key centres, or at least began in some key. The problem of notation in such situations has no easy solution. The outer movements are deeply felt, the first using the piano in a linear way, thus resulting in four moving voices, whilst in the last movement, the keyboard is more a chordal function. The middle movement is a jaunty interplay between 3/4 and 6/8, with perhaps some reference within it to some of Bliss's own music. I liked the trio very much.

We also found a short piece for clarinet and piano called *Pas de Deux*. Perhaps there is a balletic connotation? This short piece in a clear A-flat major consists simply of a melodic line in the clarinet and arpeggios in the piano. The piano takes the tune once, with counterpoint in the clarinet.

We would not have bothered with this piece in its duo guise, but for the fact that it reappears in a much bigger and ambitious piece for winds and piano: *Pas de Quatre*, for wind quartet and piano.

The structure of the work merits notice

1. 'Allegro Vivace', scored for the full ensemble
2. an 'Andante' link goes to 'Variation A', for flute and piano
3. 'Pas de Trois', for bassoon and piano
4. 'Variation B', for flute, oboe and bassoon
5. short link to 'Pas de Deux', for clarinet and piano; this is the movement also published separately
6. 'Adagio' link to 'Coda'.

There is obvious symmetry that emerges from this scheme, as well as variety of scoring. Williamson ensures thematic continuity between movements; the principal theme is a driving, energetic figure in fourths, a little reminiscent of Hindemith. Some movements have key signatures. The 'Coda' is the fastest movement and has a brilliant, loud ending, with a final reference to the theme. I make reference to the key signature issue again, because it seems to me to be a part of Malcolm's versatility as well as musical ambiguity; in the long run, it is quite possible that it contributed to his personal angst.

Quintet for Piano and Strings is a different animal altogether. Where the wind quintet was energetic with a balletic connotation, and generally high spirited, the quintet with strings is a huge, often sombre work, with a score of 68 pages. The level of detailed craftsmanship is high, and the whole has obviously been most carefully notated and considered. The first movement is an adagio, full of eerie harmonics; this serves as a kind of introduction to the second movement, which is really a substantial allegro—the heart of the whole quintet. This is largely a perpetual motion of unceasing semiquavers, and a turbulent, heaving feel often made up of fast, undulating scales. The contrasting worked idea is a more angular and violent one, with the piano predominant and strings either holding pedal tones or abruptly commenting on the piano gestures.

Example 4.24 M. Williamson, *Quintet for Piano and Strings*, mvt 2, six bars after letter G (pp. 17–18)

Eventually and inevitably, the two thematic groups are combined in varying fashion, with the scalar idea triumphant at the end. The last movement returns to the mood of the first. This is Williamson at his best; the work was written in the late 1960s, when it seemed that everything was possible to this composer. Malcolm played the piano part himself and there used to be a fine recording on the Argo LP label. Whether this is now available is unknown.

There also is music for piano, wind and strings—notably, the *Serenade for Flute, Violin, Viola, Cello and Piano*, also written in the 1960s. It was commissioned by the Australian flautist Douglas Whittaker, who came back from England soon after to take up an appointment at the School of Music in Canberra; sadly, he died soon after arriving here. The pianist at the premiere was another personal connection: the Australian Geoffrey Parsons, pupil of Winifred Burston (also my teacher) at the Sydney Conservatorium. This is a much lighter work than the quintet. The titles of the movements suggest the kind of music that we can expect: I) 'Puppet Theatre'; II) 'The Doll Left in the Rain'; III) 'Carousel'. As to be expected, the composition features the flute, and would have allowed full reign to Whittaker's virtuosity.

Finally, the *Variations for Violoncello and Piano*, also from Malcolm's 'golden age' of the 1960s. This is a genuine duet between the two instruments, consisting of an 'Introduction' (really a first variation on the not-so-far-heard theme), an 'Andante Theme' followed by nine variations. The material is abrupt, angular, almost Webernesque.

Example 4.25 M. Williamson, *Variations for Violoncello and Piano*, bars 1–4

The variations are terse and to the point, with the last variations acting as a serene coda. Like so much of Malcolm's music, this has disappeared off the radar. It is to be hoped that Williamson's undoubted place in Australian music can somehow now be reinstated. We do not have so much quality music that we can afford to jettison this composer.

Richard Meale (1932–2009)

Richard Meale died just a few days before I sat down to write about him, so it might be appropriate to say a few general things about his habits as a composer, for I had known him since 1951, when we met at the NSW State Conservatorium of Music, where we were both students of the legendary Winifred Burston. Richard had already begun composing as a student and showed early promise. There were already pronounced traits in his approach to composing a piece. He seemed to need opportunities to talk about the still-embryonic piece at great length, theorising about it in every possible way, often before a bar was composed. He had a most lucid mind and clarity of expression; however, this method of bouncing ideas off whoever was available among his friends did not actually produce a quicker result; indeed it often slowed the project to a topic to be discussed. Quite often, too, the first bars never progressed anywhere, and he certainly had far more beginnings than endings. This characteristic persisted throughout his life and he became well known for his inability to meet a professional deadline, or even complete a work. I hasten to add that of course there are many complete pieces, often with a very fine finish. He realised himself that he had this attitude to composition and, in a phone call late in his life, he said to me that he now understood that he was an amateur at heart, using the word in its best sense; and in a way, he was right. On another occasion, he confessed to me that he was running dry and was devoid of ideas, which was something that I never thought to hear from him; but many composers such as Sibelius and Bax, for example—both admired by Meale—dried up. The rate of works, later in Meale's life, certainly slowed to a trickle and eventually dried up.

Richard had too much pride as a composer to rework old pieces (it would have bored him to tears), or to revert to a used methodology; silence was preferable as an option. He continued reading philosophy to the end of his life and his enthusiasms were transferred to this new field of interest. Looking back over his output, it is clear that he was swayed by the currents and eddies of fashion, either his own personal passion or something that struck him from elsewhere in the musical world; there are very few works that demonstrate a developing trend; rather a succession of sudden stylistic changes followed by abrupt stops and new beginnings. The musical profession was especially puzzled when he suddenly reverted back to a neo-romantic language: was this a yearning for his lost youth, or yet another start? We do live in a free world, of course, here in Australia, and although there might be a kind of musical mafia and trend-setters, I rather suspect that Meale looking backwards was another example of him tiring of a way of expression and attempting something that was new for him. The one constant factor in his output was an infallible sense of colour, which is there for all to see in his orchestral music, and to a lesser extent in his smaller works. Some songs and violin/piano pieces from his younger years now appear to be lost, as he was not good at looking after his own manuscripts. For example, I recall a piece for violin and piano entitled *Mosaic*, which was written for his then fellow student Stan Ritchie, who went on to become the leader of the Metropolitan Opera Orchestra. Stan and I premiered the work in what was then called 'Diploma Class' in front of Sir Eugene Goossens, who received the new work with some warmth. During some of Meale's personal moves, the manuscript seems to have vanished, along with some vocal music and some other material, such as the *Flute Concerto* written for Peter Richardson. An equally early *Rhapsody for Violin and Piano* from 1950 (according to a recent typesetting of the work) has survived: a substantial one-movement essay with thematic material full of fourths and fifths, recalling Hindemith, who was an early preoccupation, even aping his *Tierce de Picardie* arrivals in cadential gestures. Meale is an interesting figure in Australian music, tinged with tragedy; those who knew him on a personal level have long recognised that he did not fulfil his own potential.

The piano was his instrument, and he composed at it. As a performer, he was severely limited by being double-jointed, which meant a huge physical effort to produce a sound; nevertheless, he was at home at the keyboard and understood it well.

I have before me his very early *Divertimento for Violin, Cello and Piano*. The manuscript has no date, but this is obviously an early work from the 1950s; I would hazard a guess at 1952 or 1953. Indeed, if my memory serves me correctly, it was composed for a birthday party held at Richard's residence in Marrickville in Sydney. Quite a few fellow students were present, and the work was played through on this occasion. The clean piano and string writing, with crisp rhythms that are nevertheless always alive and taking unexpected twists and turns, are very typical of the early Meale style, as is the strong arrival on tonal centres. The European avant-garde was yet to impinge on Richard's consciousness, and there was little or no information easily available to music students. The work is in a fairly conventional layout of movements: 'Tempo Giusto-Deciso'; 'Adagio Tranquillo'; 'Scherzo', 'Trio' (tranquillo), 'Scherzo'; then a short reference to the opening of the work (only six bars), entitled 'Reprise', moving into the last movement, which is a set of 'Variations on a German Folk-Tune'. The tune is a modal melody, followed by six variations, featuring different instruments and added counterpoint, as well as a controlled accelerando to a flashy ending. The world that this composition inhabits is that of Martinu, Hindemith and maybe even Vaughan Williams—all early preoccupations of the composer. The slightly humorous play with form—that is, the short reference to the opening of the work in the 'Reprise', followed abruptly by the 'Variations' section, is similar to a gesture employed in his solo piano work *Sonatina Patetica* from the same period.

The first work that shifted gear into a new mode was the *Sonata for Flute and Piano* (1960). I met Richard in San Francisco at about the time he wrote this piece. I was there studying with Egon Petri, he was in transit to some university on a special visiting scholarship; we went to a pizza place, I remember, and he startled me by declaring that Elvis Presley was a great singer. It was a point of view that I had not expected from him, since there had been no obvious interest in the newly emerging rock scene at the time; as well, it seemed a huge leap from what I thought were our common interests. But it is quite evident in the flute sonata that obsessive repeated patterns and rhythms from rock music are present, especially towards the end of the piece. The other very pervasive presence is that of Messiaen. The repeated notes, asymmetric rhythms and trills could be straight from one of Messiaen's bird-inspired works, such as the piano solo opening the fourth movement.

Example 4.26 R. Meale, *Sonata for Flute and Piano*, mvt 4, bars 4–8

Strongly accented, compulsively repetitive bass chords are another feature. Meale had obviously studied the Messiaen writings on his own technique and the sonata is also full of controlled increasing and decreasing durations. Curiously, the repetitions (both literal and gradually embellished by playing with durations, or by the additions of new pitches into the gestures)—whether from rock and roll or from Messiaen—seem to work together within the sonata, despite the disparate origins. But what seems to concern Meale the most here is the tension between strict notation and freedom of flow. He tackles this problem in a few ways in the score—not always successfully, although the prefatory notes to the score try to stress that he wants flexibility of phrasing to be coupled with observance of durations. But if you ask the players to count semiquavers strictly, it is close to wishful thinking to also demand that 'it must not sound rigid'. Sometimes, the bar lines in the two parts do not coincide—another attempt at what is described above, and probably with equally ambiguous results. But, in the hands of virtuoso performers, the sonata has undeniable raw power and impact.

Example 4.27 R. Meale, *Sonata for Flute and Piano*, mvt 4, bars 26–8

This wrestling with control versus freedom is explored in a different way in *Las Alboradas*, for flute, violin, horn and piano. Meale has moved on from Messiaen to Boulez. The fully written-out sections certainly look, feel and sound like the heavily systemised Boulez of that time (the mid-1960s). This flirting with the world of serialism—very much a fashion of its day, and now sounding a little tired—is accompanied by another type of writing, allowing the composer to extend his search for control and freedom simultaneously. The work has two large sections of totally free, unbarred fragments, with the players given various choices embedded into the score. Although only a quartet, *Las Alboradas* actually requires a conductor to have some overall supervision over all the free sections, and the introduction to the score has a full page of instructions as to what the conductor needs to do. It was at about this historical period that the American writer Edward Cone suggested somewhere that there should be formed a Society for the Performance of Twentieth-Century Music Program Notes; Cone's argument was that quite often the notes were the most interesting part of the score! The compulsory long-winded prefaces to scores, as well as the trendy notations of free-floating fragments and aleatory structures (which interested composers such as Boulez and many others), are all present here, as are the constant time changes, with the usual profusion of triplets and quintuplets. The work brought much attention to itself, and was possibly the first of its type by one of our major composers. Whether it has worn well is still an open question.

Example 4.28 R. Meale, *Las Alboradas*, bars 41–3

The French obsession probably reached its peak with Meale's writing of *Incredible Floridas*—a powerful work inspired by Rimbaud. The ensemble is fairly large, and the role of the piano is consequently minimised—in general, we have avoided writing about such works, applying a roughly numerical consideration to keep the number of scores considered under some restriction. My memory of playing this piece—which certainly needs a conductor, and is a kind of chamber symphony—is that the keyboard part fulfils a sort of continuo role, filling in and adding to the chordal progressions, or acting as a member of the percussion section. The recitation of French text by the ensemble, required by the composer, is generally somewhat of an embarrassment, given the Australian accent and most players' non-acquaintance with the French language.

Meale recognised the regressive qualities in his very late output, and the title *Palimpsest* (1998) must have been chosen very deliberately, signifying a kind of 'overwriting' on an old manuscript. Scored for flute, clarinet, violin, cello, vibraphone/marimba and piano, this chamber work, too, requires a conductor. Despite the beauty of the scoring and the general mastery over the sounds themselves, I must confess, however, that I found myself puzzling over the sheer necessity of writing a piece that would sit comfortably in the nineteenth century. The piano part, yet again, is somewhat like a romantic continuo and is full of tonal arpeggio patterns, over which the melodic lines are 'overlaid'. There is a flash of the old fire in a dance movement, but on the whole, the slow repetitions of arpeggios in the piano part bespeak a resigned world-weariness.

Donald Hollier (1934–)

Donald Hollier is a flamboyant figure in Australian music; I have written about him at some length in *Australian Piano Music of the Twentieth Century*. I might say here that, speaking generally, instrumental chamber music is not Donald's natural world of expression; he is far more at home in the world of opera (he has written an impressive number of them), and large-scale choral works, often with multiple choirs and large instrumental forces accompanying them. Needless to say, in today's timid world of music making, Hollier's extravagant scores are unlikely to be programmed; apart from the great expense, the content of these large works can also be confronting or controversial. Hollier is a brilliant organist and pianist, and much of his background has, therefore, strong connections with the world of church music as well as the secular world of the concert platform. He has also proved himself to be an inspiring producer and director of operas, ancient and modern. But paradox is part of the Hollier make-up and, coupled with the musical extrovert, there is also a rather private person. Over the years, far from seeking the limelight, Donald Hollier has, seemingly deliberately, withdrawn into a personal world. This has happened gradually, starting with a departure from academic teaching (he was an outstanding lecturer at the School of Music at The Australian National University), then more and more from public concert appearances, whether as organist, pianist or conductor, and constantly loosening previous links with the personnel of the music world. He then began to spend large amounts of time in hideouts in Greece and Wales, all the time incessantly composing. A man with a lesser will would have by now dried up or given up. Very few of us have the moral strength to create in a vacuum; but Hollier has continued to produce. He said to me once that not having to worry about seeking performances or self-promotion had in fact given him the utmost freedom; he answers to one, and can allow his imagination totally free flight, since practical considerations are simply not part of the equation.

As one work is completed, it is put into a desk drawer somewhere, and the next work commenced. The scores themselves are quite often oversized, and storage and preservation are ongoing problems. It is my hope that one of our State or national libraries will seek him out and archive what must by now be a formidable amount of material. The oversized physicality of the music is not just the product of utilising massive forces; quite a few works for smaller forces, even some of the solo piano works, are on large sheets. Donald often rules his own lines where he wants them, since various aleatory elements are often at play, so the scores have arrows and blocks involving choices and possibilities.

Due to his preferences, and once one takes away the solo piano and organ music, as well as the many operas and choral blockbusters, there is less left than one would perhaps expect. Because Hollier has worked with singers all his life, most of his music that falls within the scope of the present book is in fact song settings for voice and piano. The piano part is always composed with the composer's obvious presence at the keyboard.

Thus, the very early *Sonata for Trombone and Piano* (1953) commences with an authoritative declaration by the composer at the keyboard.

Example 4.29 D. Hollier, *Sonata for Trombone and Piano*, bars 1–2

The style of piano writing has stayed with Hollier ever since those early years. Hollier played the work with the dedicatee Ronald Smart (who became Director of the Conservatorium in Sydney) in what was called Diploma Class, with Eugene Goossens presiding. It must have been a nerve-racking experience for the young composer, but Goossens praised the work and congratulated the performers. I remember the afternoon vividly, because premieres of works by students were unusual—composition was not formally offered by the institution at that time. Donald was always something of an Anglophile, and much of the work has a cast reminiscent of Vaughan Williams in the parallel triads.

Example 4.30 D. Hollier, *Sonata for Trombone and Piano*, bars 3–4

The sonata is in the traditional four movements: a rather grandiose 'Allegro', a concise 'Adagio' and 'Scherzo', and a quasi–perpetual-motion finale, with a cadenza for the trombone. The work brims with confidence, and should finally be published.

The many song settings from later years encapsulate in miniature the characteristic's of Hollier's music in general. Thus, if one opens the score *of Five Songs to Poems of Christopher Brennan for Soprano Voice with Piano* (the score is dated 13 June 1976), the first event is a silent pressing of a chord locked with the third pedal. The piano writing is florid and quite often rhythmically free from the vocal line, which in itself is rhapsodic and difficult.

Example 4.31 D. Hollier, *Five Songs to Poems of Christopher Brennan*, 'Song 1', stave 3, p. 3

The piano has frequent and virtuosic outbursts in the whole cycle. Hollier's use of the piano has links with European art song, but has pushed the role of the piano well beyond setting the mood. It is not just an equal, but is often the dominant partner in the music.

The five settings are

1. 'Was it the Sun, that Broke My Dreams' (1896)
2. 'Scant Majesty of Stars'
3. 'O White Wind' (1906)
4. 'O Mother'
5. 'Sweet Silence after Bells' (1913).

Brennan's poetry is, of course, highly dramatic, vivid and eminently settable. There is a note on the score that alludes to a Christopher Brennan album consisting of 20 songs in all, for soprano, alto, tenor and bass, with piano.

One of the songs from the soprano album uses a quasi-blues style. The flirting with popular music occurs now and then in this composer's output. For example, in *Sonnets Book 4, A little blue music for male voice and ensemble* (which comprises alto saxophone, piano—doubling harmonium or synthesiser—percussion and strings, either orchestra or string quartet), the composer asks for a 'blue movie' to be shown during the performance of the songs, specially created from the poems. Since some of the poems have a rather liberal use of various four-letter words as well as explicit descriptions of sex acts, what Hollier wishes for is probably a porn movie using Allen Ginsberg's text. Whether this has ever been performed is doubtful. In a fairly large ensemble, the piano is less important, but it is nevertheless ever-present as well as assertive in its part.

But to return to the Brennan settings, which form an important part of the Australian repertoire for voice and piano: the *Six Songs to Poems of Christopher Brennan for Baritone or Mezzo-Soprano and Piano* (1998) use the following texts

1. 'The Banners of the King'
2. 'Disaster Drives the Shatter'd Night'
3. 'Dead Starts'
4. 'But on the Zenith'
5. 'Pale Absence of the Ruin'd Rose'
6. 'Fairy Tales'.

The pianist is asked to sweep across the strings with a plastic plectrum, as well as to play various clusters. Donald could always do the 'insides' of the piano without moving from his seat, as he has very long arms and is very tall to boot. Some of us lesser mortals have to get off the piano stool and grope under the piano lid in a fairly undignified manner, but he always brought off these effects with simple aplomb. There are aspects of the score that are unclear: a few small cues marked 'Vla' or 'Vln', as well as the puzzling instruction to wedge (lock with third pedal?) 27 different keys between the second and third song. It is unclear how this can be done without drastically interrupting the performance; even with the participation of the page-turner, one would still run out of fingers!

Nigel Butterley (1935–)

When I opened the Nigel Butterley folder to view what we had found, the first thing that sprang to my attention was the song cycle *Child in Nature*—a set of seven songs. What we have now is a lovely typeset edition from Wirripang, issued in 2008. But way back in the dim 1950s, I had played this cycle from Nigel's own hand; it was in San Francisco, where I was studying with Egon Petri, and had arranged a concert of Australian music at the conservatory. One of the items was this song cycle, and it was very well received; so the score brought back a flood of memories. We performed the cycle a number of times in the Bay Area—a beautiful part of the world. The song titles might give some idea of Butterley's relationship with nature

Australian Chamber Music with Piano

1. 'The Child'
2. 'The Bird'
3. 'Brown Jack'
4. 'Spider's Web'
5. 'The Cricket'
6. 'The Wind and the Song'
7. 'A Dark Glow about Me'.

The words, by Robin Gurr, are anything but sentimental. Nature, to the poet, and perhaps more importantly, to the composer, is not about feeling warm and fuzzy. Butterley's relationship with nature, and with the world in general, is mystically inclined. His music is driven by this attitude, and he has said that the world would be a much bleaker and poorer place without man's mystical sensibilities. Whether announced openly in the title or not, Nigel's music is contemplative and lyrical. In this cycle, both the vocal and the piano writing are marked by refinement and transparency; everything is reined in, rather than proclaimed loudly.

Butterley's choices of poetry for setting and inspiration are also indicative of his approach: Walt Whitman, William Blake, Kathleen Raine, the Dead Sea Scrolls, Thomas Traherne, to name the ones I am aware of.

Child in Nature is one of Butterley's first steps in a long evolution, heading towards a complex chromatic language, somewhat akin to that of Michael Tippett. But in Nigel's textures, everything is clear and clean. Take, as example, his setting of *Frogs* by Emily Dickinson.

Example 4.32 N. Butterley, *Frogs*, bars 1–3

At the end of the song, Dickinson's words reveal something about Butterley's own attitude to the outside world: 'I'm nobody! Who are you? Are you Nobody too? Then there's the pair of us? Don't tell! They'd advertise you know! How dreary to be somebody! How public like a Frog, to tell one's name the livelong June, to an admiring Bog!'

The choice of words also reveals a sense of humour, the presence of which I can personally attest, but which is clearly perceivable in another set of seven pieces, this time for flute and piano, named *Conversation Pieces*. These are obviously lighthearted, and akin to teaching material. The titles again say it all

1. 'Let's Decide'
2. 'I Can't Get a Word in Edgeways'
3. 'Secrets'
4. 'Listening'
5. 'A Foreign Language'
6. 'Phoning a Friend'
7. 'Making Plans'.

The music wittily follows the idea behind the title, and uses some modernist compositional techniques in the process.

In a more serious vein, also for flute and piano, is *Evanston Song* (1978), which explores the acoustic idea of the wind instrument playing into the open grand piano, with the pedal depressed, thus creating an echo-chamber effect. The piano part is mostly single-line counterpoint to the flute.

Example 4.33 N. Butterley, *Evanston Song*, bars 23–5

The two large-scale pieces for solo instrument and piano are *Forest I for Viola and Piano* (1990) and *Forest II for Trumpet and Piano* (1993). In the trumpet/piano piece, much of the solo part is concerned with the development and growth of a very simple cell, which can be seen to start the process right at the opening. As well, the harmonic world of the piano part is heard at the very opening so that much of the chordal writing (not usual with Butterley) is based on the octave and third sound superimposed on the two hands. The piano also, later, moves into the more normal Butterley approach of contrapuntal lines, which become woven with the octave and a third sonority. As always with Nigel's music, what is occurring is very clear: the counterpoint in any one part tends to be most active when the other part is quiescent. The language in this work is remarkably consistent.

Example 4.34 N. Butterley, *Forest II*, bars 1–3

Both of the *Forest* pieces fill much-needed gaps in the trumpet and viola repertoire. The viola piece is the larger of the two, written for Simon Oswell, the well-known Australian viola player. Both instruments are treated in a virtuosic manner, with plenty of exciting double-stopping for the viola.

Example 4.35 N. Butterley, *Forest I*, bars 57–61

The use of the piano as a single-line instrument—so characteristic of the Butterley approach—is used with great effect in some of the soft, more eerie moments of the piece, especially in one passage where the two instruments are rhythmically together, but not playing unisons.

Example 4.36 N. Butterley, *Forest I*, bars 71–2

Finally, we also unearthed the rehearsal copy of a concert aria, *The Owl* (words by James MacDonald); this is in Nigel's hand, but I am uncertain whether it is meant for public performance as a soprano/piano setting. I am unfamiliar with the full score, but it is an obviously substantial piece, and my guess is that it requires instrumental colour to succeed in public performance. What we have here is purely utilitarian, although it fits the piano quite well.

Helen Gifford (1935–)

Unfortunately, we have only two works by Helen Gifford in our overview. This is a matter of personal regret to me, because I regard Helen as one of our genuine composers, with always something interesting to say, as well as with a sense of direction and evolution. Her scores are highly crafted and the two mentioned here are no exceptions. The first, *Fantasy*, for flute and piano, is an early work going back to 1958. Helen describes her music of this time as her 'French period'. This is not a serious remark, but there is truth in it. The figurations and ornaments do have something of the world of the heavyweights Debussy and Ravel as well as the lighter weights Satie and Françaix embodied in them. There are strong thematic links throughout the work, and, to my ears, the piano part is begging to be scored for a small ensemble. The mood is captured right at the opening.

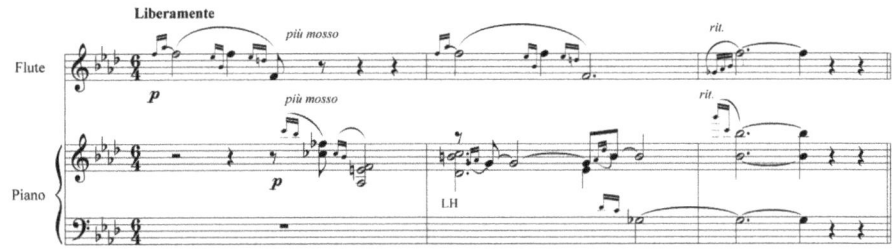

Example 4.37 H. Gifford, *Fantasy*, mvt 1, bars 1–3

The first movement still uses key signatures abandoned or deemed unnecessary in the second and third parts. The flautist enjoys a cadenza in the second movement, and then the third begins with a sweep of colour.

Example 4.38 H. Gifford, *Fantasy*, mvt 3, bars 1–3

Time and Time Again was written one-quarter of a century on. It was composed for the Seymour Group, which for a time held an important place in performing new Australian music. The ensemble here is flute, clarinet, large suspended cymbal, maracas, vibraphone, piano and cello. This is how Gifford lists the ensemble on the score, and it is how the score is laid out. The piano is really merely a member of the percussion line-up in this work, and is treated as such. The composition consists largely of layered ostinatos and repeated patterns, achieving some lovely sonorities through the interplay of these mostly repeated patterns. As in the *Fantasy*, here Helen declares her hand right from the start.

Example 4.39 H. Gifford, *Time and Time Again*, bars 1–12

The title, of course, is hinting at the nature of the composition. Helen Gifford is primarily a composer for the theatre, and probably regards herself as such, hence the relatively few chamber works. Both of these do display theatrical flair, directness and immediacy.

Derek Strahan (1935–)

It is always interesting to write something about Derek Strahan, for here is a composer who is, one might say, obsessed with the legend of Atlantis, and a huge part of his output is directed at exploring aspects or specific events of that legend. So, if one opens the score of *Atlantis, A work for Flute/Alto Flute & Piano* (1991–94), one is first faced with the famous quote from Plato, in which most of our legend is embedded. The composer then says:

'ATLANTIS' is the first of a series of projected smaller scale works which are preparatory to the composing of a cycle of operas on the topic of Atlantis. Thematic material and leitmotifs are introduced and their structural potential explored. 'ATLANTIS' is a 3-part work further subdivided into 13 sections. The notes which follow give programmatic references for each section and indicate how these influence and determine the thematic and structural nature of the music.

So far, so good. What follows next is a detailed 'explanation' of each piece. For instance, the first is named 'Dolphin's Ridge'. The composer gives the geographical location for this site, then goes on to explain that the area is prone to volcanic activity, which mythology would have us believe was in the province of the god Poseidon, who wielded a trident and was reputed to have been the first ruler of Atlantis. If we look further, we find a page of leitmotifs of a few bars each, 11 in all. Each leitmotif has a title; thus we find 'Poseidon', 'Trident', 'Atlantis', 'Atlas', 'Pan', and so on.

When we open the actual score, we immediately find the 'Trident' motif, rumbling away in the bass, presumably suggesting the beginning of an earthquake, or even *the* earthquake; the flute, meanwhile, announces the 'Poseidon' theme. The movement then goes on, using other themes—always labelled—and even describing specific events, such as 'Eruption 1882'. In other words, the music is driven to some extent by an internal program; the composer obviously feels that this kind of information is important, otherwise, why divulge it? He even provides a short bibliography on Atlantis at the end of his introductory essay.

What interests me (as I, too, often use mythology as a springboard for new music) is the dilemma, which can be posed in a series of questions.

- Does the labelling of themes improve our understanding of the work?
- Could it be that it in fact colours our understanding (positively or negatively)?
- Is this what Strahan is after?
- Does the title of a theme make it mean exactly that to the listener?

- Does the music make sense without the 'calling cards' being paraded in front us?
- Is the 'program' driving the music?
- Is there self-sufficiency in the music of the themes and in their contrapuntal combinations as well as in their own evolution?

These are all vital questions for both the listener and the composer. I am not being original in posing them, as the argument has been with us for a long time. My personal view is that the sound has to be coherent on its own. If one needs an 'explanation' of the music, without which it might falter, the composer has failed. Having said all that, I do not believe that Strahan has failed. He displays impressive technique and control over his raw material, whatever the raw material might mean to him. In an opera, the motivic ideas would be accompanied by visual information and action, giving the composer's view of 'meaning' some immediate, quasi-Wagnerian result. The abstract 'pure' music needs more exposure before some critical judgment can be expressed. The language can sometimes be surprisingly tonal, with long pedal notes, indeed invoking some association with Wagner. Here, for example, is a depiction of what Starahan calls 'New Island'—presumably volcanoes pushing land up and out of the water.

Example 4.40 D. Strahan, *Atlantis*, bars 75–7

The music is painted with broad strokes and would certainly lend itself to dramatic or cinematic use. Later in the piece, this note from the composer precedes a flute cadenza:

The following scene takes place between two lovers. The setting is the terrace balcony of a white Arcadian villa on the coast of Atlantis. It is a bright, moonlit night, the air is warm, and the sea is calm. The lovers, locked in each others' arms, embrace as they gaze out at the expanse of the Atlantic Ocean.

It probably takes longer to read the description than to play the music. If the composer's inner eye sees his Atlantis scenes with such clarity of detail then perhaps it is indeed apt to be proceeding towards an opera. Large slabs of the score are extremely tonal, even with key signature, but most of it is in a free rhapsodic style. It ends with triumphant restatements of thematic materials, marked 'The Golden Age'.

A related work is also for flute and piano, but now with the addition of a vocal part. *Eden in Atlantis* is, in effect, a massive concert aria (63 pages), composed in 1996. The score heading says 'Music and Libretto by Derek Strahan', so this could very well be an actual part of the projected operatic cycle. Now, it is easier to see how the words shape the music. Being part of the Atlantis project, the thematic materials are already familiar from the earlier work and, I would hazard a guess, are common material to all the related Atlantis pieces and possibly the forthcoming operas too. The piano and flute seem to suggest a larger orchestra yet to come, and much of the music is word painting in a polystylistic manner, sometimes even verging on Hollywood clichés. The vocal line is often delivered in parlando fashion, and the music contains many long pedal passages with figurations and melody floating above. There are echoes of Wagner, Liszt, Scriabin and the French impressionists. There is a flute cadenza similar to the earlier work. Playing through it at the piano, I feel it is begging to be orchestrated, and perhaps this version is a transitional stage of the aria. There is another large-scale vocal work, a song cycle entitled *Rose of the Bay, A song cycle about Sydney* (1986). I found it far less interesting, with the subject matter prosaic and thus less inspiring. I do not know the timing, but the score is 135 pages!

Escorts, Trio for Piano, Alto Saxophone & Flute is another programmatic work, clearly driven by a story-line. The movement names make it clear: 'The Quarrel'; 'Rough Trade'; 'The Tourist'; 'The Chauvanist'; 'The Reconciliation'. Much of this piece is controlled by varying the subdivisions of long beats in different ways, playing off these fractions one against the other.

There are two works involving clarinet: *Trespassers Will Be Prosecuted*, a short, frenetic piece written in telegraphic style, and *Voodoo Fire, Trio for Clarinet, Percussion and Keyboard(s)* (1995). Having recently composed a piece myself relating to voodoo ceremony, I was naturally curious to look at this work in three movements. The trio is, however, really outside the province of this book, as it asks for electric piano and the composer states in the score that he imagines the keyboard part as a 'tuned percussion instrument', and the various presets include brass sounds. The work is dedicated to the Australian virtuoso Alan Vivian.

Australian Chamber Music with Piano

Jennifer Fowler (1939–)

Jennifer Fowler, like David Lumsdaine, has spent most of her working life in England, and, although known as an Australian, she has not been an active participant in Australian musical life. Her attitude to the piano is well known (see my *Australian Piano Music*) and is quite naturally manifest in her chamber music. Quite by chance, her small collection of scores for my perusal also contained a song cycle, *And Ever Shall Be* (1989), for mezzo-soprano and eight instruments (flute, oboe, clarinet, trombone, percussion, violin, viola and cello). I looked at it, although there was no piano, simply to reacquaint myself with her linear, controlled, contrapuntal style of writing; there was a valuable lesson to be learnt from looking at this score (see below).

We found three works with piano. *Invocation to the Veiled Mysteries* (1982) (written for the Seymour Group) is for flute, clarinet, bassoon/contra-bassoon, violin, cello and piano. The keyboard part is severely restricted, limited to some As and Es in different octaves of the instrument. In effect, Fowler treats the piano as a big xylophone/marimba; she is adamant that there be 'absolutely no pedal', making certain that the resemblance to a percussion instrument is even more strictly upheld. Given this restriction, and the fact that the piano is not used very much at all, the interest lies in the other parts, though the piano acts like a rhythm section.

Example 4.41 J. Fowler, *Invocation to the Veiled Mysteries*, Letter F, p. 12

The mosaic of the other instruments is often complex and fascinating; using simple means such as repeated notes and scales, Fowler manages to evoke a variety of moods from her ensemble.

Line Spun with Stars (2006) is for flute, cello and piano. Once again, the composer deliberately restricts her options:

In view of the vast choice of notes which one could use in a particular piece, I like to set myself some limits: in this piece I have limited myself to drawing a line, i.e. the piece is almost entirely monophonic (one note at a time).

Some episodes of the piece have a characteristic pattern: a cluster of notes which revolve around a central note; a kind of 'star' pattern, in which the central note exerts a gravitational pull on the surrounding notes. Leading from one 'star' pattern to another are episodes which have a strong sense of direction, or line (hence another sense of the word 'line' in the title). The line pulls the stream of notes downwards or upwards, until encountering another star pattern.

The main preoccupation of the piece is concerned with movement. An impetus is generated which propels the piece either towards faster movement, until it reaches a burst of rapid notes; or towards slower movement, when it reaches a passage of long notes. The rate of movement is constantly changing within each cycle. As well as that, the cycles themselves vary in length and are also expanding and contracting.

Because this preoccupation with rhythmic expansion and contraction is so important in the piece, it will help to explain the decision I mentioned earlier. The piece is limited to a monophonic line [Fowler means a single line in each instrument, not overall], so that by a single stream of notes the patterns of tempo and direction can be etched more distinctly.

I have let the composer speak for herself here. Each of the instruments has quite a long cadenza unaccompanied, reinforcing her idea of line. Although there are a few fleeting moments where more than one note is sounded in the piano part, the great part of it is truly monophonic. The three instruments almost never play together, so the maximum texture at any given moment is two parts. The piano part this time does contain some pedal indications, but this, too, is infrequent.

Letter from Hawarth (1984, revised 2005) is for soprano, clarinet, cello and piano. This, particularly, was a score in which looking at a work *without* piano earlier on was instructive. If one covered the piano stave on the left of the page, the piano part looked like two linear instruments. Hardly a chord in sight!

Example 4.42 J. Fowler, *Letter from Hawarth*, bars 121–3

Moreover, the style of the moving parts in the piano was consistent with Jennifer's usual flow of line. I do not mean this comment in a critical sense; after all, Bach wrote some rather nice music in two moving parts! *Letter from Hawarth* is a setting of a letter that Charlotte Brontë wrote to Monsieur Heger, containing what Fowler labels a 'contained intensity', which she sought to emulate in her score.

5. Retrospective Composers

Miriam Hyde (1913–2005)

Miriam Hyde passed away between my last book on Australian piano music and the writing of this one. She remained active to the very end, keeping up a lively correspondence as well as playing the piano in public and composing. When I last wrote about her, it was in some senses easier, as I was describing her own instrument and the various works she composed for it, both on a concert level and many pieces used for teaching. In chamber music, her output is smaller and the role of the piano is quite different. She still produced voluminously, but it was for other musicians; she seemed very fond of wind instruments, and much of the chamber music involves flute and clarinet. But, because she was also a poet on the side, she wrote many song settings using her own and other poets' words. Miriam reacted strongly to the written word, and reading her introductions concerning her own music, one senses a sort of infatuation with the English language. In recent years, Hyde had a number of pieces published. For many years, everything was in manuscript, and, prior to photocopying, getting a Hyde score was a real difficulty. She had amazing patience and stamina, and would often make handwritten copies of complete works for colleagues. But it was with the advent of computer typesetting that she finally found it possible to get some of her instrumental and vocal pieces into print. The Keys Press and Wirripang have been major initiators in this welcome direction.

The problem of Miriam Hyde is twofold. Her style of composition was already outmoded when she began her career; she seemed incapable of shifting, or even wanting to shift, direction, and stuck to her personal aesthetic all her life. For a long while she must have felt the forgotten woman of Australian music, as a few generations of composers regarded her as a total anachronism. The other problem is that, writing about her, one is aware that everything is of one kind, and one would only seriously repeat oneself. The issue of style is probably less important now, and if we pretend that she was born earlier and is simply a prolific composer in the nineteenth-century way, perhaps we can view her in a more positive light. After all, content is no doubt more important than style. What is harder to deal with, though, is the fact that the style itself became an immovable object, and the date of composition does not seem to matter, as development or change of direction just did not happen.

We gathered a large representation of her output. The songs—whether settings of her own words or taken from English literature—are almost without exception quasi-pastoral in character, and deal with descriptions of nature and moods provoked by nature. Hyde's music is generally melody and accompaniment—counterpoint is rarely encountered in her output. When writing for solo piano, this was a very convenient formula, and one could show considerable ingenuity weaving the two elements together and shifting them between the hands. When setting words, the melodic element was shifted to the voice, and this left the piano part purely as accompanying the voice, supporting it harmonically. There is of course the introductory gesture from the keyboard and the link between verses, but the piano does not go beyond that. It is as though what was originally in the left hand now becomes material for both hands. For a virtuoso pianist, Hyde's song accompaniments are surprisingly reticent. I found it odd, given Hyde's oft-proclaimed admiration of Rachmaninoff, that she apparently chose not to emulate the master, who wrote elaborate and demanding piano parts in his songs. Hyde takes much of the Russian's harmonic language and key shifts, but the melodic writing in the songs is more often English, tending to the modal. The choice of words is lyrical rather than dramatic.

The works for solo wind and piano are of much the same cast, although, taking the words away, the composer is sometimes forced into some contrapuntal movement. In fact, there is a *Canon and Rhapsody for Clarinet and Piano*, in which, obviously, the first movement depends on polyphony; but even the second still has vestiges of this approach, as the raw material for both movements is closely related.

Example 5.1 M. Hyde, 'Rhapsody', from *Canon and Rhapsody*, bars 1–4

What occurs on this first line is symptomatic of the whole piece: when not imitating the clarinet, the piano becomes a purely accompanying instrument. So, in the *Cradle Song*, for oboe and piano, the composer's approach is typically pure melody and pure accompaniment.

Example 5.2 M. Hyde, *Cradle Song*, bars 1–6

There is much in this vein, such as pieces for flute and piano, or viola and piano; although *Legend*, for clarinet and piano, does allow the piano a more extrovert role, but only in flashes: there is a cadenza for clarinet, but not for the piano; it is as though the virtuoso performer has discreetly retired into the background. *Sonata for Clarinet and Piano* has similarity of treatment. I feel that Hyde regarded the flute as a much more gentle instrument than the clarinet, so did not allow herself to push matters. The oboe lay somewhere in between in her mind, judging by the treatment of this instrument.

There are sonatas for many other instruments, such as the fine flute sonata and the early viola sonata. The forays into trios and quartets are less frequent, and are probably related to performance opportunities, so it is interesting to observe what happens when Hyde is faced with more than one linear instrument. A look at the opening of the *Trio for Flute, Clarinet and Piano* provides an instant reply.

Example 5.3 M. Hyde, *Trio for Flute, Clarinet and Piano*, bars 1–4

The result is a sizeable and significant work of some 30 pages. There is a shorter trio for the same combination, consisting of a 'Prelude' and 'Scherzo' (the composer here explored the whole-tone scale in an unusual departure); in a lighter trio for violin, viola and piano—in actuality a *Fantasia on Waltzing Matilda*—the string instruments quite often move in parallel rhythmic motion, but here the pianist is given a more exuberant role and has to play fast octaves and repeated chords; there are a number of versions of this *Fantasia*. But, in a quartet for winds and piano named *Sailing Boats*, Hyde returns to the familiar, and there is always a solo line and accompaniment provided by piano or by piano and two winds. Old habits die hard.

Formally, Miriam was content with using existing forms and her larger works go back to the sonata form, garnering rondo form and variations form on the way. Neither was she at all adventurous harmonically, relying on unexpected key shifts to hold the listener's attention. She was a thorough professional and very fine pianist, and I am certain that she will be remembered for these qualities.

Lloyd Vick (1915–)

When I played through Lloyd Vick's piano music some years back, there were some exciting discoveries for me, and I thought that the music had real energy and verve about it. The material on hand for the present book is fairly slight: some solo songs such as *Eggs to Sell* (1995), for soprano and piano, *How Slowly Through the Lilac-Scented Air*, the only survivor of a set of four songs from Longfellow, and a unison choral song with piano titled *Tuesday* (1983). All three are surprisingly tame and English folk-song like, reminding one of the song tradition of figures such as Grainger and lesser figures from that circle and time. I wish I could be more enthusiastic, but I need to call it as I hear it. *The Miller's Daughter*, although coming from the same sonic stable, is a little more interesting because, with the soprano and piano, there is what Lloyd calls an optional 'Shadow Chorus' that 'should be the merest "feather" of sound. It may be hummed, or sung on any suitable soft sound such as "oo" or "ah", or, if preferred, on ad. lib. combinations of soft sounds.' This shadow choir had the potential for an interesting effect, but unfortunately, Vick chose it to sing basically the same chords as played by the piano—a rather staid four-part accompaniment in D major, complete with diatonic passing notes. Regrettably, there is only one instrumental piece, a cello/piano work entitled *Rebecca* (1986), using the musical equivalents of the letters of the name. It is in a similar vein to the songs, with a tinge of Schumanesque texture and melancholy

Eric Gross (1926–2011)

At a distance, Sydney as a city seems to produce so much superficiality and glitter, so much that is politically correct, so much pretty music, that it is always a relief and pleasure to look at products from Eric Gross, who just composes honestly, without pretentious titles or pose. Eric is a prolific composer; the three works we chose to represent him are Opus 216, 268a and 258! Not many of us can match that output. To my ears, there were always two Erics: one producing masses of light music, including film music, and the other, the more Germanic side of his musical persona, writing the series of piano pieces that I have written about before. The three works in front of me fall somewhere in between these two sides. Both the *Three Inventions for Clarinet and Piano* (1997) and *Clamorosa*, for the same combination, as well as another wind piece, *Euphonics II for Bassoon and Piano*, have a number of common characteristics. The lighter side manifests itself in the texture and predominantly linear writing for the piano, punctuated with the occasional chord. The wind parts are virtuosic, with wide leaps and constant changes of articulation. The language is highly chromatic and rhapsodic; some gestures from the 'lighter' Eric have leaked through into this music, making it more palatable. Gross's sophisticated language does not seem interested in extended techniques, and I suspect that it is part of his work ethic not to be self-consciously avant-garde!

Example 5.4 E. Gross, *Three Interventions for Clarinet and Piano*, No. 1, bars 19–21

Geoffrey Allen (1927–)

The Keys Press is currently the most prolific publisher of Australian music, accumulating a catalogue that now numbers several hundred scores. It is also responsible for the Heritage Series of Australian music, which has produced more than 70 scores as a direct outcome of a research grant from the Australian Research Council, and I happen to be the general editor of that particular series—the outcome of many years of research into Australian solo piano music and chamber music with piano. This very book is another outcome of the same research process. I thought it best that I declare my association with Geoffrey Allen, who runs the Keys Press, as we have been working together for many years. My exposure to his music has been limited to his solo piano works, and at times I was a little puzzled by the unexpected twists and turns of the music, though there was much that I admired, especially in the sonatas. This book has now given me an opportunity to look at Geof's output from another angle. I began with the songs, because they represent his very first compositions, written in England while he was still a student. Since then, and especially after he retired from his work as librarian in Western Australia, Geof has been very productive. I looked at a good selection of his songs: *Two Chinese Songs* (1948–49, after Li-Po); *Two Browning Songs* ('A Lover's Quarrel' and 'Home Thoughts from Abroad', 1950–51; the second song was written when the composer was already away from England, in New Zealand, probably feeling homesick); and *Nursery Rhymes Nine* (1959–62), also for voice and piano. These are all English nursery rhymes, and gave me a first clue about Geof's compositional approach. Even rhymes that everyone knows, such as 'Wee Willie Winkie', 'Simple Simon' or 'Humpty Dumpty', all begin innocuously enough but then begin to get distorted and asymmetric. I started to follow the thread of how the music moves unexpectedly, helped by the familiar rhymes and melodies; the settings actually aurally demonstrate how the composer's mind works. The songs vary in their strength of tonality and bar regularity; some have key signatures throughout. As I played through *Two Songs for a Wedding* (2008, Walt Whitman's 'Smile O Voluptuous Cool-Breath's Earth' and John Shaw Nielsen's 'Love's Coming'), then *Songs that Mother Never Taught Me* (1993, the often quirky and amusing words by Geof himself: 'Love Letters', 'Heart Attack', 'The Vampire's Lullaby' and 'The Dangers of Love'), my sense of understanding the flow of the music grew. There are four more collections of songs: two books of songs set to poems of Kevin Crossley-Holland, entitled *Speaking of the Snow* and *Stile and Stump* (2007), another book to poetry of Geoffrey Grigson called *Remembered Love* (2005) and the most ambitious of all, *Bredon Hill* (eight songs for tenor and piano; 1995). Grigson and Crossley-Holland were students from Oxford and were resident at St Edmund Hall, where Geof Allen was himself in the late 1940s. The song settings sit well within the English song tradition, and the vocal lines, the piano writing and the choice of words all belong to that group of composers whom we think of as English songwriters.

The instrumental pieces with piano are of a number of types. *The Watercolors Suite* (1989), for instance, is a set of pieces for flute and piano, with interludes for solo flute and for solo piano, making up a set of nine pieces in all. They are all short, linked by the motif of water, and written for a conference on water resources. Geof's music for wind instruments and piano has a distinctly French approach, with finely etched lines and restrained piano part. Other pieces for wind include *Pastoral for Bassoon and Piano* (1999), *Outback Impressions* (2005), pieces for clarinet and piano, and *Contain for Bassoon and Piano* (1999). Mixed with the Gallic lightness, the pieces are also in the English pastoral tradition, and Geof seems happy enough to stay within these confines. All the works with piano, whether vocal or instrumental, give the piano important material, creating an ever-unfolding contrapuntal interplay between the solo instrument and the keyboard. Allen is a composer who works thematically, and motivic coherence is the glue that holds much of his music together, given its waywardness in matters of key centres. There are three small works for strings: *A Little Suite for Double Bass and Piano* (1999), *Soliloquy for Violin and Piano*, and *Cantilena for Violoncello and Piano*—the last being the slow movement for an intended, but never completed sonata. A *Sonata for Flute and Piano* (2004), however, does exist; in four movements, it brings to mind Geof's admiration for Poulenc.

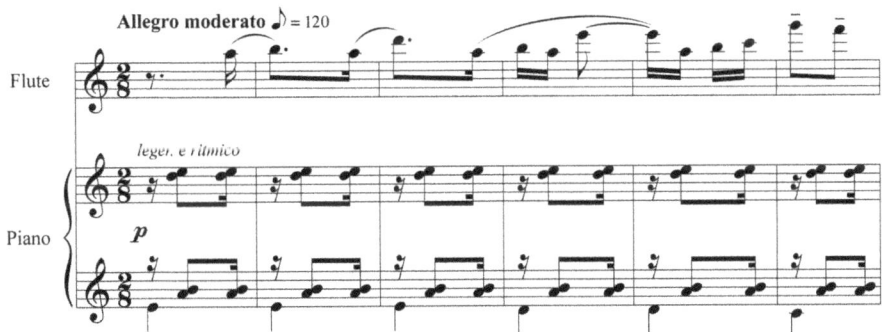

Example 5.5 G. Allen, *Sonata for Flute and Piano*, Op. 56, mvt 1, bars 1–6

Finally, there are two larger-scale works: *Trio for Violin, Violoncello and Piano* (2006), and *Fantasy Trio for Flute, Clarinet and Piano* (2009). These four-movement works contain piano parts that are bolder, less reticent than in the solo wind/string works, and seem to contain more quasi-improvisatory gestures, especially in the *Fantasy Trio*.

George Dreyfus (1928–)

We collected a number of scores by George Dreyfus. They included the *Seven Songs for Bruce Knapped* (1987), for voice and piano, *Carboni* (1979), for a show based on Raffaello Carbone's *The Eureka Stockade*, followed by *Ein KaffeeKonzert*, for piano trio and voice. This last is a set of fixed-form pieces such as a 'March', 'Waltz' and 'Gavotte'; the settings are in German and no doubt are meant to be humorous or even a send-up. I missed the point because of the language. The musical language, however, is consistent with the other pieces that we looked at. Thus, *Grand Aurora Australis*, for oboe, piano and optional percussion; *Songs for Manning Clark's History of Australia, The Musical*; *Tender Mercies*, for French horn and piano; and *Larino, Safe Haven*, for trumpet and piano, are all essentially miniatures that join the previously listed works in that the atmosphere pervading all the music is essentially music hall, from the end of the nineteenth century, with a smattering of a kind of manufactured Australian folk music. Even in *In Memoriam, Raoul Wallenberg*, for clarinet and piano, written for a documentary film on Wallenberg and therefore dealing with a very tragic incident from World War II, George cannot seem to shake the shackles of this style. I have no idea whether Dreyfus is seeking to challenge the definitions of what constitutes 'serious' or 'concert' music. I am certainly not entering the debate, and can only say that these scores do not fit the overall picture of what we are looking at in this book. As is well known, George is a fine bassoon player, so the piano parts are almost inevitably of the 'vamping' variety. Amusingly, George was a postmodernist years before the term was even invented!

May Howlett (1931–)

May Howlett's output includes many short works for wind and piano, as well as vocal settings, often to her own words. The music has a gentle, lyrical exterior, but sometimes things are not quite what they seem, and lurking behind the lilting, almost cabaret exterior of some of the work there is a sting in the tail, an unexpected turn of phrase. So, in *Exhibits*, a suite for flute and piano (I. 'Mobiles', II. 'Veil VII', III. 'Electric Mouse', and IV. 'Streeton's Noon'), we find in the first movement a static harmony within a Debussy-ish framework, whilst in the third there is an explosion of cluster-related chords. Even in the last movement, the essentially pentatonic piece takes unexpected rhapsodic byways. This is probably typical of May's output as a whole. She is not interested in barnstorming, so everything is held in check. The feminine dream world appears mostly in the shorter pieces such as *Lahara's Stream*, for clarinet and piano, *Nocturne*, for horn and piano, or *Sacred Grove*, for bassoon and piano. Howlett's sense of humour is ever present, however, as in a sudden breakout of a vamping bass in a march section in an asymmetric 9/8 rhythm; it is especially evident in *Secrets*, a kind of song cycle dedicated to Marilyn Richardson, that extraordinary soprano for whom much Australian music has been composed. In *Secrets*, we begin with the line: 'Juliet, Juliet! Have you found your Romeo yet?' This is answered in the next song by a rag-doll Romeo, who 'woos (how he laughs and jokes and woozy, woozy woozy)', with the piano thumping away

5. Retrospective Composers

in quite virtuoso fashion in rag tempo. A short song entitled *The Rose Mystery*, set for voice and oboe, reveals May Howlett's melodic gift. 'The Cat' shifts into a more hypnotic world, with strange colouration.

Example 5.6 M. Howlett, 'The Cat', from *Secrets*, bars 9–11

The cycle ends, unexpectedly, with solo voice singing 'The Chataka Bird'.

There are more settings to her own words, such as *Songs of a Watchful Man* (1986–89), comprising 'Horatio' (whose bridge has become an overpass), 'Angothra' and 'Seagulls'. A separate song, *To Beauty*, has an almost Rachmaninovian feel to the lush harmony and vocal line.

Finally, I looked at *Wings of the Wind*, for flute and piano ('Thermals', 'Mistral' and 'Ah! Sirocco'). Here, modern playing techniques for the piano are grafted onto an essentially conservative, though volatile, temperament. One last comment: May Howlett's music is strong on thematic unity and control.

Ralph Middenway (1932–)

Having never seen Ralph Middenway's *The Letters of Amalie Dietrich, Opera in One Act for Vocal Soloists and Piano* (libretto by Andrew Taylor), I had to imagine it all unfolding as I played through the score. First, I wondered whether the piano score was a reduction, but apparently it is not; everything that is written can be done on the keyboard, although just very occasionally, the music seems to beg for orchestration. Given the almost impossible task of getting a new opera staged, it is little wonder that composers, even accomplished and experienced composers such as Middenway, turn to the easier expedient of using the piano in this fashion. It is, then, regrettable that the sound of the piano lasting through a whole opera, even a shortish one, does become wearying. Staging, singing and lighting would no doubt enhance everything and disguise the use of a single instrument. The piano writing is secure, though not extravagant; for my taste, too often it merely comments on what is going on and what is being said or sung, and I waited in vain for the piano to leap up, come to life, and overwhelm everything, but that does not happen in this piece. The second problem is the idea itself: making an opera out of reading letters. Very little actually happens, and the drama is further weakened by repeating what the composer sees as important lines, sometimes over and over. His setting of the text tends to be glued to the actual speech rhythms, and this restricts the musical flow to an extent. I thought that the words themselves—whether in the letters or in actual conversation—are too prosaic and deal with very mundane matters; this would hardly inspire the composer to push his music towards some kind of acoustic explosion. Middenway certainly knows what he is up to, and his control over thematic material and cross-referencing in the music is exemplary, but perhaps he needed to be more ruthless with the words instead of being governed by them. The music itself is a rich palette of chromatic writing, often ending or skirting round tonal centres, such as the long E pedal in the opening music. Superimposed triads are another feature of the palette. Naturally, this is all subjective reaction to playing through the score, and it would be good to see an actual production!

We also looked at *The Stream of Time, Songs of Acura, for Soprano, Bass Clarinet and Piano* (1984). This is another instance of Middenway's interest in Japanese culture, like his piano sonata of 1990. Here the text (in translation) comes from Yamanoue Okura, the famous poet: 'one of the three greatest poets of his time, much of his work was included in the Man'yoshu, the Collection of a Myriad Leaves, dating from 794 A.D., the first great Japanese anthology' (composer's program note). The settings are both refined and restrained, befitting the poetry. Middenway's score is made much more readable by including the actual (concert) sound of the clarinet, as well as the part in B-flat.

David Morgan (1932–)

David Morgan has lived in South Australia for many years now, and produced much music. I am a little mystified as to why he is not better known, and would hazard a guess that as a composer he lies in that middle ground between modernity and light music. In some ways that is the most difficult place to be, for the followers of either 'side' find you a problem. I could be quite wrong about this, of course. We accumulated a good sampling of his works, favouring more recent times.

So, a piano quartet from 1999: marking the death from cancer of someone obviously close to David in 1996. I have already commented before on Morgan's propensity to constantly interrupt the flow of the music by a cadential gesture; it is here as well, and is just something that is native to the composer. He favours parallel fourths and fifths in the two hands of the pianist, moving in conjunct or disjunctive motion, forcing the arrival point of the cadence. This creates a kind of bitonality, but it is rarely over-harsh because of the open intervals used. Morgan's chamber works use titles that are descriptive, and contain obvious clues as to what is driving the music. Here, we have the following movements: 1) 'Apprehension'; 2) 'Crossroads'; 3) 'Toll'; and 4) 'Vale'. The last is very tonal, whilst the second movement, following the clue of the titles, plays with the interaction of 2/4 and 6/8. There is kind of 'death-chord' that appears:

Example 5.7 D. Morgan, *Piano Quartet*, mvt 2, bars 199–206

The *Piano Quintet* (2000) (also commemorating, sadly, more deaths caused by cancer) is not dissimilar in style. The fourths and fifths tend towards a Hindemith-ish sound, here and in other pieces. The titles in the quintet are: 1) 'Slow March'; 2) 'Sunshine and Shadow'; and 3) 'Unmasking'. The second movement perhaps owes something to Bartók in its asymmetric rhythms. The first movement is strongly tonal—something we find in some of David's works—and contains an almost banal trumpet-like call. The *Suite for Horn & Piano* (1998) is a lighter, more playful work written for his daughter. Again, the movement titles tell us something of the compositional approach: 1) 'Ditty's Dump and Dash (this opens with a 12-tone row, which provides the raw material for what follows); 2) 'Groundlet'; 3) 'Scherzo'; 4) 'Pastorella'; 5) 'Capriccio'; 6) 'Post-Haste'. The last movement juggles different tempi in a structural manner, whilst the first movement is full of time changes.

David Morgan's *Violin Sonata No. 4* is a work that dates from 1959, but was completed in 2005! This is a feat in itself, which I personally cannot imagine even attempting. Is this because Morgan's style has not changed much over all these years? Is the phenomenon uncovering a drying-up occurring in the composer's life? Certainly, the landmark fourths and fifths are here, as well as a reliance on old forms: 1) 'Toccata'; 2) 'Sarabande'; 3) 'Ground'; 4) 'Wild Waltz and Melancholy March'; and 5) 'The Lonely Art' (perhaps the composer musing in an autobiographical manner). The writing is fluent and contrapuntal. David has always known his instruments.

The *3 Cabaret Songs* (1999) are scored for soprano, clarinet, cello, piano and percussion. The songs are: 1) 'A Welsh Wife'; 2) 'The Scorpion and The Bull'; and 3) 'Saint Peter and the Pope'. The settings are folk song-like in style and the whole is obviously light, but colourfully set in a most attractive frame.

And so, we are now left with a collection of trios. The *Trio for Violin, Clarinet & Piano* is a recent work (2005). The first movement is a 'Rondo on the Name Charles Edward Ives', containing some of the most grinding chords I have ever seen in David's music, partly the result of deriving note equivalents from Ives' name. These are mostly three-note adjacent notes, widely spread out. The second movement, 'Tranquillity and Frenzy', has some adroit tempo shifting, with a wry, Shostakovich-like humour. This is followed by a 'Mad March', which begs the question: is Morgan more at home, more natural, in lighter, more miniature forms of expression? The last movement is called 'Magpie Rondo, Groundlet and Coda'. The magpie appellation must refer to a high bird-like call that is important in the rondo.

We are left with some piano trios. The first trio was composed in 1952 and revised in 1997. A very tonal, early work, with a 'Theme' and 'Variations' to begin with—the variations most skillfully handled—a 'Pastorale' and a 'Scherzo'. Perhaps there is an over-reliance on sequence, but the appearance of different tempi is another by-now familiar trait. These tempo changes are closer to Tippett than Carter, and are used more structurally, to create blocks. The second trio (1999) is yet again in memory of a cancer victim, which accounts once more for the sequence of movements: 1) 'Elegy'; 2) 'Days of Wrath, and Remembrance of Innocent Happiness' (again smacking of Shostakovich at his most ironic and angry); and 3) 'Simple Song'. The third trio (2005) opens with 'The Naming'. Here again, I felt that the more compressed form resulted in a more successful composition. The remaining movements all deal with other composers: 2) 'Variations on a Theme by Mozart'. Here, the wilder the departures from the theme, the more interesting is the music. The key of A major dominates the movement, and one has the impression that the composer became enslaved by the theme. The remaining two movements are: 3) 'A Walk in the Woods (whilst thinking of Bruckner)'; and 4) 'The Woods So Wilde (*Divisions on an Air* after William Byrd, 1590) and Orlando Gibbons'. There are 18 divisions (a free variant of the theme) and a coda.

The last and most recent piano trio—the fourth—is probably my favourite from the selection. It, too, has quasi-programmatic titles: 1) 'Sound'; 2) 'City: Heinrich Schutz, Dresden and Coventry'; and 3) 'Silence'. The second movement has, as part of the score: 'Don't mention the war! (Basil Fawlty).' The trio is deft and colourful, with the first movement's strong superimpositions of triads, and the last movement's very static E-major tonality showing effective contrast.

Colin Brumby (1933–)

Looking back to what I wrote about Colin Brumby in the last book, I felt both vindicated and puzzled. What motivates a composer—with a firm hold of the postwar avant-garde language, who took his place in Australia as one of the generation that broke with tradition—to change gear and go into reverse, and drive in reverse for quite a long way? Of course, I do not know the answer, neither do I condemn the composer who did this; I just wish that the mental processes were a little clearer to me! Brumby, from the mid-1980s, not only returned to a soft-edged romanticism, but, not content with that, also went even further back, so that much of the music sounds like a late nineteenth-century exercise in style. My impression is that Colin became weary of the constant battle with critics and audience alike—especially in Queensland, which at that time was conservative—and chose the easier path. If I am wrong about this, I am happy to apologise to the composer; the decision might also have been related to an aesthetic disenchantment with what the avant-garde of the day stood for, and how it eventually itself became dogmatic and intolerant of anyone not toeing the party line. Most of the pieces we gathered are miniatures, in which the piano has some form of arpeggiated accompaniment, and the solo instrument or voice carries the 'tune', largely diatonic, in four-square rhythm and overarchingly diatonic. I list here the pieces that I played through: *Aria*, for solo violin and piano; *A Little Romance*, for alto saxophone and piano; *A Little Waltz*, solo for violin and piano; *Mudoolun*, for cor anglais and piano; *Menteith*, for flute and piano; *Sospiri*, for clarinet and piano; and some vocal music—a solo song, *Malinconia, Ninfa Gentile*, with words by I. Pindemonte, set in Italian, and sounding like a popular Italian tenor number; a *Serenade* (words by Aubrey de Vere); and finally *A Poor Young Shepherd* (words by Verlaine), set in French.

Playing through all of these, the thought crossed my mind: did the composer finish up in the wrong place in the profession? Should he have begun in the light-music sphere? Did all that 'classical' training actually get in his way?

Of more substance is the *Bassoon Sonata*, with touches that hark back to figures such as Schumann and Brahms, in the richer piano sonorities and the structure with its climaxes. The second movement might be slight, but the last has interesting cross-rhythms between the solo instrument and the piano. Yet another Germanic work is the *Piano Quartet*, written between December 1983 and January 1984. I liked it less than the *Bassoon Sonata* because of the unremittingly thick texture, but there is certainly a sense of the big romantic sweep in the music.

The work that appealed to me the most was *Chiaroscuro*, for clarinet, cello and piano, where tritonal tensions, such as E-flat minor against A minor, lend spice to the language. There is a more vital rhythmic drive in this three-movement work—with its Satie-esque waltz as the second movement—than in any of the other works that I looked at. The three instruments have an equally colouristic and even combative role in this fairly short and terse composition.

Example 5.8 C. Brumby, *Chiaroscuro*, mvt 1, bars 1–4

Mary Mageau (1934–)

Mary Mageau embodies an elegant, spare style, whether she writes for the keyboard or for instruments or voice. The music relies on its building blocks based on folk-like turns of phrase and exotic scales, whether constructed or taken from some ethnic source. Parallel with that, she likes to explore popular music of the past, as we will see. Her violin and piano piece *Calls from the Heartland* (1995) is in five short movements, alternating tempi and moods. The raw thematic material is often pentatonic and is obviously founded in an affinity with folk music. She does not write technical difficulties into her scores, and performers no doubt find it graceful to perform. Even when Mary writes for a professional ensemble such as the Darling Downs Trio, the texture remains clean and lucid. This particular trio is named *Concert Pieces for Piano Trio*, with named movements—that is: 1) 'Il Penseroso'; 2) 'L'Allegro'. The music itself in the first movement even looks 'white', as few accidentals appear, resulting in a piece that is centred on the note A. The second movement is longer and more virtuosic; it also has a return to the first-movement tempo close to the end, giving some sense of reprise. But even the second movement, with constantly running semiquavers, is still marked on the metronome with a modest q = 112; so it is more playful than driven, cooler than passionate.

Mageau likes to add subtitles at times, and, in *Dialogues* (1992), for clarinet, viola, cello and piano, we get: 1) 'Hot Gossip'; 2) 'Whispered Secrets'; and 3) 'Affirmative Replies'. The titles no doubt give both performers and audience some clues to the work's 'meaning', or at least inspiration. *Dialogues* is a highly energetic, colourful piece. The piano scampers in similar motion scales, treated as a single line. Chordal passages are few and far between.

There is another reference point in Mageau's music, which is rag music from her native America. And so, in *Ragtime Remembered* (for oboe, clarinet, horn, bassoon and piano), we have three movements based on ragtime and tango. This is an obviously light piece, and the piano part now acquires the texture and feel of the original dances of this genre. Mageau has a real feel for this kind of music, and the work, using the piano as a kind of continuo and the instruments sharpening and spicing up the sound, really works and cannot fail to get the audience involved. There is a related work, named *Suite with A Beat*, in a similar vein. Here the piano can be substituted with harpsichord, as the other instruments are three recorders, playing three movements titled: I) 'Ragtime', II) 'Blues', and III) 'Quick Step'—all originating from Mageau's country of birth.

We also uncovered two songs: *She is a Cat* (1998, words by Mocco Wollert), a joyful and exuberant vocal number, and a more serious setting: *Son of Mine* (for soprano and piano, 1992, words by Oodgeroo Noonuccal), with some dark moments, the piano quite often playing in the bass register.

Example 5.9 M. Mageau, *Son of Mine*, bars 5–8

Australian Chamber Music with Piano

Michael Bertram (1935–)

It was a great pleasure for me as a pianist to discover Michael Bertram's music in my last book. I found it free, rhapsodic, with often-extravagant gestures and a very rich palette that was not frightened to revert to tonality when so desired. Here, the scope of the music is smaller, and we have three works to look at. First, *I Will Write to You, Three Love Songs for Soprano* (Op. 11, 1992), with piano accompaniment. The songs are introduced by a piano slowly building towards a cluster with wide cross-hand leaps for the melodic line, finishing with a quiet, rolled A-minor arpeggio. Generally, Bertram, in his music, has the feel of a melody with accompaniment—a typically pianistic way of viewing the act of composition—and, given the task of writing a set of songs, this is very much to the fore here as well. The words come from Rupert Brooke (song 1: 'Oh Lovers Parted') and Robert Graves (2. 'I Will Write', and 3. 'Bird of Paradise'). The composer avoids time signatures as much as possible, evidently trying for an improvised effect rather than a metric feel. This is not always possible, of course, but even when forced to bar, the free effect continues since the bars are rarely of the same duration. The end of the first song illustrates how Bertram achieves the rhapsody that he desires.

Example 5.10 M. Bertram, 'Oh Lovers Parted', from *I Will Write to You*, ending

Note the ambiguous A-minor, A-major ending. Enriched traditional harmony is certainly a feature of this composer's work, but, interestingly, here he is more reluctant to do what he did in the solo piano works. Perhaps matters of balance had something to do with such compositional decisions. The second and third songs approach text setting in a similar way. The climax of the third song is not given to the voice, but to a passionate outburst from the solo piano, with proportions such as 10 against nine, and such others, enhancing the climactic point, and the piano ending the set, as it did at the very opening, with an A-minor rolled chord.

The second song cycle that we found is *The Green Castle, Five Songs for Soprano* (1994). These use variable settings, thus: 1) 'Not To Sleep' (Robert Graves), with piano; 2) 'Justus Quidem tu es' (Gerard Manley Hopkins), with string quartet and piano; 3) 'Silence of the Night' (Christina Rossetti), with piano; 4) 'Up-Hill' (Christina Rossetti), with string quartet; and finally 5) 'The Green Castle (Robert Graves), with string quartet and piano. In this way, Bertram squeezes the maximum contrast out of the combination. The quartet is never broken up as an entity. The approach of melody and accompaniment is here taken to a kind of maximum, as the background comprises a consistently saturated palette upon which the composer superimposes the voice. The sound is reminiscent of songs by Rachmaninoff and the ecstatic moments of Scriabin. I suspect that this is what I found attractive about Bertram's music in the first place! But the chromaticism is under constraint here, perhaps because of pitching considerations for the soprano.

The *Variations for Flute and Piano* (Op. 10, 1991) is a somewhat curious work, in that the composer generally avoids the problem of writing for piano and flute simultaneously, and huge chunks of the work are for one instrument or the other. 'Variation 1' is largely for flute—the piano only interjects, as in an operatic recitative. 'Variation 2' begins with a waltz-like bar set up by the piano and repeated many times; the flute plays over it. 'Variation 3' is for unaccompanied flute. 'Variation 4' again uses the piano for a simple, repetitive 5/8 background, written on one stave, with flute superimposition. 'Variation 5' is for solo piano, in a flashy and showy cadenza. 'Variation 6' has the instruments shadowing each other, with the piano part very restrained, in a single-line, softly pedalled role. 'Variation 7' is again largely flute and 'Variation 8' is another showy cadenza for the piano, featuring double octaves. 'Variation 9' is consequently mostly flute and the final 'Variation 10' uses some prepared piano effects behind the flute. This is a virtuoso work for both players. Bertram milks the rather sparse theme for all its worth, both melodically and harmonically.

Richard Peter Maddox (1936–)

Maddox's vocal settings and instrumental sonatas have confirmed the views I held about his music when I wrote about his piano works. He is obviously very fond of Shakespeare as there are numerous settings: *Beauty Herself is Black*, which consists of Sonnets CXXVII, CXXX, CXXI, CXXII (1998); Sonnet XVIII appears in *Four Songs of the Far Side*; *The Marriage of True Minds (Shakespeare on Love), Op. 103, A Duet song cycle for Soprano and Bass* includes Sonnets CXVI, Ferdinand and Miranda from *The Tempest*, Beatrice and Benedick from *Much Ado about Nothing*, Demetrius and Helena from *A Midsummer Night's Dream* and Sonnet LX. Then there are either settings of real folk songs or Maddox's own quasi folk songs. We have the *Five Australian Songs* for voice and piano (1. 'Botany Bay', 2. 'Morton Bay', 3. 'Click Go the Shears', 4. 'The Streets of Forbes', and 5. 'Waltzing Matilda') grouped with *Two Songs for Teenagers Op. 105* (2004), consisting of: 1) 'Drama Queen', and the jaunty 2) 'A Sailor's Complaint'. *The Stranger in My Skin* is for voice, oboe and piano, and uses words by Bruce Dawe: 1) 'Stranger', 2) 'Looking Down from Bridges', 3) 'The Swimming Pool', 4) 'Bedroom Conversations', and 5) 'A Peasant Idyll'. *Four Songs of the Far Side* includes settings from Dawe ('Sleight of Hand'), F. T. Macartney ('Bargain Basement') and Dame Mary Gilmore ('The Pear Tree'). There are commonalities in this profusion of songs. Maddox is a composer strongly rooted in tonality, and the many imitations and sequences that make up the music are never far from a tonal centre. Maddox tends to use a more dissonant language when the songs are concerned with humour or the words suggest triteness. To my ears, the music of such settings is more interesting than the usual, more staid settings. Otherwise many of the songs have long pedals recurring, with chords shifting further and further away from home base and then either returning or finally modulating to a new centre. The accompaniments often incorporate imitative figures, thus suggesting a flow of counterpoint, which usually does not last very long. The folk settings have, characteristically, a mild taste of dissonance about them, as the familiar tunes are clothed in a fleeting unfamiliar setting. 'Waltzing Matilda' is a good example of this, and here, as elsewhere in Maddox's output, the piano parts are not easy. The composer says of this setting: 'a commission from Dorothy Williams in (as she put it) "the style of Benjamin Britten" to be sung at a reception at the Australian Ambassador's residence in Brussels.' In the middle of the Macartney song, Maddox suddenly asks for a 30 cm wooden ruler with which to play chords or else tap on the keyboard without sounding notes; this reinforces my impression that the most interesting moments in this composer's music occur when he is less earnest and allows his quirkier side to emerge. *Letters from Armidale* (1997), with words by Mary Hewes Buck (1. 'Lovely Day', 2. 'Figs', 3. 'Letters', 4. 'News Flashes', 5. 'Rain'), lies somewhere between the serious Shakespearean sonnets and the folk settings.

There are three sonatas for oboe and piano, a rondo for the same combination as well as a clarinet sonata. The composer's thought processes can be readily gleaned from the program note for the third sonata (incidentally, the oboe music is linked to the fact that Maddox's brother is an oboist):

The first movement starts with a reference to a well-known tune from Handel's *Judas Maccabaeus*…the piano then embarks on a passage…in the relative major key (C Major). When the oboe joins in, there is a transition to C-Sharp minor, which eventually leads back to the opening march theme. After the rising chord sequence the second main theme is introduced but it is muddled up with references to the opening theme until the theme is restated in C minor. This leads to a turbulent middle section where the two main ideas seem to buffet each other around until the…passage returns to E-Flat. This modulates back to the original A minor for the re-entry of the oboe.

The quote demonstrates very clearly both the formal and the tonal attitudes of the composer. I should add here that Maddox seems content to establish a time signature and generally stay within it. Resultantly, the rhythmic/metric aspects of his scores lend an additionally conservative air to his output. There is a playful set of *Variations on a Nursery Song*, for cello and piano, based on 'Pat-a-Cake', with affectionate pastiches of composers such as Bach, Beethoven, Schumann, Chopin and Brahms; a short *Viola Sonata* from 2002, and finally, *Wayne's Farewell*, for trumpet and piano (2002).

Ann Carr-Boyd (1938–)

Ann Carr-Boyd's chamber music did not contain any particular surprises, in that, like her music for solo piano, it consists mostly of miniature pieces and songs— strongly tonal, light in style and sometimes verging on cabaret in approach. We looked at a number of pieces for solo instrument with piano accompaniment to begin with: *Ann and Del* and *Ann and Del in Oz* (2004)—two pieces for flute and piano composed for a radio program and deliberately meant to evoke music from the Glenn Miller era. But, Glenn Miller aside, Carr-Boyd's own language is still very much in the same vein, without the big-band beat. Thus, *Beneath the Yellow Moon, a Suite for Violoncello and Piano* in three movements ('Beneath the Yellow Moon', 'Billabong' and 'Dreamtime Haze', 2004)—composed for the noted Australian ethnomusicologist Alice Moyle's ninety-sixth birthday, and inspired by John Moyle's verses—is another work in which the solo line carries the tonal melodic material, whilst the piano part is largely based on arpeggios based on triadic patterns, often with sixth notes added. A slightly earlier piece, from 1996, *On the Shores of Aswan*, for clarinet and piano, allows the keyboard part a little more participation in the thematic unfolding. In *Fabia's Fantasy* (2003, for horn and piano), the instruction on the score asks for the mood of 'gentle rock'—another way of describing her compositional approach.

Carr-Boyd's vocal music is exemplified by the song cycle *Museum Garden*, consisting of five songs for soprano and piano (2002, words by Mark Doty). The vocal line must be gracious to sing, and is mildly sentimental, with some melismatic writing and a long piano introduction in the fourth song. In the last, the composer uses the word 'cabaret' as part of the performing instruction, which corroborates not only what I feel about her music generally, but, more importantly, what she herself requests from her performers. *Brown Pansies* (1997, words by Corrine Laird), for voice and piano, likewise opens with a lazy drooping figure reminiscent of nightclub song.

There are a number of folk-song settings, such as *Folk Songs '76*, from various countries, set in a variety of languages, for soprano with small ensemble (seven songs in all); *Moreton Bay*, for flute, violin, piano and cello; a traditional *Railroad Gallope* (1971, original composer not given on score, but rearranged from voice and piano); and *Song of the Women of the Menero Tribe*, originally by Isaac Nathan, also for voice and piano, rearranged for flute, piano and cello.

An original trio for flute, clarinet and piano, *Julian Turns Night into Day*, started life as a piano solo named *Blues in Orange*, and once again hints at a lighter origin of the composer's music. We found a tiny piece—possibly meant as an encore—for violin, cello and piano named *Moonscape Remembered* (1991). A *Dance for Strings*, with piano accompaniment (1978), is likewise of a folk character.

A work that did not seem to fit the composer's overall output, and was perhaps tried out as an experiment, is *Combinations*, for violin, cello and piano, with aleatory elements and small clusters, not precisely notated either, in the piano part. The two strings act as a unit pitted against the free-flowing piano part. Even though many of the written patterns do have strong tonal origins, it does seem a one-off in the composer's output—commissioned by the Musical Society of Victoria. I was personally attracted by it and was sorry that Carr-Boyd did not seem inclined to try more in the same vein and beyond!

Philip Bracanin (1942–)

Philip Bracanin's *Eternal Image* (1998), for soprano, clarinet, horn and piano, is his most significant work that we located for this book. It is a setting of a portion of Byron's *Childe Harold's Pilgrimage* and consists of one solid movement, split into sections, as governed by the changing mood of the words. The piano lays the background for the action, by an ostinato moving in quavers in 5/4 and generally consisting of added sixth chords, giving a kind of radiance to the music. Most of the piece is firmly anchored in G major, although the piece ends in A major. On top of the piano harmonies, the voice and instrumental parts move in a constantly unfolding counterpoint, some of it strict and canonic, some rather more rhapsodic. But for a piece that is essentially static harmonically, the movement of the single lines and words maintains the interest.

Another work we found is *Three Bagatelles for 2 Treble Instruments & Piano*. The movements are: 1) 'Canon', 2) 'Slow Waltz', and 3) 'Allegro'. These are essentially easy pieces, meant for teaching, and really outside the scope of this book. More in keeping with what we were after is *Three Pieces for Violin and Pianoforte* (1976). This is really like a sonatina for the combination, except that it opens with the slow movement, and then, each successive movement becomes faster. The language is freely chromatic but economical and refined. It is a short but most effective work. A more substantial and serious composition is *Of Thoughts Unspoken*, for clarinet, viola, violoncello and keyboard (does this mean piano?). The choice of instruments gives the sound a dark patina. The first movement is essentially slow, but harmonically more conservative than the violin/piano work. The second movement is really a scherzo, with a wistful, melodic and slower tempo trio; the piano here is reduced to sparsely spaced rolled chords. After the scherzo returns, the tempo suddenly drops to an andante, and an emotional summing up of the work occurs here, before we return to the scherzo tempo, this time heading towards a fast coda to end with. The work, though conservative in some ways, has an essential honesty about it, with a refinement that I usually associate with Phil's work and a strong emotional element.

6. Pluralism

James Penberthy (1917–99)

James Penberthy lived a long and active life; he was involved with a huge spectrum of genres and musical forces and his biography is long overdue. Jim was very outspoken and various Establishment places and figures had trouble coping with him and his honesty. For a while, he also wrote newspaper columns and music criticisms, so, in parallel with the Establishment's unease in its dealings with Jim, there was probably a little fear that he might say uncomfortable things in a very public way. Ultimately, it is his music that has to be the final arbiter of what we think about him. Since he was prolific, what appears here is only a tiny representation of his output and it is my fervent hope that a large book about James Penberthy will appear one day.

Jim did not have any particular aesthetic axe to grind. He regarded himself as a professional composer and would produce what was required; his music covers many styles, and it is difficult to say what was closest to his artistic heart. Personally, I feel that we get a glimpse of the essential Penberthy is some of the string music and some of the vocal music, especially the later Zen-like settings. Penberthy was a man with a well-developed sense of humour and flashes of this side of him appear in his scores.

For instance, in his *Six Violin Pieces* (1971), the titles of the movements read

1. 'Doris' (Miss Bendigo 1934, 'Wow')
2. 'May' (Was in my class at school. She had red hair and will probably end up in Hell.)
3. 'Marie' (Her lover died practicing Tchaikovsky's Piano Concerto No.1)
4. 'Mary' (this is one of those girls about whom only doctrinal archbishops can complain.)
5. 'Coral' (A girl who was very good and very gay; or was she?) [Note: in 1971, the word 'gay' meant exactly that!]
6. 'Rose' (She was 24. She taught me at Violet. Had I been 24 she would have taught me more.)

The music is light textured, but not light in substance. Jim was not a concert pianist, but he felt very comfortable at the keyboard, and the writing displays someone who trained at the piano, and made compositional discoveries at it as well. Thus, many of the chord formations are often bitonal combinations of triadic chords, plus more subtle derivations. The composer's hand could span one-tenth, as is clear from the writing. But even when a C-major triad is sounding in the left hand, over and over again, the context and other activity of the music not only deny the tonality, but also use it as a tension point. This is Penberthy still attached to his past, but moving away from it at the same time. Jim was not afraid to experiment; quite the contrary, he saw it as one of the functions of art. I remember an occasion when he wrote a string quartet in which each player had a computer screen, and responded to what was flashed on the screen: some random instructions. He was possibly the first Australian composer to use computers in this creative fashion, right at the start of the computer era. That he did not pursue this line of work was a purely personal choice. Possibly it was too clumsy for him at the time.

The many songs and cycles consistently use the piano to set a mood and to either maintain or disrupt it with the keyboard. Quite often the piano announces important thematic material immediately. Penberthy's choice of words is extremely diverse. In his song cycle on words by Nancy Paine, *Love Wine and Flowers*, he addresses rather prosaic everyday subjects side by side with more traditional subjects for settings, such as nightmares; but there is also the question of the sound of a typewriter and taking the Toyota to the service station; it all seems grist for his mill. Penberthy's long experience with music making shows itself constantly in the word settings—concerns about how the singer finds pitch, and layout of the tessitura of voice versus piano.

Example 6.1 J. Penberthy, *What Bird is That*, bars 1–3

In *Bedlam Hills*, for chorus and piano (words by Vivian Smith, and dedicated to his old friend Rex Hobcroft), Penberthy enjoys alliteration in the dedication—it reads 'To horny Hobcroft'. But the setting is deadly serious: the bleak landscape depicted in Smith's poetry is mirrored in the chromatic lines of both the chorus and the piano.

Another dramatic and powerful work is the *Sonata for Violin and Piano*, commissioned by Jan Sedivka, and obviously intended for performance by Jan and his wife, Beryl. The work is in two movements, and there is a strange occurrence in the manuscript: the ending of the first movement is missing, as the manuscript cuts off at the end of the top system of the page. We have been unable to locate sketches for the missing portion, which must be the ending, as a kind of recapitulation is occurring; I have composed a usable ending for this first movement, as the work is definitely worth saving.

Example 6.2 J. Penberthy, *Sonata for Violin and Piano*, mvt 1, bars 1–5

There are probably a number of incomplete works in the Penberthy archive. A work in fairly rough manuscript entitled both 'Oboe Sonata' and 'Oboe Sonatina' (Penberthy is dithering here because the work tends towards something more substantial than a lightweight sonatina) needs some editorial and compositional attention, but would seem to be a very fine addition to the small oboe repertoire. Most of the manuscript is complete, but there are a few rough and sketchy pages that would need to be studied and completed, or slotted into place. This might be a work from his Paris days. On one page we find scribbled 'Editions de Minuet, 7 Rue Bernard Palissy, Paris 6, France'.

A very fine work is the *Perihelion Quartet*, written for the distinguished ensemble of the same name. Penberthy defines and separates the movements by solo cadenzas. These tend to bring the pixie out of him, as in the cello cadenza he suddenly writes: 'Pizz all over the instrument at random [though some shapes are given] plus any other brilliant tricks and finish on bottom C.' The clarinet cadenza has a little fragment underneath which he has written 'that is the song of the Butcher Bird'; then the opening motif from Beethoven's *Fifth Symphony* is sounded, but underneath he writes: 'So is that possibly accurate?' Similarly, after a multiphonic: 'I slipped that in for a lark.' But the piece is serious stuff, with a deeply felt lament appearing near the end of the quartet. This is yet another work that needs publishing and disseminating. It is very clear now—some years after Jim's death—that his larger-than-life personality and refusal to kowtow to the Establishment had negative effects on his perceived stature as a composer. When the extraneous nonsense such as PR fades away, only the music is left behind.

His *Trio for Flute, Oboe and Piano (Lament for a Kangaroo)* could easily have descended into maudlin sentimentality, but does not. The composer writes:

The first (angry) movement contains an introduction by the oboe of the theme. The associate[d] ideas are chromatic or derived from the opening piano accompaniment. The second is a scherzo with a short introduction which also serves as a coda. The two themes are a brief staccato figure, used antiphonally and developed, and a short parody of a popular air. The third movement is an extended, freely developing lament, in which there is some degree of pathos.

It is the last sentence that is telling: the scherzo movement has a texture and approach allied to Shostakovich in its treatment of material.

In passing, I would like to mention the settings of short poems by Dan Chadwick in *Odyssey 71*, for voice and piano. These songs—reflections on nature—are stepping-stones on the way to the many collections of Zen settings from late in Penberthy's life.

The Zen settings (Penberthy calls them 'Zen Epigrams') are a distillation of a lifetime of experience. The piano writing is sensitive and refined, the vocal lines delicate and restrained. Everything is understated.

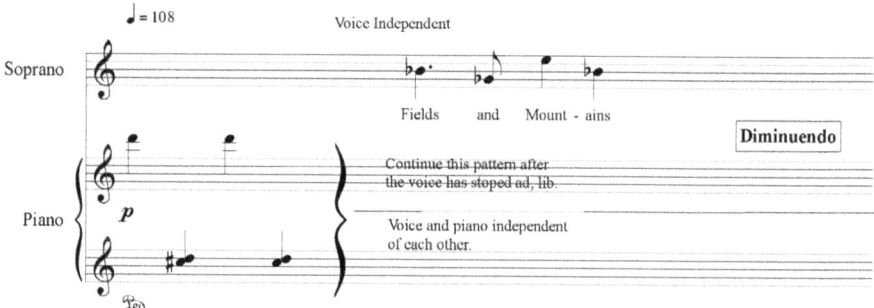

Example 6.3 J. Penberthy, 'Fields and Mountains', from *Zen Epigrams*, opening

Penberthy's musical journey was long and the milestones and arrival points significant. He is clearly a composer who in due course will be studied and surveyed in detail. There is a typescript of an autobiography in his archive that must surely be the starting point for such a venture. It is a story that some lucky musicologist/biographer will tell one day.

Moneta Eagles (1924–2003)

Eagles' output within the proscribed boundaries of this book is small and lightweight. There really is little to report. An unpublished *Conversation* (1961), for clarinet and piano is certainly worth rescuing and publishing. As the title suggests, the work is imitative, with two principal ideas bandied about between the two instruments: one is playful and short phrased, the other more sombre and longer legato phrased. The two parts are of equal significance. The piece is quite short. A song from 1950 to words by Robert Bridges, *I Love All Beauteous Things*, for voice and piano, is a little too sentimental for my taste. There is also a *Lullaby* (1956), for clarinet and piano, which won the prize in a competition run by the ABC jointly with APRA in 1956. Eagles won a similar competition with her piano sonatina. Here we have a piece lasting 3.5 minutes in a lightly lyrical idiom. Her other work for clarinet and piano, *Two Sketches* ('Scherzino' and 'Soliloquy'), is designated as a teaching piece (1964). We found two vocal pieces: a two-part song with piano for children's voices named *Night's Thoughts*, and a setting of Dorothea Mackellar for soprano, mezzo-soprano and piano (1954): *The Dreamer*. Both of these part-songs are pretty enough, but hardly of much consequence. What is surprising is that Eagles managed, in those times, to get most of her work in print with English publishers—no mean feat for an Australian composer.

Peter Sculthorpe (1929–)

Most of the material that we gathered by Peter Sculthorpe for this book turned out to be miniaturist. As well, works tend to reappear in differing guises over the years. Thus, *Darwin Calypso* was first written for a revue and first named *Manic Espresso*. Then it was arranged for the Darwin Guitar Festival for two guitars and strings; later, Sculthorpe 'lovingly re-worked it for the Australia Ensemble'.

Djilile, a work for cello and piano, also appears in *Dream Tracks*. *From Saibai* is an arrangement of *Songs of Sea and Sky*. *Parting*, for cello and piano, was originally for soprano and piano. There is also a tenor version of the song 'lovingly dedicated' to the singer (incidentally, *Sydney Singing* also '*lovingly*' describes the composer's feelings about Sydney).

The works themselves cover a good span of the composer's life, and are thus representative of his approach. The reworking of old material suggests that the essential musical thought has not changed that much over all the years. *Darwin Calypso*—no matter how thoroughly reworked—is still a feeble attempt at the genre, best left to skilled hands such as Darius Milhaud or even Arthur Benjamin.

The work is in simple ternary form, with the middle section describing 'the languor of tropical nights by the city's harbour'. Sculthorpe has always had a keen sense for pretty colourations, and here the cello glissandi (asked to sound like 'sea-gulls') at the coda of the piece are a case in point.

In *Djilile*, the atmosphere of the piece is created by a rocking, repetitive ostinato-like piano part, with the main motif in the alto part of the right hand, with the cello playing simple folk-like counterpoint against it. Sculthorpe's 'Aboriginal' pieces favour semitones with the occasional tritone. This is a short work, but the *Djilile* tune reappears in *Dream Tracks*, for violin, clarinet and piano. The work is in four sections, with *Djilile* essentially forming the second and fourth sections, whilst a children's song from the Torres Strait is used in the first and third. The piano part, though important, is essentially simple: it provides a constant restatement of the tune or is used in soft background patter, or equally soft chordal interjections.

This use of the piano to provide a pedalled background of simple diatonic patterns reappears in *From Nourlangie*, for piano quartet. The technique is by now familiar: the occasional high glissandi in cello and violin to produce 'seagull-like sounds', an overlay of an equally simple folk-like melody, somewhat syncopated, possibly an attempt to copy the slight irregularity common to folk-music performers. *Landscape II*, also for piano quartet, is in four short movements, and is largely an essay in colorations, with harmonic slides, plucking notes inside the piano, repeating patterns in independent rhythms and free improvisations. The melodic element appears to be Japanese in origin, at least to my ears.

Both *Songs of the Sea and Sky* and *Saibai* are based on the same Torres Strait melody. The latter, for violin and piano, is somewhat shorter than the original version for clarinet and piano. The opening motif provides the raw material for a dance-like section for piano solo, which is then overlaid with the slower legato idea. The piano parts in Sculthorpe generally, although fairly simple, sometimes present a curious hand distribution, which I suspect most pianists would alter.

There is an early *Pianoforte Trio*, of which only the first movement survives, as movements II and III have been withdrawn. The surviving movement is somewhat reminiscent of the composer's unsuccessful sonatina for solo piano. Another early piece is *Sea Chant*, for unison voices and piano, set to words by the music critic Roger Covell. It is a highly derivative version of the English sea shanty and need not concern us further here. Generally, Sculthorpe's word settings—deprived of ethnic sources—tend to be rather undistinguished. *Parting*—whether for voice/piano or cello/piano—is equally ordinary. So is *The Stars Turn* (words by Tony Morphett).

At least in *The Song of Tailitnama*, for soprano and piano, the folk element gives a sense of direction to both the melody and the accompaniment. But *Three Shakespeare Songs* are once again a predictable and rather clumsy pastiche of what we imagine is the music that Shakespeare would have been familiar with. Sculthorpe has, in recent years, revived other earlier works and added didgeridoo parts to them. One wonders how this reflects on the integrity of the original music.

Instrumentally, something similar occurs. *From the River*, a kind of reminiscence of childhood, is based on a rather trite quaver figure in 12/8, no doubt representing the river in motion; again, as used before, there is a short, slower middle section, and we return to the opening idea. The introduction by the composer strengthens the programmatic drive of the piece. *Sydney Singing* is similarly naive, complete with quasi bugle calls of *The Last Post* played on the oboe to remind us of the El Alamein fountain at King's Cross, as well as imitation ship's horn blasts in the movement based on Circular Quay. The movement depicting Bondi Beach is embarrassingly akin to past Australian kitsch depicting places in Australia, of which we already have a plethora.

I have left comments on *Eliza Fraser Sings* to the end, since it is the biggest work of the ones we located. We are, however, once again faced with a work that is built up of small pieces—six of them this time. Much of the word setting is measured recitation, and the melodic writing lacks character and distinction; there is much reliance on the performers' abilities to improvise, and the piano writing tends to be mostly arpeggiated chords. The work, which should be highly charged and dramatic, is certainly not that. After playing through all these pieces, it seems to me that Sculthorpe's music basically lacks passion.

Betty Beath (1932–)

Betty Beath writes in a very accessible idiom that is lyrical, often verging on the pentatonic and with some exotic overlays from Asian culture. Thus, *From a Bridge of Dreams*, for flute and piano, and *From a Quiet Place*, for viola and piano, are related pieces that can be played separately or together. In the second piece, the pianist can (ad lib) also strike a Nepalese singing bowl, which immediately adds colour and some suggestion of the oriental into the mind of the listener. A third work of similar duration is *Lagu Lagu Manis*, for cello and piano, based on scales and melodies from Java and Bali. The cellist sometimes plays on the body of the instrument, using it like a bongo. Once again, there is an effect of colour from another culture. The music is technically of moderate demand and rhythmically fairly simply constructed.

Moon, Flowers, Man, for flute, voice and piano, is another example of Beath's orientalism. This time, the text—although sung in English—is from Chinese literature. Once again, the music is a combination of pentatonic and whole tone. Another work we looked at, *Nawang Wulan—Guardian of Earth and of Rice*, for alto flute and piano, is of the same cast. Interestingly, there is also a vocal work, set in Indonesian to words by Subajio Sastrowardojo, which is musically substantially the same work.

There are some slightly bigger works such as 'The Lament of Ovid' (song number three from the cycle *Towards the Psalms*) as well as *Points in a Journey, A cycle for voice, flute and piano*. Here the sources are non-oriental and the writing is more adventurous, maybe as a result of being free from another culture and its influence. The second work contains five songs, but the composer declares her intention of adding to it 'as I discover poems which relate to the theme: points in a journey'. The copy we perused was from the late 1980s. Perhaps there are now more songs in the cycle? I thought these were the more interesting and questioning pieces from the totality of what was available by this composer.

Beath's music does open up the question of what might happen when a composer delves into essentially foreign cultures. I leave the question open, but it is a matter of importance.

Don Kay (1933–)

Since my last book, *Australian Piano Music of the Twentieth Century*, was released, Don Kay has continued to work and produce and in fact has blossomed as a composer following his retirement from active teaching at the Tasmanian Conservatorium of Music. His music has developed and strengthened, on the evidence of what we gathered for the present tome.

We begin with a work named *Coolness*. There are six versions of this work, most of which do not concern us here, as they are for solo oboe or solo clarinet—intended for use principally for a ballet concept. We are using the latest version, which is for voice, clarinet and piano, based on a haiku. A very witty effect occurs in the setting, whereby, we hear the slow unfolding of the words

> How very cool
> How very cool it feels
> How very cool
> Cool
> Cool
> Taking a noonday nap
> Taking a nap

6. Pluralism

> Cool cool it feels
> How very cool it feels
> How very cool it feels taking a noonday nap, to have a wall against my heels!

Each line is separated by music—sometimes quite elaborate and virtuosic—so the whole haiku takes about 4.5 minutes to unfold. The word 'cool' has a modern connotation, and the composer—knowingly or unknowingly—plays with it, suggesting a different meaning. The final line is heard only once, and certainly has a surprising and humorous effect. The writing is consistently alive.

Example 6.4 D. Kay, *Coolness*, bars 22–6

The latest version, from 1994, is 20 years after the original work was written for solo oboe, so obviously Don kept seeing further potentialities in the original single line.

Evocations, for violin, clarinet and piano, comes exactly in the middle of this period, dating from 1985. The composer's preface describes the work and partly its technique:

> This work seeks to convey suggestions of memories—sometimes vague, sometimes intertwined as in a half sleep and sometimes slightly more substantial, perhaps of visual images or associated emotions. The pervading mood is one of fleeting reminiscences and delicacy. Techniques include long held sounds, brief, but often repeated and seemingly unrelated ideas interrupting each other, and their occasional drawing together to allude to moments of greater substance.

Although in one movement, the work is more than 260 bars long, and reaches its most intense moments roughly in the middle; the beginning and end are very remote and soft, with the piano playing a *permutating* four-note cell, the clarinet concentrating on a repeated note idea, and the violin using a short pizzicato motif.

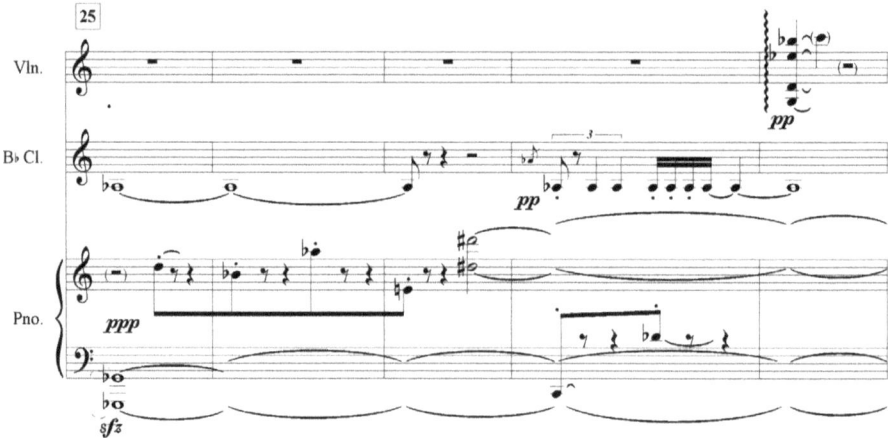

Example 6.5 D. Kay, *Evocations*, bars 25–9

Although seemingly illogical, the work hangs together very well, given the ingenuity of combinations of the disparate ideas and the satisfying overall shape of texture and dynamics.

Hastings Triptych, three pieces for flute and piano, was written the following year (1986); the movements are: 1) 'Hastings Bay'; 2) 'The Caves'; and 3) 'Lune River'. Hastings is on the edge of a remote region in southern Tasmania, and Kay is obviously reacting to the beautiful landscape. The first movement is delicately handled, with soft sevenths and ninths in the flute part; one might argue that the effect is somewhat spoilt by the few obvious and intrusive chromatic scales in both flute and piano parts. The second movement is more concerned with colour.

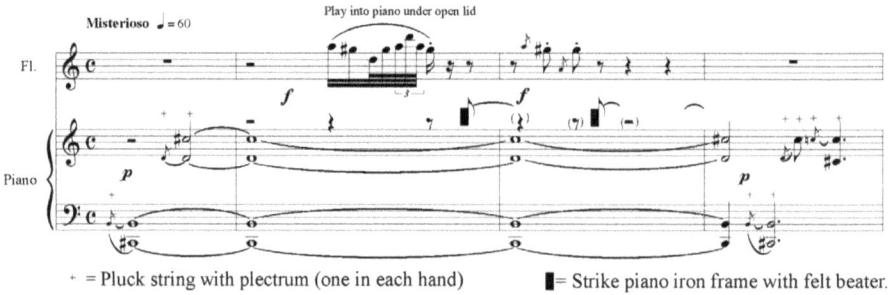

Example 6.6 D. Kay, 'The Caves', from *Hastings Triptych*, bars 1–4

The third movement is probably the most conventional, with a persistent flute idea containing a falling tritone, and the piano using an equally persistent drooping chromatic figure in octaves.

Finally, a somewhat later *Piano Trio* from 1996 is also inspired by the southern Tasmanian wilderness. It is subtitled 'The Edge of Remoteness' and the composer finds a parallel in this region with his own inner landscape. Perhaps Kay, in this work, is expressing the sense of being on the edge of Australia—something I have heard voiced by many Tasmanians generally! But of course they are privileged to live in one of the most beautiful parts of the country. Kay's language here does not contain any surprises. The two string instruments counter the two hands of the piano. Mostly they move as two distinct units, the hands often in octaves, just as the strings often move at least rhythmically together, if not in parallel lines. Thus, although technically a trio, this is structured more like a duo of bowed-against struck sounds. The beginning establishes the bleakness of the mood immediately.

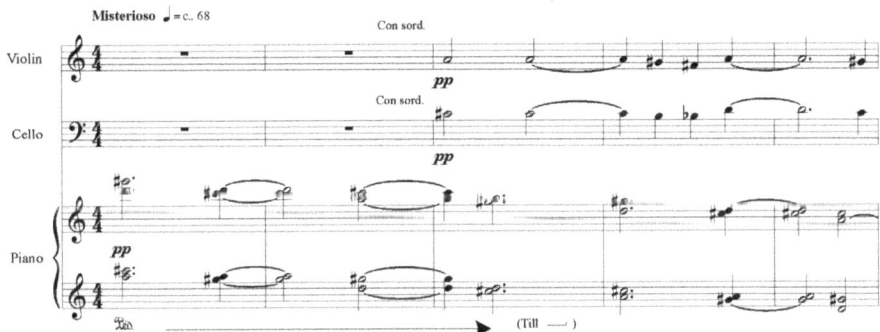

Example 6.7 D. Kay, *Piano Trio*, bars 1–5

This is another one-movement work, this time of more than 300 bars. It does erupt into violence, but most of it is creepily still.

Don Kay is an individual voice in Australian music. Since he has lived and worked in Tasmania almost all his life, the so-called 'mainland' has yet to recognise his worth. But he has produced steadily and convincingly, the remoteness helping him to find his own language.

Wilfred Lehmann (1929–)

It was doubly refreshing to come across a group of pieces for violin and piano by Wilfred Lehmann. I had heard Lehmann play his violin a number of times, but had no idea that he was drawn to composition. The group of pieces that we saw is all from the end of the twentieth century, so he either kept it all a dark secret, or, more likely, this was a late interest. The pieces are obviously written by a violinist, and a good one, for the solo part is certainly demanding. The compositions are rather naive formally, but Lehmann is not afraid to experiment with sound, and he uses the piano to create cluster-like aggregates of sound, which, with the pedal down, lend a heavily impressionistic air to the pieces. The first, from 1987, is *Forest Evening*. Here, the piano plays 'bird-call' figurations with the pedal constantly held down. Against this background, the solo violin plays long legato lines. From the previous year (1986) comes *Polish Variations*. The theme is in the style of a mazurka, but an original not borrowed theme. This is followed by a series of variations. In 'Variation I', the violin performs double-stops; when the piano joins it, parallel seventh chords are the result. 'Variation II' is labelled 'Scherzo' and the violin has fast semiquaver figures across the strings; the trio section of this scherzo is pizzicato and percussive in both parts. 'Variation III' is largely unaccompanied, and is called a 'Nocturne'; with the 'Coda', the double-stops return. Lehmann must have enjoyed the experience of writing these pieces, for now two sonatas follow them.

The *Sonata Seriosa* (1998) begins with a 'Prologue' in the low register of the piano in octaves moving in sevenths, setting the dark mood of the work. The middle of this prologue gives way to wide arpeggios in the piano with the violin part floating high above; then the opening returns. The second movement is called 'Intermezzo', and Lehmann combines double-stops in thirds with high piano figures, much like we had already observed.

Example 6.8 W. Lehmann, 'Intermezzo', from *Sonata Seriosa*, bars 2–4

The instruments swap roles later in the movement. The third movement is 'Violin Cadenza in Free Time', which speaks for itself; the piano does join in after a while and again provides a cushion for the violin. The cadenza movement is in itself in sections and allows the piano a cadenza as well. The following year (1999) Lehmann wrote his *Sonata d'Estate*. This begins with a languido section in which the piano essentially plays a series of cluster-like chords to set up the blanket on which the violin superimposes its line. The second movement is a 'Summer Waltz' of a somewhat Ravelian cast, which, as he has done before, is constructed on an ABA basis. The droopy chromatic lines of this waltz give it a somnolent characteristic, and reminded me at least of the opening of the Ravel 'La Valse'. The third movement is a 'Theme and Variations', and Lehmann returns to the very opening of the sonata. It is because the chord structures of the piano are very similar throughout all these pieces, the formal structures are rather traditional, and Lehmann is fond of sequences that these all say to me, apart from the hand itself, that these are experimental pieces, rather than the result of many years of experience. But I stress that I found the pieces interesting and worthwhile. I hope they can be published and performed. It was a buzz for me to 'discover' them!

Eugene Goossens (1893–1962)

I feel that I cannot let this book go to press without some material on Eugene Goossens, who was Director of the NSW State Conservatorium of Music and Chief Conductor of the Sydney Symphony during my student years. We all know, of course, that his connection with Australia was not a long one, and ended in tragedy when he was forced to resign from his position and go back to England a broken man—due largely to the post-colonial, narrow-minded, puritanical society that was Sydney at the time. While Goossens was director, many students took the opportunity to play chamber music by him for the composer; there was a weekly class that he took, and his imposing presence was both an inspiration and somewhat scary. But his comments to the performers were always helpful, so I found myself, as a pianist, often asked to play his chamber music and songs. I will not pretend to know every piece of his in this category (and one can consult reference books for a complete listing), but I do know quite a lot of his music, and every piece mentioned below comes from my own library, and I have performed most of them. I believe that the first piece of his that falls into the chamber music category that I encountered is the *Three Pictures for Flute & Piano*. The writing, both for flute and for piano, is rich and chromatically saturated—like so much of his music. The movements have subtitles: 1) 'From the Belfry at Bruges'; 2) 'From Bredon in the Cotswolds'—a particularly beautiful setting of a simple folk song that is the basis of the movement, sung to him by Philip Heseltine (Peter Warlock); and 3) 'From a Balcony in Montparnasse'. At the height of his compositional career, as against his conducting career, Goossens was invariably mentioned in various books in the same breath as Stravinsky, Bartok, Martinu, Bax, Vaughan Williams and others. He had a huge influence and seemed to know everyone. Thus, he transcribed—for Jascha Heifetz no less—the 'Romance' from Act III of his opera *Don Juan de Manara*. There is also his *Lyric Poem Op. 35* for violin and piano. I was asked to play these two pieces a number of times, and grew very fond of them. Slightly lighter and shorter, for either flute or violin and piano, are the *Five Impressions of a Holiday, Op. 7*. The subtitles are: 1) 'In the Hills'; 2) 'By the Rivers'; 3) 'The Water-Wheel'; 4) 'The Village Church'; and 5) 'At the Fair'.

The *Suite for Flute, Violin and Harp (or two Violins and Harp or Piano) Op. 6* is far more effective with harp, and I suspect that the use of the piano was just an afterthought or convenience. The 'Impromptu', 'Serenade' and 'Divertissement' that make up the suite are more tonal, less chromatic and tend to be folksy, unlike most of his chamber music. In a similar vein is his *Islamite Dance* for oboe and piano. There is also a light-textured work for flute, oboe and piano: *Pastorale et Arlequinade*. These works have a spiritual link to his set of piano pieces entitled *Kaleidoscope*, some of which he recorded on piano rolls. Speaking of piano rolls, Goossens composed a *Rhythmic Dance* originally meant for performance on the pianola, commissioned by the Aeolian Company in London. Subsequently, with the decline of reproducing pianos, Goossens transcribed the work for two pianos (dedicated to the famous two-piano team of Maier and Pattison) as well as for orchestra. It makes an excellent two-piano piece, but, given its origins, the music is machine-like, and runs in continuous semiquavers, contrary to his usually expansive, rhapsodic way. But, we return to the more familiar Goossens with his *Rhapsody for Violoncello & Piano Op. 13* (an early work revised late in his life). Finally, there are his splendidly atmospheric violin sonatas, dedicated to Albert Sammons and Paul Kochanski, once again illustrating the circles in which he moved; the second sonata is especially effective. I am truly surprised that this fine music has been allowed to fall into obscurity. There is as well a compact *Quintet Op. 23*, for string quartet and piano—a rather grand piece in one movement.

Of the songs for voice and piano, probably the most important are the six settings from James Joyce, entitled *Chamber Music*. Singers often asked pianists to perform the *Three Songs Op. 26* ('The Appeal', 'Melancholy' and 'Philomel') and also the *Deux Proses Lyriques Op. 16* (settings are in French). Other songs that I have before me: *Four Songs* (1. 'Threshold', 2. 'A Winter Night Idyll', 3. 'A Woodland Dell', 4. 'Seascape'), words by Bettie Holmes; *When Thou Art Dead* (words by Margaret Kennedy); *Two Songs Op. 9* (setting of Musset, in French); *Persian Idyls Op. 17*, words by Edwin Evans; and *Three Songs Op. 19* (1. 'Afternoon', 2. 'Epigram', 3. 'Tea Time'). Finally, there are a few English folk-song settings. All the songs and instrumental works require complete pianism to succeed.

I hope that this brief note on Goossens and his chamber music with piano will inspire musicians to search for and perform his work. Although most of the material is out of print, in recent years various reprints have begun to be available.

7. Sitsky's Chamber Music

Edward Neeman

Larry Sitsky's sound world is characterised (in his own words) by the 'intense expressionistic style, the improvisatory aspects, the ejaculatory phrases, the abrupt changes of dynamics with its associate expressiveness'.[1] As a pioneer of modernist music in Australia in the 1960s and 1970s, Sitsky is often—and quite rightly—grouped with his fellow travellers from the same period, composers such as Richard Meale and Don Banks who had grasped the importance of the earth-shaking changes taking place in American and European musical circles and fought against the odds to foment a similar re-evaluation of the power and relevance of music in Australia.

In Sitsky's wide and multifaceted output, there are two overarching themes: mysticism and melody. Sitsky is captivated by the mystical quality of music, and its power to touch the innermost reaches of our soul. The expression of spiritual yearnings lurks just beneath the audible surface, giving his music a constant sense of purpose. As a scholar of Busoni, he credits the Italian composer's music and writings as important influences on his mystical outlook. Sitsky describes the late works of his mentor in his book *Busoni and the Piano*:

> These works seem to move on a plane divorced from reality, from everyday experience. Busoni's music can be legitimately described as a record of a mystic journey, and as the journey comes to fruition, the message to be deciphered in the record demands an understanding of the mystic vision from the listener. This withdrawal from reality is without doubt the largest single obstacle to the popularisation of Busoni's music.[2]

He views the role of composers as 'magicians, we play with sounds, we create a world'.[3] The majority of Sitsky's works from 1965 onwards have titles borrowed from mystical texts, which is Sitsky's way of acknowledging his sources of inspiration. As he says: 'I decided fairly early that I was going to be honest about the sources of my inspiration. And the fact is that most of my pieces happen because I'm reading a particular text or poem, and that generates a piece of music.'[4]

---

1 Sitsky, Larry 1971, 'Sitsky on Sitsky', *Music Now*, (April), p. 7.
2 Sitsky, Larry 1986, *Busoni and the Piano*, Greenwood Press, New York, p. 6.
3 Cotter, Jim 2004, *Sitsky: Conversations with the composer*, National Library of Australia, Canberra, p. 74.
4 Sitsky interview, 2 July 2009.

While spiritual and philosophical elements are often the starting points for his works, Sitsky does not allow this to become a substitute for compositional technique. The source and effects of music might touch things outside the physical realm, but their message must be intelligible to the performers and the audience to have the desired effect. As Sitsky says, 'the music has to exist on its on strengths and weaknesses, and its own logic. If it depends on storytelling, it's a fizzer.'[5]

Sitsky has a natural gift for fluid vocal lines, and an effortless ability to express poetry in melody that is clear even from his earliest songs. Sitsky's explorations with serial technique led him to develop a highly personal style where the row assumes the role of the melody so that the serial transformations and fragmentations are clearly audible in the cantilena.

Sitsky's melodies are not beautifully proportioned, symmetrical, or nostalgic. Their function is not to seduce, but to express. They are craggy, often widely spaced, and rarely have a sense of metre or cadence. Where there is polyphony, it can often be resolved into a primary melody and a textured accompaniment, or into separate and unrelated layers of sound. A narrative unfolds through the rhetorical line, a narrative whose simplicity and inner beauty are revealed gradually, as the thematic repetitions elucidate the multiple faces of the primary source material.

Chamber Works

Sitsky began primarily as a vocal composer. His intuitive ability to express words in music meant that his earliest songs have an assurance not present in the purely instrumental works of the same period. Sitsky's finest and most ambitious works from the 1960s and 1970s are his operas, written in collaboration with the Tasmanian poet Gwen Harwood. She knew how to shape the libretti to provoke Sitsky's natural inclination towards sensuality, lurid shapes and bold gestures. When Sitsky adapted these operatic instincts into purely instrumental works, he would give the declamatory vocal lines to a solo instrument, while the rest of the ensemble would provide a fluid backdrop.

The *Sonatina for Oboe and Piano* (1962) is Sitsky's first mature chamber work, and many of the hallmarks of the later works are already hinted at here. He has always felt that the piano works best as a supporting instrument in ensembles; here, the pianist offers inside-the-piano effects, using his fingernails, palms, a coin, and a metal pencil while the oboist takes the centre stage. Rhythmically, Sitsky likes to contrast rhetoric with rhythm; here, the amorphous opening

---

5   Ibid.

movements are a foil to the complex polyrhythms based on additive patterns in the third movement. Much of the first two movements are written without metre, coordinated by cues that allow the players more room for rubato.

Example 7.1 L. Sitsky, *Oboe Sonatina*, mvt 1, p. 2, first stave

The polyrhythms appear in the third movement, with irregular metrical patterns: the piano divides the 14-beat cycle into 2+5+1+6, whereas the oboe part is divided 3+2+4+2+3.

Example 7.2 L. Sitsky, *Oboe* Sonatina, mvt 3, first stave

Note: In all the examples of Sitsky's music, accidentals apply only to the note they immediately precede.

Sitsky makes use of a 'patchwork' recapitulation in almost all his instrumental music, where fleeting glimpses of previous material reappear in ghostly succession at the end of a work. This sonatina is one of his first works to do this; a few bars of each of the previous movements are heard in the fourth and final movements. Finally, that mystical spark—the audible desire to connect with a higher plane of consciousness—seems to be present here almost for the first time in Sitsky's instrumental music. He hints as much with a musical quote from Busoni's *Sonatina Seconda* in the fourth movement.

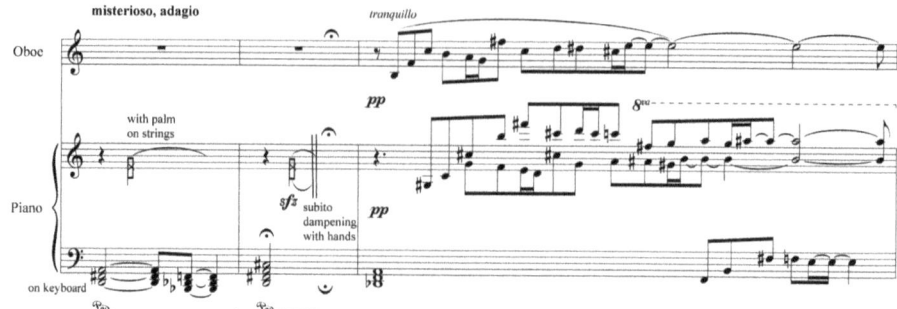

Example 7.3 L. Sitsky, *Oboe Sonatina*, mvt 4, first stave

Example 7.4 F. Busoni, *Sonata Seconda* (Breitkopf and Härtel, Leipzig, 1912), p. 9

Note: Accidentals apply only to the note they precede.

Just as Busoni intended this sonatina as a sketch for his opera *Doktor Faust*, which is the culmination of his fascination with the occult, the experimental oboe sonatina sowed the seeds for the young Sitsky's later compositional and mystical development in his music.

As Sitsky is fundamentally a melodic composer, for whom the line is the overriding element, many works focus on the possibility of organising the melodies using very long rows. As he says:

> [T]here was a period when the Second Viennese School was very interesting, whereas earlier I would have thought it a bit academic. I discovered that it didn't have to be and that it was very powerful and it suited me in a couple of the operas to write in a kind of expressionistic way. There was the discovery of the kind of lyrical 12-tone music in the visage of people like Dallapiccola, for instance. It didn't all have to sound angst-ridden, angular Germanic.[6]

---

6   Cotter, *Sitsky*, p. 94.

Sitsky's earliest ventures into 12-tone writing in his opera *Fall of the House of Usher* (1965) and the *Twelve Mystical Preludes* (1967) already show Sitsky's preoccupation with melody and broader lines. By the time of his piano trio *Atman* (1975), he had abandoned all pretence of using the 12 tones of the chromatic scale as the basis of his rows, using freely constructed melodies instead and relying entirely on the expressive power of the gestures and intervals contained within these melodies over the course of the transformations. The cello part has a row that is 22 notes long, with two similar 11-note halves.

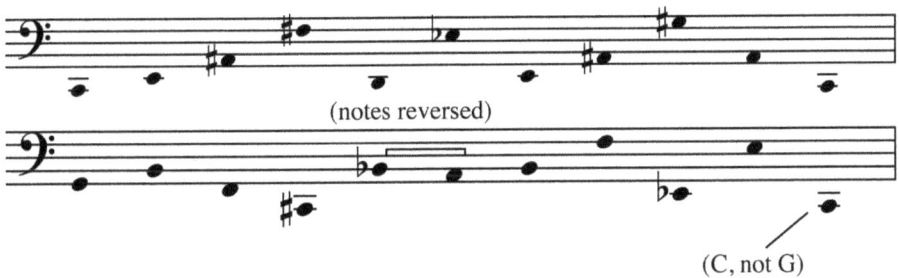

Example 7.5 Tone row from *Atman*, with similar 11-note halves

The second half is a transposition at the fifth of the first half, with the sixth and seventh notes reversed and the last note of the second half transposed down a fifth to match the last note of the first half.

The warm intimacy of the low cello opening notes is a fitting introduction to a row that is more 'whole tone' then chromatic—nine of the first 11 notes belong to the C whole-tone scale—and the repeated low Cs in the original row hint at a tonal centre, perhaps the 'absolute abiding centre' of the self that is the 'Atman' of Buddhist thought. Sitsky bases the cello part almost exclusively on this row, carefully sculpted so that the cello gradually rises from its lowest register to the highest by the end of the work.

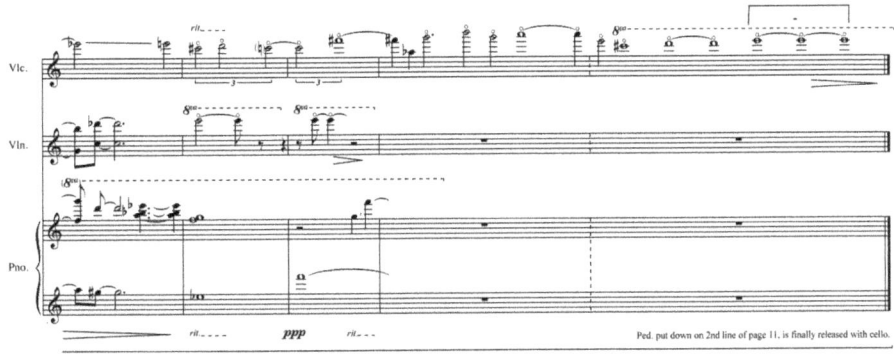

Example 7.6 L. Sitsky, *Atman*, p. 14

The ending, with the solo cello rising above the lingering resonance of the piano, might represent the triumph of one's personal Atman against the impurities of the outer world.

The idea of the row as a melody—incorporating the processes of transformation and fragmentation—remained central to Sitsky's composition, even as his imagination took him further away from the traditional serial idiom. The year 1984 was an astonishingly prolific one for Sitsky. He had become fascinated with Armenian chant through the music of the mystic George Ivanovich Gurdjieff, and pared down his style to focus squarely on melody. His gift for musical rhetoric shone as he explored the full emotional range of this oriental music, relying on the power of pitch contour to convey meaning beyond the possibilities of ordinary language.

The *Trio No. 4, Romantica for Violin, Cello and Piano* (1986) combines these Armenian-inspired melodies with row technique. The initial themes are richly ornamented, as they circle restlessly around a pitch centre of E.

Example 7.7 L. Sitsky, *Trio Romantica*, bars 1–3

As they become fragmented and transposed with different 'rows' unfolding simultaneously in counterpoint, the sense of tonality is gradually obscured, as is the Armenian influence of the melodic material.

Example 7.8 L. Sitsky, *Trio Romantica*, bars 200–2

The violin line is a development of the violin/cello lines beginning in bar 15, with octave transpositions; the cello line is a further development of the scale motif (see, for example, bars 40–50, 142–5); the right hand of the piano comes from the opening cello line, transposed down by a third; while the ostinato bass, now in arpeggios, has a root of G instead of E as in the opening. Sitsky references the romantic era with sweeping arpeggios, strident octaves, rippling accompaniment figures and such piano textures that blend into each other; he combines sections of anguish, of grandeur, of pathos, and of humour in a single, sweeping movement.

Sitsky never intended great things for the *Tetragrammaton*, for violin and piano (1987). When his friend the violinist Jan Sedivka asked for a work for violin and piano, Sitsky struggled with the idea before eventually giving up and putting his sketches aside. These sketches later became the epic 12-movement quartet for flute, viola, cello and piano, *The Secret Gates of the House of Osiris*. As Sitsky wrote: 'The extended colour and development of the basic materials in the quartet seemed to answer my dissatisfaction with the original concept.'[7] Only after completing this larger work did Sitsky realise his original idea of a smaller, four-movement form for only two instruments, and he would continue to view the duo work as a compromise of the grander quartet. Nevertheless, the *Tetragrammaton* would prove to be a pivotal work for Sitsky, as he rediscovered the potential for a solo instrument with piano accompaniment—a combination that he had avoided for 25 years! He followed it with an outpouring of duo works including *Sharagan II*, for cello and piano (1988), *Necronomicon*, for clarinet and piano (1989), and one sonata each for violin, oboe, and double bass with piano accompaniment.

---

7 Sitsky, Larry 1997, *Tetragrammaton: Four pieces for violin and piano*, Seesaw Music, New York, program note.

With these works, Sitsky's harmonic language expanded to take advantage of the unique importance of the piano in a duo ensemble. In his earlier works, the texture seems more important than any specific harmonic moment, as layers of sound collide and drift apart. In the duo works, Sitsky allows the natural dialectic between a single-line instrument and the piano to dictate a dynamic relationship between the melody and the harmony. Certain motifs might be associated with certain harmonic colours, and the melody seems to respond to the suggestions of the accompanying chords. In *Tetragrammaton*, the opening melody is similar to the row from *Atman*: it is a long, winding melody with hints of the whole-tone scale. As the work unfolds, however, it becomes clear that the melody is not as autonomous as it was in the earlier trio, as the harmonies underneath drive the music development. In the opening, Sitsky lets the violin carry the melody alone, accompanied only by occasional shadows in the piano. As this theme is reprised in each of the four movements, the accompanying piano chords become gradually thicker.

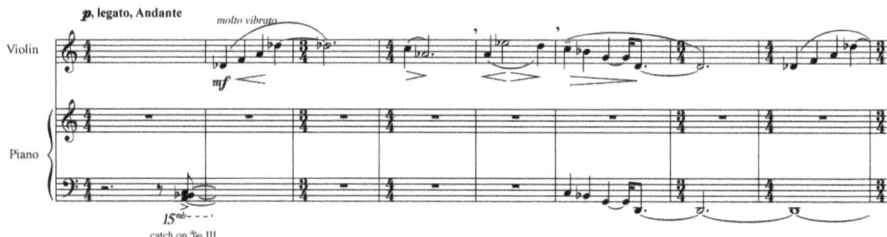

Example 7.9 L. Sitsky, *Tetragrammaton*, mvt 1, p. 1 (original manuscript version)

Example 7.10 L. Sitsky, *Tetragrammaton*, mvt 2, p. 10 (original manuscript version)

7. Sitsky's Chamber Music

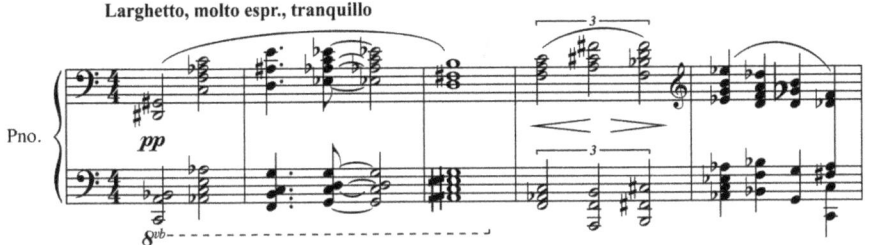

Example 7.11 L. Sitsky, *Tetragrammaton*, mvt 3, p. 15 (original manuscript version)

Example 7.12 L. Sitsky, *Tetragrammaton*, mvt 4, p. 25 (original manuscript version)

Sitsky uses chords based on fourths and fifths—dramatic, commanding chords. He frequently juxtaposes two unrelated chords against each other in different registers of the piano, causing a bell-like jarring of overtones. The final reprise uses the lower registers of the piano, and the richness of the harmony becomes formidably opaque—a dark mass against the searingly bright light of the soaring violin line.

Sitsky's temperament always fought against the restrictions of strict serial technique. Sitsky characterises this internal battle as one between the 'right brain' (creativity) and the 'left brain' (order). As he says:

> If you ask me what my ideal music is, I would say it's one that pleases both sides of the brain. But it's a tall order. I want it to sound as though it was springing into life at that moment, but I also want it to sound logical. I suspect it's impossible.[8]

The fourth violin concerto, *The Dreaming* (1998), was Sitsky's first work to use no 'rules', with a coherent musical form constructed entirely by instinct. Whether remarkable or inevitable, the sonic landscapes and musical narratives of his more freely composed works are not much different from the earlier, stricter

---

8   Sitsky interview, 2 July 2009.

pieces. Among his chamber works, Sitsky comes closest to free composition in the *Sonata for Oboe and Piano, The Nine Songs* (2005). While he still uses a row, he fragments it and allows himself to bend it with chromatic alterations, resulting in an almost limitless range of melodic possibilities. The 'rightness' of the music is immediately compelling as it evolves naturally out of the oboe's first utterance.

Sitsky almost always composes with specific performers in mind. The Czech emigré violinist Jan Sedivka was the dedicatee for four violin concerti and *Tetragrammaton*, and Sitsky's violin writing is ideally suited for Sedivka's richly romantic playing. Sedivka's recordings of Sitsky's music are among the finest, due in part to their similar musical styles; both have a fascination with mysticism and the philosophies of Gurdjieff, and, as Sitsky says: 'Jan and I both play like gypsies.'[9]

His acquaintance with the Russian virtuosos Alexander Ivashkin and Oleh Krysa inspired works in a leaner, more athletic style. The *Enochian Sonata*, for two cellos and piano, begins rather cheekily with a nod to Prokofiev's cello sonata.

Example 7.13 L. Sitsky, *Enochian Sonata*, bars 1–6

Example 7.14 S. Prokofiev, *Sonata for Cello and Piano*, Op. 119, bars 1–5

---

9 Beaumont, Rosina 1987, 'Words, music merge in mystery', *Mercury* [Hobart], 31 October 1987, p. 23.

The oboe sonata would be a daunting challenge to perform, not only because of the technical difficulties, but also because of the almost total lack of expression marks. It is hard to imagine how someone unacquainted with Sitsky's musical language would be able to make sense of the score. Perhaps this is because Sitsky wrote the piece for David Nuttall—a close friend with whom he has collaborated for more than 20 years. As Sitsky explains, the paucity of markings 'wasn't conscious, but maybe I was thinking that we'd be playing it, so if necessary we'd add and subtract whatever'.[10]

Vocal Works

Sitsky was a budding poet in his youth and has retained a special affinity for the power of the spoken word. He is careful to preserve the natural inflections and rhythms of the language in his songs, judiciously colouring and highlighting single phrases. He prefers imagery to narrative, which has naturally led him to set poets who imply much more than they explain. As he says: 'For me the structure of the poem immediately dictates the structure of the music…Most of my settings are shortish. I'm looking for something that has a self-contained form, so the music will provide a frame for the poem.'[11]

This desire for epigrammatic poems has frequently inspired Sitsky to set shorter Chinese poems. In the works where he does set the Western romantic poets, he frequently chooses only a fragment of a much longer poem for his setting. The refrain from the cantata *Deep in My Hidden Country* (1984) is an excerpt from Christopher Brennan's poem *The Wanderer*—an extended meditation on physical and metaphysical journeys. The four lines that Sitsky uses encapsulate the restless nature of the wanderer without reference to specific events:

> Go: tho' ye find it bitter, yet must ye be bare
> to the wind and the sea and the night and the wail of birds in the sky;
> go: tho' the going be hard and the goal blinded with rain
> yet the staying is a death that is never soften'd with sleep.[12]

These enigmatic lines that refer only obliquely to the subject of the poem, yet somehow capture the essence and the beauty of the poetic language, are typical of Sitsky's settings.

---

10 Sitsky interview, 1 September 2009.
11 Sitsky interview, 2 July 2009.
12 Brennan, Christopher 1966, *Selected Poems of Christopher Brennan*, A. R. Chisholm (ed.), Angus & Robertson, Sydney, p. 50. Sitsky changes tho' to though, ye to you, and soften'd to softn'd.

As Busoni writes in his *Sketch of a New Aesthetic of Music*:

> When the scene presents the illusion of a thunderstorm, this is exhaustively apprehended by the eye. Nevertheless, nearly all composers strive to depict the storm in tones which is not only a needless and feebler repetition, but likewise a failure to perform their true function. The person on the stage is either psychically influenced by the thunderstorm, or his mood, being absorbed in a train of thought of stronger influence, remains unaffected. The storm is visible and audible without aid from music; it is the invisible and inaudible, the spiritual processes of the personages portrayed, which music should render intelligible.[13]

This perspective—that the music should not express the meaning of the words directly, but should rather be complementary to it—resulted in a number of unorthodox settings of poetry in many of Sitsky's works. Sitsky uses Christopher Brennan's unusual translation of *Recueillement* by Charles Baudelaire in *Deep in My Hidden Country ('from Baudelaire')*:

> Learn wisdom, O my Grief, and hold thy peace,
> The evening thou didst long for nearer grows:
> The blurring vapours o'er the city close,
> Dispensing care to some, to some release.
> Now that the mortal mob without surcease
> Beneath the hangman lash of Pleasure goes
> To pluck remorse where fruit of tempting glows,
> O give me thy hand and, when their gibberings cease,
> Come hither. See from heaven's balconies
> The lost years lean, in robes of antique shape;
> Regret, with smiling look, thro' waters rise:
> Beneath its triumph arch the sun lies dead;
> And trailing o'er the East a shroud,
> O Hark! The Night with stealing tread.

Brennan (1870–1932) was heavily influenced by the French symbolist poets. His original poetry is exuberant and loquacious, and he favours expressions that would have been quaint even at the time, giving his poems a faded quality even as they sprang to life. Sitsky's romantic sensibilities and his taste for art that spurns a limp 'naturalness' in favour of strongly etched personality would lead him to consider Brennan 'that most settable of Australian poets'.[14]

---

[13] Busoni, Ferruccio 1911, *Sketch of a New Aesthetic of Music*, Theodore Baker (trans.), Schirmer, New York, p. 14.

[14] Sitsky, Larry 1984, *Deep in My Hidden Country...Cantata for soprano, flute, percussion, cello & piano*, Distributed by the Australian Music Centre, The Rocks, NSW.

Sitsky uses vivid colours in the instrumental parts: brilliant runs in the piano, expressive melodies contrasted with snap pizzicato in the cello, and piercing gestures played with very hard mallets on the vibraphone to mirror the garish imagery of the first two stanzas of the poem.

Example 7.15 L. Sitsky, 'Recueillement', from *Deep in My Hidden Country*, opening

As 'Regret, with smiling look' and 'The Night with stealing tread' rise to the surface, the initial instrumental turbulences settle into a rocking, polyrhythmic ostinato.

Example 7.16 L. Sitsky, 'Recueillement', from *Deep in My Hidden Country*, pp. 30–1

The song concludes with a tranquil instrumental chorale harmonised entirely in G major.

Example 7.17 L. Sitsky, 'Recueillement', from *Deep in My Hidden Country*, pp. 32–3

Over this, the singer twice repeats a word like a mantra: 'wisdom'. Wisdom. This word comes from the beginning of the poem, and Sitsky must have been intrigued by the implication that wisdom is a balm for grief to emphasise it in this way.

Such emphasis—magnifying certain words or phrases to bend the poetry in unusual directions—is a common device in these songs. Sitsky often assigns a fixed pitch to certain words. The first of the songs from the Whitman cycle, 'Out of the Cradle, Endlessly Rocking', highlights two simple words: 'out' and 'from'. The text of this poem is the introduction to a longer poem about the death of a nightingale and its resonance in the soul of a young boy, awakening his inner poetic instinct:

> Out of the cradle endlessly rocking,
> Out of the mocking-bird's throat, the musical shuttle,
> Out of the Ninth-month midnight,
> Over the sterile sands and the fields beyond, where the child leaving his bed wander'd alone, bareheaded, barefoot,
> Down from the shower'd halo,
> Up from the mystic play of shadows twining and twisting as if they were alive,
> Out from the patches of briers and blackberries,
> From the memories of the bird that chanted to me,
> From your memories sad brother, from the fitful risings and fallings I heard,
> From under that yellow half-moon late-risen and swollen as if with tears,
> From those beginning notes of yearning and love there in the mist,
> From the thousand responses of my heart never to cease,
> From the myriad thence-arous'd words,

From the word stronger and more delicious than any,
From such as now they start the scene revisiting,
As a flock, twittering, rising, or overhead passing,
Borne hither, ere all eludes me, hurriedly,
A man, yet by these tears a little boy again,
Throwing myself on the sand, confronting the waves,
I, chanter of pains and joys, uniter of here and hereafter,
Taking all hints to use them, but swiftly leaping beyond them,
A reminiscence sing.[15]

As the words 'from' and 'out' appear regularly at the beginning of the poetic lines, Sitsky structures the vocal line so that these words are emphasised by always recurring on the same pitch.

Example 7.18 L. Sitsky, 'Out of the Cradle, Endlessly Rocking', from *A Whitman Cycle: Six songs for low voice & piano*, bars 2–7 (vocal line only)

Example 7.19 L. Sitsky, 'Out of the Cradle, Endlessly Rocking', from *A Whitman Cycle: Six songs for low voice & piano*, bars 19–26 (vocal line only)

---

15 Whitman, Walt 1921, *Leaves of Grass*, Modern Library, New York, p. 213. Sitsky cuts the following lines: 'From the myriad thence-arous'd words,/From the word stronger and more delicious than any,/From such as now they start the scene revisiting'; 'Borne hither, ere all eludes me, hurriedly'; and 'Taking all hints to use them, but swiftly leaping beyond them'.

In *Music of the Mirabell Garden*, Sitsky took this idea a step further. He unified the cycle of six poems by selecting 62 'recurring image words'—words such as 'dark', 'sky' and 'blood' are always set to the same pitch in the vocal line and similar accompaniment in the instruments. Sitsky ordered the poems so that the density of these image words would gradually increase; while the first poem, 'Winter Nightfall', contains only 14 image words, the final poem, 'Grodek', contains 35.[16]

As the instrumental music treated pitch organisation more and more liberally from the 1980s onwards, the vocal music became less stylised and more varied; the driving force of the text inspired Sitsky to represent the emotional qualities of each song with their own sound world—often radically different from each other.

The *Shih Ching (Book of Songs)* (1996) is more of a collection of songs then a song cycle *per se*, as Sitsky writes:

> These twelve settings are of words that had long sat on my library shelves, waiting to be set. Finally I decided that, rather than attempt to incorporate them into some kind of cyclic format and unified concept, I would in fact go the other way, and give the *Book of Songs* cohesion via diversity.[17]

The enigmatic, mystical quality of 'Napoleon' (Walter de la Mare) recalls the earlier *Whitman Cycle* with rich sonorities and clusters on the piano.

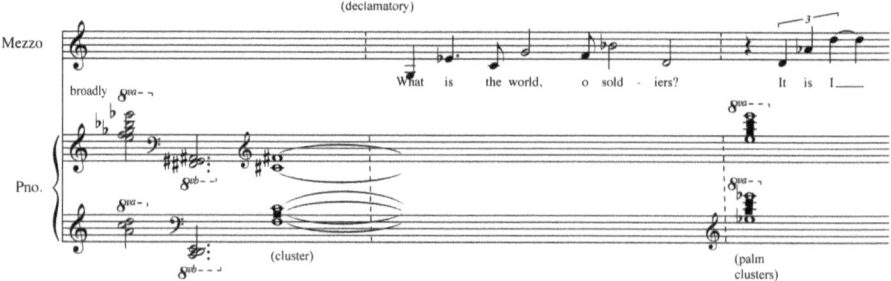

Example 7.20 L. Sitsky, 'Napoleon', from *Shih Ching*, first stave

The 'Sands of Dee' (Charles Kingsley) is unabashedly tonal, in a strophic form with variations in the piano accompaniment. The setting of Alexander

---

16 See Whiffin, Lawrence 1987, 'The use of recurring imagery as a structural device and a free approach to serialism in the song cycle "Music in the Mirabell Garden" for soprano and eight instruments by Larry Sitsky', *Musicology Australia*, vol. X, pp. 31–40.
17 Sitsky, Larry n.d., Shih Ching (Book of Songs): 12 settings for alto and piano, Unpublished ms., program note.

Blok's 'She Burst in from the Cold', in a translation by Sitsky, is set to violent *Sprechstimme*, accompanied by a virtuosic and kaleidoscopic piano part. Sitsky specifies that the *Sprechstimme* should be 'closer to speech than song'.

Example 7.21 L. Sitsky, 'She Burst in from the Cold', from ***Shih Ching***, p. 5

Sitsky's latest song cycles embrace this same diversity. *Bone of My Bones* (1998) concludes with another turbulent setting of Blok in Sitsky's translation, 'When We Parted', but the other songs use rich, ornamented vocal lines ('Introduction'), tapping on the lid of the piano ('Down by the Salley Gardens'), and there is even a 'Cabaret Song'—a setting of Elizabeth Barrett Browning's familiar love poem *How Do I Love Thee?Let me count the ways....*

Example 7.22 L. Sitsky, 'Cabaret Song', from ***Bone of My Bones***, bars 1–6

The Jade Harp (2005), for voice and fortepiano, also uses *Sprechstimme* and speech, but is firmly couched in the darkly brilliant harmonic and freely lyrical language of works such as the *Nine Songs* (2005), for oboe and piano.

The Piano Writing

As melody is Sitsky's priority; the piano often plays a subordinate role to the voice and solo instruments in the ensemble. As Sitsky says: 'I like the sound of instruments unaccompanied. So when I do use the piano, I have a feeling that the integrity of the line—whichever instrument it might be—is still number one. The piano therefore provides colour, backdrop…The line itself is still the predominant thing.'[18]

He loves to exploit the resonance of the piano by building up sonorities on the sustain pedal. Chords are left ringing (see the *Tetragrammaton* example above) or through ostinato (see *Romantica*, Example 7.7). In the oboe sonata *The Nine Songs*, he gives 'The Great Lord of Destinies' a rich halo of overtones with thick bass runs, pierced by a lament in the oboe.

Example 7.23 L. Sitsky, 'The Great Lord of Destinies', from *Nine Songs*, bars 49–51[19]

And he brings out the dazzling beauty and ornate attire of the 'Lady of Hsiang' with brilliant but edgy piano writing that hints also at her capricious temperament.

Example 7.24 L. Sitsky, 'The Lady of Hsiang', from *Nine Songs*, bars 30–4

Percussion has always played an important role in Sitsky's music—an element that he attributes to his early exposure to Chinese opera.[20] The pianist is often

---

18 Sitsky interview, 2 July 2009.
19 This movement is largely a transcription of the 'Prologue' from Sitsky's 40-minute piano piece *The Way of the Seeker* (2004). In the solo piano version, the pedal should be held throughout the movement—an indication that Sitsky replaced with 'con Ped.' in this oboe and piano version.
20 Holmes, Robyn, Shaw, Patricia and Campbell, Peter 1997, *Larry Sitsky: A bio-bibliography*, Greenwood Press, Westport, Conn., p. 4.

expected to recall the sounds of drums, bells and gongs—sounds that Sitsky uses to build up raucous and primevally exciting climaxes. He calls his song 'Desolation' from *The Jade Harp* a 'rhythmic recitation', as the spoken words in the voice are accompanied by relentless drumming clusters in the fortepiano—perhaps a moment when Sitsky comes closest to capturing the sound of Chinese opera.

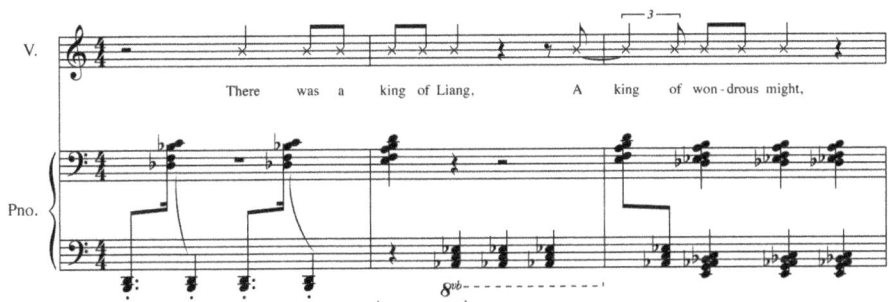

Example 7.25 L. Sitsky, 'Desolation', from *Jade Heart*, bars 6–8

Although the chamber and vocal works use the piano primarily for colour, Sitsky is a virtuoso pianist in his own right—a fact evident from the technically fiendish piano parts in works such as *Narayana*, the *Enochian Sonata*, or the violin sonata *Omnia Exeunt in Mysterium*. One of his most striking piano moments is the earth-shattering outpouring of energy in the brilliant piano cadenza from *Narayana*.

Example 7.26 L. Sitsky, *Narayana*, mvt 4, system 1, p. 16

Sitsky does occasionally allow the pianist to shine as a soloist—for example, at the end of the first movement of the *Enochian Sonata* where the combination of the thick, late-romantic piano texture and the rich harmonies allows the piano to shine in all its glory.

Example 7.27 L. Sitsky, *Enochian Sonata* (Keys Press, p. 12)

Performing Sitsky's music

In his book *Busoni and the Piano*, Sitsky approvingly quotes from Busoni's *Sketch of a New Aesthetic of Music*:

> Notation, the writing out of compositions, is primarily an ingenious expedient for catching an inspiration, with the purpose of exploiting it later. But notation is to improvisation as the portrait to the living model. It is for the interpreter to *resolve the rigidity of the signs* into the primitive emotion.[21]

For Sitsky, the innate nature of the music is far more important than the notes on the page. He never hesitates to adapt another composer's work to suit himself, and he expects his music to receive the same treatment. The revisions of his piano concerto *The Twenty-Two Paths of the Tarot* (1991, revised 1994) in collaboration with Roger Woodward show Sitsky's openness to quite substantial reinterpretations of his music as well as the fruits of an aesthetic dialogue between these two fiery musical personalities; the later version's fleshed-out solo part and streamlined structural arc are perhaps more convincing than the original.

Rhythm in Sitsky's hands is a wild and untamed beast, far from the regular tempos and polished rubatos of today's pianists. His favourite recordings are those by the legendary pianists from the dawn of the recording era such as Busoni, Rudolph Ganz and Ignaz Friedman—pianists whose rubato might be considered old-fashioned today. He has startled many a young student diligently playing in time by asking whether they are counting the beat. On an affirmative

---

21   Busoni, *Sketch of a New Aesthetic of Music*, p. 15 (emphasis in original). Quoted in Sitsky, *Busoni and the Piano*, p. 295.

reply, he will invariably say, 'Well, you must stop it at once!' Nevertheless, tempo and proportions of time on a broad scale are crucial for Sitsky, and he composes with a metronome and a stopwatch for this reason.

Sitsky's recordings form an essential guide for performers wishing to understand the full force of his musical personality. The recording of the piano sonatas by Roy Agnew is one of his finest, demonstrating his thorough command of melodic line and dramatic thrust.

Some basic elements should be borne in mind: in Sitsky's mature scores (from the oboe sonatina onwards), accidentals apply only to the notes they immediately precede. There are rare exceptions: the earlier *Oriental Love Songs* (1960) uses normal accidental rules in sections with bar lines, but unmeasured sections have an accidental on every sharp or flat. Some typeset or engraved scores follow normal accidental rules, even where Sitsky did not intend this. An example is the hand-copied score of *Music in the Mirabell Garden* (Seesaw Music, New York, 1996), or the separately engraved piano part of the piano concerto *The Twenty-Two Paths of the Tarot* (typeset September 1997, Peter Mapleson for Symphony Australia). In his handwritten scores, Sitsky writes sharps and flats even on tied notes; many of the typeset scores do not include these.

In the handwritten scores, repeated notes are often written using noteless stems. The pitch of a note can usually be determined by the shape of the notehead; Sitsky writes in the staff spaces with horizontal noteheads, and on the staff lines with vertical noteheads. Oversized sharps and flats apply to all notes in the following chord.

The slurs in the string parts are almost always phrase marks and have nothing to do with bowing. Occasionally short (usually two-note) slurs are meant rhythmically; here the notes under the slur can be played on one bow, with an initial accent and a separation at the end. A sensitive but liberal approach to slurring and portamento will bring Sitsky's melodies to life and heighten the emotional intensity of the wide intervals. The bowings in the following example help the ornamental gestures to flow around the central melody without disrupting it.

Example 7.28 L. Sitsky, *Sharagan II*, mvt 1, Example—bowings by David Pereira

Sitsky composes with few drafts or sketches, and he is reluctant to return to a work after he has completed it. For the performer, this cuts both ways: while Sitsky is open to novel interpretations or even rearrangements of his music, it can be hard to work out the original intentions. The recent typeset scores of Sitsky's works, published by the Keys Press, are a boon to performers, but as the scores go to press with minimal revision or proofreading, there are many errors and ambiguities. Performers using the typeset version should also refer to the manuscript copies available at the National Library of Australia, with the caveat that for works after 1996, Sitsky did not intend his final handwritten draft to be published in facsimile, so that any errors are often fixed only in the typeset publications.

Part 3: The Third Generation

The 1970s marked what might be regarded, in retrospect, as a golden period in Australian music. The battles that the previous generation had fought were over and done with, and the new generation could embark on their careers with a fresh sense of optimism about the viability of earning a living as a composer. Generally, government support for the arts was at its highest, and various organisations directly supported composers, such as the Australia Council and the Australian Music Centre. Commissioning from the major educational and concert-giving organisations was also peaking, so there was money for the commissioning as well as the performance of new scores. Publication became a reality probably for the first time in our history—that is, publication of serious art music, not just commercially viable educational material, kitsch (nationalistic and other varieties), or fairy floss. Suddenly composers were employable as composers, reversing previous trends where composers were employable only if they taught something else. New compositions were recognised in academia as products of serious personal research. As for music by composers who were concert pianists—this was a breed that was rapidly dying out, so the importance of the piano in chamber and vocal music began a slow decline as well. Cultural historians will be writing about the changes to our society, and about the new political awareness that came from involvement in conflicts in the Pacific and Asian regions. Some composers were passionate about this kind of engagement and it influenced their music; others, as usual, simply jumped on that particular bandwagon and used it to be continually fashionable and trendy. The sad cause of the Aboriginal people was yet another cow to be milked, one way or another. The 'golden age' did not last long, historically speaking, and the realities of being an artist in Australia returned all too soon, with all of its attendant evils and cynical exploitations.

8. The Next Wave of Modernism

Ann Ghandar (1943–)

Ann Ghandar is a fine pianist, so, in her compositions, the piano parts tend to be assertive and vital to the musical discourse. *Autumn Chimes* (1995) is probably best described by the composer herself:

> *Autumn Chimes* was written in the autumn, and it uses a selection of scales from garden chimes on display in a shop in Federation Square, Canberra. I used different combinations of the five instruments (flute, oboe, violin, cello and piano) only using all of them in the last piece, and making two of the pieces for a solo instrument (flute, piano). Two of the five pieces are based on Egyptian folk tunes ('Gentle Waves of the Sea' and 'The Nightingale').

In fact, Ann Ghandar's studies of music of the Middle East have affected her approach to composition, and over the years I have noticed a softening and an increasingly gentle lyricism appearing in her scores. Two of the pieces of *Autumn Chimes* are named after birds: 'Cormorant' and 'Ibises'. The first movement is titled 'Rain', which neatly takes us to another set of pieces, for flute and piano: *Birds in Light Rain*. Each of the short pieces is named after an Australian bird

I. 'Eastern Rosellas'

II. 'Crested Pigeons'

III. 'Galahs'

IV. 'King Parrot'

V. 'Lone Crested Pigeon'.

By a curious coincidence, as I write this, I have just completed recording the complete series of 73 *Bird Impressions* by the South Australian composer Hooper Brewster-Jones, written in the early 1920s. It is good to see that this tradition is still alive and well in Australian music. The Ghandar (Ann originally comes from Adelaide, too) pieces are one-page miniatures—lightning sketches of our feathered friends; unlike Brewster-Jones, Ghandar does not incorporate the bird's call into her pieces.

Her *Sonata for Clarinet and Piano* seems to me to be full of Eastern scales (perhaps taken from her studies of Egyptian music). More a sonatina in scope than a sonata, the work is cast in the traditional fast-slow-fast, three-movement format.

Australian Chamber Music with Piano

Gerald Glynn (1943–)

Gerald Glynn says of *Interplay* (1980), for cello and piano:

> Interplay began as a composition for harpsichord and cello, but as the work progressed something acoustically bigger and stronger than the harpsichord seemed necessary to counterbalance the assertiveness of the cello writing.
>
> And so the piano took over, thereby considerably widening the dynamic and pitch range through which the piece was to move. The influence of the harpsichord is still to be felt however in the constant arpeggiating of the opening chord, one of the recurrent unifying characteristics of the work, which is heard in many different guises before the piece finishes...
>
> Repetition with variation is in fact one of the salient features of the writing; another is the cat-and-mouse-like interaction between the two instruments, which is implicit in the title.
>
> Like two athletes in a relay race, there is a passing to and fro of the baton, often using a common pitch to do so. There is a jostling and friendly rivalry between the two, repeated attempts to have the last word on a given subject, and an occasional bit of devilry.

Example 8.1 G. Glynn, *Interplay*, bars 1–4

Like all of Gerald's music, here organic growth and development are ever-present characteristics. Even in his early (1971) *Music for Clarinet in B-flat and Piano*, it is there to be discerned. This particular work is especially interesting in that Glynn uses a mixture of graphic and standard notation, giving the players free rein when he thinks it desirable to create a more rhapsodic effect, and tightening the control when he wishes to be more in charge of proceedings. Thus, notes given a specific duration are always at crotchet = 60; otherwise the notation is graphic, with 1 cm being equivalent to one second. This clever mixture of notations results in a free-flowing but powerful work.

Glynn's *Strata for Violin and Piano* (1994) is a different kind of music altogether. It consists of three discrete movements, called, quite naturally, 'Stratum 1', '2' and '3'. Each stratum movement is basically an exploration of a single kind of texture or idea. So, 'Stratum 1' is essentially long notes with varying dynamics, the piano often playing at the extremes of the keyboard. 'Stratum 2' is directed scales and arpeggios, with the two instruments not often together, but jostling for room. 'Stratum 3' has elements of both previous movements juxtaposed. The writing for the instruments in all of the mentioned works is virtuosic and requires command of the instrument. There is nothing here for the faint-hearted. The pieces are full of an admirable energy.

Gerald is a fine poet himself, so it is not surprising that he would be attracted to word settings and, moreover, that his choice of words would be dictated by a refined taste for language and its inflections. This is immediately apparent in *Love's Coming* (1986), a song cycle for medium voice and piano on six poems by John Shaw Nielsen. Since Nielsen is an important Australian poet, I list the titles of the settings for the reader's interest

1. 'Love's Coming'
2. 'Surely God was a Lover'
3. 'The Hour of the Parting'
4. 'Love in Absence'
5. 'So Sweet a Mouth had She'
6. 'When Kisses are as Strawberries'.

The settings are a model of clarity and balance between the piano and voice. The piano part sets the mood, as in traditional lieder/art song, and then develops under the vocal line, both supporting the setting and growing in its own right. Unlike the purely instrumental music, where the keyboard writing is often fierce, here Glynn holds the piano part in check, and always with due deference for the vocal part. In *The Rose of Amherst* (1991), a song cycle for medium voice and piano on poems of Emily Dickinson, the piano part is a little more elaborate, but the same sensitive balance between voice and keyboard is maintained. The songs are

1. 'I'm Nobody, Who are You?'
2. 'Exultation'
3. 'The Soul Selects'
4. 'I Sing to Use the Waiting'
5. 'Pain'
6. 'A Summer's Day'.

Example 8.2 G. Glynn, 'Pain', from *The Rose of Amherst*, bars 1–4

I caught up with Gerald recently after a long period of contact only by mail, and he told me that he has recently retired from active teaching in Paris, so I hope that his productivity will increase. We have too few composers of his calibre not to value their output for the cultural enrichment of our country.

Roger Smalley (1943–)

It is a great pleasure to once again write about Roger Smalley, our outstanding composer and pianist. His scores are a model of clarity and are musically unambiguous in their intention. What shines through everything are Roger's concern and command over form. Even in an early *Capriccio for Violin and Piano* (1966), the composer carefully inscribes the form of the piece on the title page: 'Fantasia', 'Scherzo', 'Nocturne', and 'Coda'. The first and last sections are extensive cadenzas; the work as a whole is dominated by very low, growly chords on the piano constantly interplayed with very high notes, including harmonics, on the violin. Smalley, a virtuoso himself, quite naturally writes in virtuosic fashion for his instruments of choice, and is a perfect example of what we are in danger of losing—that is, composers who are also constant and active denizens of the concert platform. Composers who are not performers often have no sense of the theatre and drama of performance.

I mention here Smalley's *Monody for Piano with Live Electronic Modulation* (1972), although it is not strictly within my personal definition of chamber music. This is a solo piece, but is really a product of its time—and the then fashion—using early synthesisers and ring modulation, mixed with the acoustic piano sound and emerging 'live' through two speakers. I cannot imagine this piece being revived in today's computer world. The title is a simple reflection of the fact that the piano line is a monody: one note at a time. The pianist is also required to play some percussion instruments with the left hand at the same time as the right hand plays on the keyboard—requiring no mean dexterity. Over the years, Smalley has moved away from electronics to purely acoustic music.

The *Movement for Flute and Piano* (1976) still has remnants of the tyranny of the European avant-garde, with its own brand of political correctness. In this case, the pianist has to constantly reach under the lid of the instrument to produce special effects. It is not much use Roger saying in his introductory notes that these 'various inside-the-piano techniques should be executed as unobtrusively as possible'. Some of us are anatomically unsuited to perform such manoeuvres without just about climbing on the piano stool. Again, Smalley has largely abandoned such writing. In this piece, concentrating on the effects, which interrupt the lyrical flute line, often hamstrings the piano part. Once again, we note the composer's preoccupation with form; this time, he writes a 'Theme' (a particularly lovely one, first given out by the flute), followed by seven variations. It is fact that when the piano is left untrammelled to do its own thing, the music takes off, as in an effects-free slab of time in variations two and three. In general, my contention is that the piece works best when it is least gimmicky. The flute is asked to play into the piano, to increase the sympathetic resonance.

The *Piano Quintet* (2003) is like a breath of fresh air in comparison—free and exuberant—the 'Overture' immediately capturing our attention and sounding like a baroque movement. The 'Intermezzo', which follows, is in effect the slow movement. The third movement is a scherzo, played one beat in the bar, and with the phrase lengths indicated in the score, and used as a structural device. The movement consists of 'Introduction—Scherzo I' (mostly three-bar phrase units); 'Trio I' (legato as against the prior staccato section); 'Scherzo II' (mostly four-bar units); 'Trio II' (pedal and harmonics); 'Scherzo III' (a mixture of phrase durations). Not content with this elaborate structure, the composer has a further highly organised last movement, labelled 'Chaconne & Variations', with each subtitle representing a particular miniature: I) 'Marche Funebre'; II) 'Waltz; III. Barcarolle'; IV) 'Nocturne (with Nightmare)'; V) 'Scherzo'; VI) 'Polonaise'; and VII) 'Berceuse'. The quintet is undoubtedly an important work in the Australian repertoire of chamber music with piano.

There are three trios that need mentioning: the first is *Piano Trio* (1990–91). This work, like some of Smalley's solo piano music, owes something to past literature that the composer has performed, and especially his beloved Chopin. Smalley says, in his introduction:

> The trio is in two parts, each of which consists of two linked movements—a short slow movement which acts as an introduction to the longer fast movement. Following my Variations on a Theme of Chopin for solo piano, this trio is the next in a continuing series of works based on material extracted from various Chopin Mazurkas (in this case an extremely chromatic 8-bar progression which occurs towards the end of the Mazurka in Ab Op. 59 No. 2).

The opening 'Prelude' presents the whole of this progression stretched over the entire length of the movement and embellished with sighing chromatic figures. This leads, via a prolonged dominant seventh chord, directly into the 'Scherzo', whose form could be represented as ABACDA—in other words, it has three 'trios' (B, C and D) but the second and third are joined, without the expected interpolation of A. The final return of A is truncated and the first part ends abruptly. This scherzo is only tangentially related to Chopin.

Part two opens with a slow passacaglia during which the Chopin progression is unfolded (from the bass up) as four superimposed contrapuntal lines, or features a common interval extracted from all four lines. The first six variations are fast and vigorous, leading to a climax in 'Variation 7': loud repeated chords in the bass of the piano out of which emerge ethereal harmonics on the two strings. The final six variations are slow and in the form of a chaconne. The music draws ever closer to the Chopin original, but the work ends ambivalently.

This trio together with the *Trio for Clarinet, Viola and Piano* (1992–99) and the wonderful *Trio for Horn, Violin and Piano* (2000–02) forms a summation of Roger's chamber music. The two last-named trios contain fast opening sections, followed by highly structured variation movements (mirror variations in the case of the *Horn Trio*). The journey by a gifted composer from a somewhat self-conscious avant-garde beginning to a personal definitive language is now complete. Playing through these scores, I was reminded of the glittery music of Roberto Gerhard, who, like Smalley, moved from a 12-tone language to highly individual gesticulatory texture full of immense energy and colour. The fast scale patterns that appear in these trios especially brought Gerhard to my mind.

Example 8.3 R. Smalley, *Trio for Clarinet, Viola and Piano*, bars 24–6

Haydn Reeder (1944–)

The collected folio of Haydn Reeder's music began with a work quite atypical of his usual style. It is a song setting (words by Gary Broadziak) for baritone and piano duet. It is obviously a lament for a lost child, and opens with a key signature of E-flat major in the piano, with moving words set in a fairly steady beat. The song is called *About Brett*. The rest of our collection of Reeder scores is what I more or less would have expected. Reeder writes in a post–12-tone style, in a dense and busy texture hovering on the fringes of maximalism. Thus, *Chants at Play with Solid Background*, for flute, bass clarinet and piano, seems to refer to a busy, close-knit, chromatically twisting figure, which is ever-present in the piece, though essentially in the piano and bass clarinet parts, providing the 'solid background', with the flute representing the 'chants at play'. Here is a characteristic example.

Example 8.4 H. Reeder, *Chants at Play with Solid Background*, bars 25–6

I could quote other like instances, but need to sum it up by saying that it is not very user friendly. *Encephalograph*, for clarinet, cello, trombone, percussion and piano, begins with a steady heartbeat (my interpretation, not the composer's) but soon shifts into irregularity of bar durations featuring much portamento and spiky piano writing.

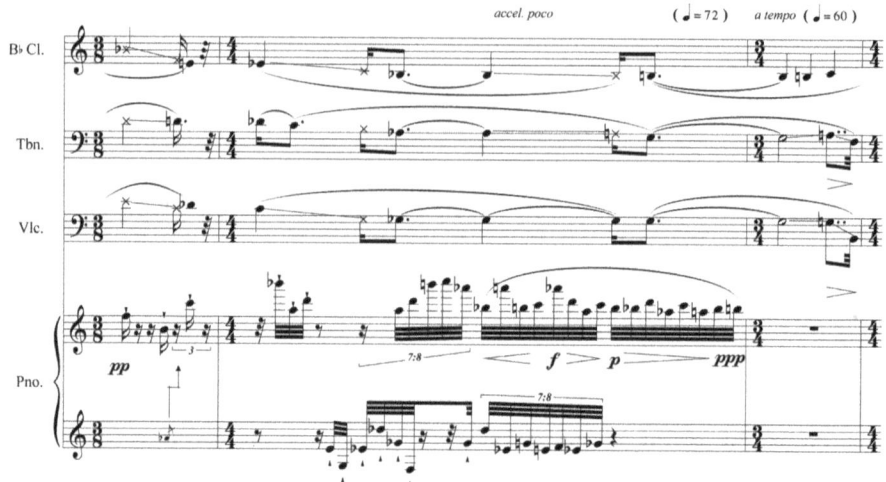

Example 8.5 H. Reeder, *Encephalograph*, p. 6, two bars after figure D

The score of *Interact* (1980), for flute, horn, viola, bassoon and piano, has a declaration of intent by Haydn Reeder:

> The composer wanted to write a work in which the characteristics of classical music were present. These appear as a balance of content and form, of pitches and rhythm, of movement and repose and a choice of instruments which blend well. The attainment of this equilibrium compelled a restriction of each element within certain boundaries, for instance, the basis of the pitch material is a symmetrical twelve-tone row. There are sections of repose analogous to the classical cadence; interaction and meshing of movement and repose sections analogous to development; and the opening idea of the work returns.

The title of *Siren's Echo* (1985), for alto flute, piano and percussion, apparently refers to the two positions of placement for the flute. Similarly, *Sonage 2* refers to a work for two pianos (mostly in a staccato pointillist fashion), whilst *Stradevarie*, for cello and piano, is an obvious play on words. *The Obstinate Flute: Perhaps it's a joke?* is a short piece wherein the flute mostly plays D-flats against the piano part.

Gillian Whitehead (1941–)

The New Zealand/Australian composer Gillian Whitehead barely makes it into this book, not due to any quality judgment on my part (I happen to think she is a terrific composer), but simply because of the limited usage of the piano and the few works that actually use the piano at all. Take *Ahotu (O matenga)* (1984), for example, with its impressive provenance of a commission by Flederman—at one stage one of our top ensembles—subsidised by the Australia Council, and premiered at the Adelaide Festival. A powerful, dramatic, deeply felt piece composed in memory of the composer's father, *Ahotu* is scored for flute/piccolo, trombone/crotales, piano, harpsichord, celeste/bass drum and a large percussion line-up. The piano is just a part of a large percussion ensemble—an array that treats harpsichord and celeste in the same manner. It is essentially outside the intended scope of this book, although I recommend the work highly.

Angels Born at the Speed of Light (1992) is in a similar situation, maybe even more so: it is scored for dancer, an improvising trio of flute/saxophones (tenor, soprano), percussion and piano (optional vibes) and narrator. Two other works are closer to what we were looking for: *Awa Herea (Braided Rivers)* (1993), for soprano and piano, and *Haiku* (1995), for voice, viola and piano. The first of these uses Maori text, some of it written by the composer; the second sets English haiku by Alan Wells. There is a strong folk basis deeply embedded in Whitehead's music—sometimes extremely close to the source, sometimes moving away from it to some degree, in one parameter or another. The long pedals often serve to highlight a most expressive and lyrical vocal line. The writing is extremely fluid and improvisational, or suggestion for improvisation is everywhere, woven into the fabric. The resultant music has a built-in and seductive paradox: it sounds improvisatory, yet has a strong thematic core—a combination I find very attractive. The composer notes that much of the vocal line for the first work, with its eight short songs, is based on birdsong. The haiku settings tend to feature instrumental solos; there is a cryptic note about a trombone solo (not an instrument listed) that I failed to understand.

Malcolm J. Fox (1946–97)

Malcolm Fox's *Six Miniatures* (1991), for violin and piano, lives in a world akin to pre–strict 12 tone—a cousin to Schoenberg's short piano pieces early in the twentieth century—except that Fox allows some improvisation (which Schoenberg would not have), and Fox also dwells on particular gestures thematically. These miniatures are highly poetic and deeply felt little pieces. From 1992, we have *Ten Thousand Years Goodbye. In celebration of frogs: their magic, mystery, humour and vitality*, for voice, clarinet and piano (text translated from Japanese by Cid Corman). The work is set out in a symmetrical fashion

1. 'Introduction': clarinet cadenza
2. 'Ten Thousand Years Goodbye': soprano, clarinet and piano
3. 'Interlude': piano solo

4. 'Five Frogs': soprano, clarinet and piano

5. 'Interlude II': clarinet and piano

6. 'Beethoven: Spring Sonata (First Impression)': soprano, clarinet and piano.

This is a most attractive and humorous work, both poetic and whimsical. The material is strongly knit thematically, well crafted and of moderate difficulty.

Richard Mills (1949–)

My suspicion is that Richard Mills is, by temperament, not inclined towards chamber music as a vehicle for his expression. He is a natural orchestral and operatic composer, and his experience as a conductor has only further strengthened these inclinations. We have only two examples of Richard's foray into chamber music: *Three Pieces for French Horn and Piano* (2002)—consisting of 1) 'Considering Spring', 2) 'Contemplation', and 3. 'Coursing'—and the *Twelve Bagatelles for Flute and Piano* (1980), which are aphoristic one or two-page pieces. The idiom of these works is generally of a light tone and fairly easy on the ear. Richard is not a pianist, but his high level of craft ensures that the writing for the instruments is idiomatic and approachable. The harmonies tend towards tonality and the broken chords are also triadic, often with additions of notes such as the added sixth.

Vincent Plush (1950–)

Plush's settings for voice and piano (or instrument and piano) are usually much more than merely that. Vincent has always been interested in historical events—especially from colonial Australian history—and many of his word settings are linked to the country's past by use of appropriate words about or by historical personages. Since he lived in the United States for a number of years, there is also in existence a work named *The Ludlow Lullabies* (1989), for violin and piano. The work involves preparing one note of the piano to imitate the tolling of a distant school bell. The work commemorates a sad but little-known episode in American history known as the 'Ludlow Massacre'. Vincent uses the 'lullaby' sections of the work with a more angry, and what he calls 'mechanistic', music to demonstrate the other side of this chain of events. A portrait in sound, with words by a famous Australian, is Vincent's *The Plaint of Mary Gilmore* (1984), for mezzo-soprano and piano. This is a lengthy work in 12 sections, the text of which comes from various historical documents, including letters. The copious introductory notes give full explanation of the sources used and their significance. Both the pianist and the page turner are also given dramatic roles to perform, such as recitation, offstage instrument playing, and so on, so this is not a staid song cycle, but in the end a piece of music theatre with a definite political message at its core. I will not list the titles of the 12 sections, since they mean little on their own and do not give much away. Suffice to say that they are discrete entities, and are easily identified in the context of a performance of this work, which would take about 40 minutes if done in full (the composer does indicate some possible shortened versions and extracts, but this is obviously not really desirable). Finally, I would like to say a few words about *The Warrant of Henry Lawson* (1988), for baritone and piano. This work—although shorter than the Mary Gilmore piece (actually, it is about half the length)—is another portrait of an eminent Australian, and, although it can be done 'straight', it is obviously conceived as a music-theatre presentation. The performers are given stage movement directions and attitudinal expressions towards each other. The singer also has to recite, and even the page-turner or pianist has a tiny singing moment; the singer also stops some piano strings from vibrating in one section by damping with the hand. Thus, Plush's works are social commentary to an extent—perhaps as important as the sounds of the pieces themselves.

Brenton Broadstock (1952–)

With Brenton Broadstock's chamber music, we witness a metamorphosis in the writing from the early works in the 1980s to turning a corner in the 1990s. The earliest work we found was *Boolee* (1984), for two pianos. It is set out in a semi-graphic way, so coordination between the instruments is not really an issue. There is much background trilling and imitation of gestures, usually at a slightly different speed, and ornate effect is quite easily achieved; with the pianists playing from a two-piano score, there is no way they would lose their places. The result is a quasi-impressionistic wash of sound. By 1986, the composer had moved on to a quintet entitled *…And no birds sing*, for flute/alto flute/piccolo, clarinet/bass clarinet, violin, piano and percussion. Written for the then active Seymour Group, this has the full paraphernalia of the then fashionable avant-garde, with graphic notation, plucking inside the piano, or using a mallet, microtones, glissandi in microtones, clusters, key slaps and detailed dynamics for just about every note. The title comes from Keats: 'The sedge is withered from the lake, and no birds sing.' The Seymour Group often used a conductor to put such works together, and I suspect that this composition was no exception. In other words, this is not so much chamber music as directed ensemble music. The writing is so ornate and detailed that players would soon become lost in the maze. Like the two-pianos piece, this is colouristic, high-plumage music, not unattractive, with a section in the middle in continuous demisemiquavers that could be exciting to witness. Similar problems beset the next piece, entitled *...All that is solid melts into air...* (1992), for alto flute, bass clarinet and piano. This is even more florid, with most notes ornamented and preceded by embellishment of some kind. Even with just the three instruments, it would be no easy task to stay together, and again, I wonder whether a conductor had to be employed, or should be employed; it is either that, or long and arduous rehearsals. The opening immediately gives the flavour of the composition.

Example 8.6 B. Broadstock, *...All that is solid melts into air...*, bars 1–4

By 1991, the composer must have *understood* the problem, for a shift begins to occur towards a simpler method of expression. *Nearer and Farther* is for horn and piano. It consists of three movements: 'Vivo', 'Intensivo' and 'Vivo'. It is only in the middle movement that remnants of the ornate style linger. The outer sections are fairly straightforward rhythmically as well as being much more tonal. Broadstock has an unfortunate liking for short note values, and some of the scores look much blacker than they need to be. It would require the movements to be rewritten in something like double values to appear much easier to read and for the eye to subdivide into beats more confidently.

By 1998, Broadstock had completely transformed his music. *I Touched Your Glistening Tears...*, for oboe and piano, is in a much simplified style and even closer to conventional tonality. It appears 'white' on the page—that is, hardly any accidentals—and is in a steady 4/4, which is a stark contrast with the earlier music. The last example we have from this composer is as recent as 2006. It is *Not Too Near...Not too far*, for alto saxophone and piano—a dance-like piece in B-flat major, having moved a long, long way from his first works. One can but wonder whether the artistic solution to the composer's earlier quest was solved by this level of revisionism or not. But I hesitate to even touch upon the subject—it is such a personal matter.

Allan Walker (1955–)

Allan Walker is a classically trained pianist as well as a splendid theoretician. His background and approach come through clearly in every score I have seen. He possesses a lucid analytical mind, and meticulous planning and pre-compositional detailing mark his works. Of the few scores that I have before me, the *Hexamiton* (1986, revised 1991), a sextet for flute/piccolo, clarinet, violin, cello, marimba/vibraphone and piano, barely sneaks into this book due to the size of the ensemble. Furthermore, Allan's layout of the disposition of players makes it clear that the work needs a conductor, so it is not essentially a chamber music score. I merely mention it here because the craftsmanship leaps out at you from the page, in addition to the other characteristics already listed above. Allan's background as well as his association with Keith Humble have generally led to his scores being essentially linked to the methodology and sound world of the Second Viennese School.

A true chamber work, however, is *Six Scenes for Flute and Piano* (1992). I will let the composer describe the piece:

> Each of these scenes briefly explores a different interaction between two instrumental characters. In the first two the flute predominates, its gestures supported and punctuated by the piano. The aphoristic third piece brings the instruments into an increasingly contrapuntal dialogue to shape a single, broken statement, while in the fourth they separate to carve out their own territory within a series of static pitch fields. The fifth is built from four elements. Those assigned to the piano, staccato chords, rapid arabesques and a slowly unfolding bass melody, jostle and collide with an animated line in the flute until some agreement is reached in the final phrase. In the last piece the characters finally, after a few unsuccessful tries, 'dance' together.

Here is the complete third piece.

Example 8.7 A. Walker, 'Scene 3', from *Six Scenes*

The others are a little longer!

Songs and Dances (2007–09), for violin and piano, written in memoriam to Keith Humble, actually uses musical equivalents to spell out Keith's name as the major thematic force of the work. I will once again quote from the composer with regard to this work:

> The idea for the piece and its title were suggested by a folk tale that surrounds a Neolithic ritual site of standing stones at Stanton Drew… the stone circle and cove were thought to be the petrified remains of a wedding party turned to stone by the Devil…According to the tale one Saturday…there was [a] wedding feast on the site of the stone circle and everybody was having a merry time. When the clock struck twelve the party fiddler refused to play because it was Sunday, the Sabbath day. The bride, who was quite inebriated by this point swore that the party would go on, even if she had to go to hell to find a fiddler. No sooner had the words left her mouth, [than] a tall dark man with a fiddle appeared and struck up a tune. Faster and faster he played and the wedding party were compelled to keep up with the tune. This went on all night and by the morning the whole of the group had turned to stone, and the Devil had made off with their souls. There was one survivor of the ordeal. The village fiddler who had refused to play at the stroke of midnight was found the following morning, cowering in fear at what he had seen during the night. Traditionally the Devil said that he would return one day to play for them again.
>
> The two parts of the piece loosely follow the narrative of the tale, the country fiddler the subject of the first part and the demonic violinist the subject of the second.

Andrew Ford (1957–)

Andrew Ford is a well-known broadcaster and writer on music. He is highly articulate and well informed, so the wider sweep of what might be perceived as eclecticism is clearly evident in his compositions. To begin with the songs, I freely admit that some of them caught me off-guard with their simplicity (triadic chords only in *And Now*, for high voice and piano, 1998, words by Catherine Strickland), as well as their proximity to folk song (*Chimney-Sweepers*, for soprano and piano, 2006, words by Shakespeare). Polystyle dominates another work for soprano and piano from 2007: *Domestic Advice*. The text varies from the Finnish *Kanteletar* (translated into English) and the Bible to *The Girl's Own Annual 1919*. There are nine songs in all, veering from prosaic to highly poetic and including an almost Hollywoodish dash of 'biblical' music complete with oriental ornaments and quasi-brass chords in the piano. *Golden Slumbers* (words by Thomas Dekker) is a sentimental lullaby, possibly written for his own child? On the other hand, *A Martian Sends a Postcard Home* (1986, words by Craig Raine), for tenor, horn and piano, employs advanced performance techniques to complement the rather quirky words. Coupled with this is the appearance of repetitive ostinato figures, which we normally associate with minimalist composers—a trait that Ford uses in other pieces we looked at—yet he is far from being a minimalist. In my book on Australian piano music, I nearly categorised Ford as a 'maximalist' composer (which he is not)! Sometimes an abundance of new technique causes a problem. *Parabola* (1989, words by Barbara Blackman), for two voices, bass clarinet, percussion and piano, did not appeal to me at all: it seems gimmicky, the words are self-consciously archaic, and the aleatory structure seems episodic and without direction. Yet another piece, named *Icarus Ascending*, for violin and piano, based on the same myth, is a successful work. Perhaps this is simply a piece that requires some staging?

Pit (1981), for three bass voices, bassoon, double bass and piano, seems more of an exercise in low textures than an actual setting. The voices are used as sound sources of a kind more akin to electronic manipulation, with isolated vowels and consonants, and the writing is rhythmically dense and complex, and would require much rehearsal. Pitch is sometimes abandoned for wiggly lines, and the Ford trait of the ostinato minimalist pitch but maximalist rhythmic overlay makes an appearance here, too. This is the kind of music that I feel is best realised via the capabilities of a computer. In 1981, this was not an option.

A more modest setting of four texts from Japanese, *A Salt Girl* (1994, translations by Kenneth Rexroth)—consisting of: 1) 'Autumn on Pine Mountain', 2) 'The White Chrysanthemum', 3) 'Snow in Spring', and 4) 'The Salt Girl'—is more successful in its spare, understated settings. But then, look at *A Terrible Whiteness* (1984, words by Elizabeth Smart), for mezzo-soprano and piano—the text dealing with writer's block—and once again the composer seems trapped by writing in an 'avant-garde' way, using a fairly ordinary text.

Personally, I liked the purely instrumental music placed before me the best. *Ringing the Changes*, for piccolo, bass clarinet and piano, and dedicated to Elliott Carter in 1990, is a good example of Ford at his best. Perhaps the Carter metrical modulation provided some modelling here, but the ostinato idea written about before is present here as well; and the rise and fall of intensity over the 10-minute span of the piece seems to work very effectively. Two short string pieces with piano complete the music that we located by this composer: *The Very End of Harvest* (2000), for viola and piano, and *A Whole Lot of Shaking* (1999), for cello and piano. They both require virtuoso players with concentrated intensity to succeed in performance. So, in the end, have I uncovered the essential Andrew Ford? I honestly do not know. Perhaps a more important question is how he feels himself about such an issue.

John Polglase (1959–)

John Polglase is a composer who deserves wider performance and appreciation, especially these days, when music organisations seem to put together lightweight programs full of fairy floss for a public that seems intent on listening to art with no challenge, and where the main criterion for program building is—to put it crudely but accurately—bums on seats. Polglase writes serious, muscular, well-constructed scores. His quintet for clarinet, violin, viola, cello and piano, *Bring Me Rain*, is a case in point. The seven movements form an obvious symmetry

I. 'Prelude'
II. 'Sonata 1'
III. 'Invention 1'
IV. 'Interlude'
V. 'Sonata 2'
VI. 'Invention 2'
VII. 'Postlude'.

The seating of the quintet is strictly prescribed, and the pianist's role is a little like the drummer in a band, whether conducting or providing the beat in the playing. The sonata movements use Bartókian asymmetric rhythms constantly and have a savage kind of intensity, especially where the hammering quavers climax in a torrent of semiquavers. The calmer sections only highlight the repeated note chords all the more, with the strings often asked to double-stop. The 'Inventions' are a commentary on prior material, in a somewhat gentler vein, and the 'Interlude'—placed in the centre of the arch form—is the slow movement of the piece. The quintet takes about 30 minutes to play, and I think it would be a most worthy inclusion in any program.

Example 8.8 J. Polglase, *Bring Me Rain*, mvt 2, bars 18–21

Falling Years is a one-movement piece for violin and piano, and, within its nine minutes, it explores a variety of patterns and textures in a rapid succession of compositional ideas. It is a virtuosic and rhapsodic piece, with a strong drive. Similarly, *Six Miniatures for Viola and Piano* is a set of aphoristic compositions, separated by silences, but not dissimilar to the violin/piano piece in effect. Given the miniscule repertoire for viola by Australian composers, it is time for these to be heard more widely.

Three Songs for Violin, Voice and Piano (poems by D. M. Thomas)—consisting of I) 'Blizzard Song', II) 'Lorca', and III) 'Elegy for Isabelle le Despenser'—is constructed so that the violin and piano tend to share and throw about similar ideas, with the voice providing a lyrical line, literally sandwiched between the two instruments (the score is even laid out in this fashion visually).

Thomas Reiner (1959–)

One of the three scores by Thomas Reiner could not be written about or even vaguely described, as it is heavily dependent on electronics. The score (written in collaboration with Graeme Gerrard in 1991) is *Encounter*, for voice, piano, flute, alto saxophone, MIDI wind controller, percussion and live electronics. The performance score excludes tape materials and electronic data, so I was totally at sea as far as the end result is concerned. *Highett Pointillism, Version 2* (2002), for flute, bass clarinet and piano, was a different matter. The idea is very simple but acoustically striking: various piano notes are doubled and held on by the wind instruments, with this amplifying them in a sense as well as negating the decay aspect of piano sound. The piano part is in itself virtually complete and self-sufficient. There are some added ornamental flourishes from the wind, which are special 12-tone rows containing all interval classes, while the piano sounds were randomly generated, so the composer is trying for a clash between high organisation and random structures. There is also a chamber quartet work by Reiner entitled *Two Children, Threatened by a Nightingale* (1985). The work is based on a painting by Max Ernst of the same title, and is for alto flute, violin, viola and piano. The composition is in six short movements

1. 'Largo Tranquillo'
2. 'Andante Giocoso'
3. 'Largo Misterioso'
4. 'Bolero'
5. 'Presto Agitato'
6. 'Adagio'.

The writing is clean and of moderate difficulty to put together. There are attractive dance-like episodes in the work. Projecting the Ernst painting could enhance a performance.

Douglas Knehans (1957–)

Douglas Knehans (another ex-student of mine) seems to prefer working on large canvases, so we found only two works that fitted our category. *Image-Shift* (1988) is for flute, violin, cello and piano. The work is in three movements: 'Grid Fantasie I', 'Sonata' and 'Grid Fantasie II'. The outer movements are clearly related, and are both quite short, framing the large central movement. The 'grid' refers to the web of sound created by the flute, violin and cello, with the piano punctuating and sustaining behind this curtain of sound. The central movement is quite complex in sound and structure and features within it two cadenzas: one for piano, and one for the other instruments. There are some striking acoustic effects in parallel and involved rhythms, tremolandi with glissandi combined and repeated-note ostinatos. It would require a virtuoso ensemble to perform it, and perhaps even a conductor might be necessary; extremes of mood, with sudden emotional changes, abound. *Soar* (2004), for cello and piano, is another big piece, this time, as the composer says: 'I set out to write a cello and piano work that I could not help thinking of as a short score for a cello concerto.' The rather wordy introduction to the score sets out other considered compositional parameters. Because the piano part is really a species of orchestral reduction, some of the writing is un-pianistic (Douglas is a flautist, not a pianist) and awkward. Though the work is highly chromatic, there is a sense of E as a centre, and it ends on a resounding E-major chord. Knehans' writing tends to be busy and driven, sometimes outright barbaric. Knehans gives a structural outline of the work in his introduction, so I will not repeat it here. If *Soar* is in fact a kind of concerto with piano, it has a roughly arch shape of five sections, compressing these tempo and mood changes into one continuous movement. Needless to say, it requires a virtuoso solo player to get through it.

Julian Yu (1957–)

The *Four Haiku for Soprano and Piano* (1992) are probably an excellent way to get to know Julian Yu's atmosphere as a composer. These delicate pieces, set in the original Japanese (although an English translation is given in the score), perhaps best encapsulate Yu's deliberately circumscribed world. Each haiku—whether based on a single note, a single chord or a single mode—is beautifully self-contained and yet contains within it just enough variation or decoration to avoid being repetitive. Much of the piano is written on one stave, and this, too, is something characteristic of the composer: an economy of means and gestures. His *Night Piece* (2007), with a setting from that famous Australian poet Ern Malley, is for baritone and piano left hand! I am not certain what the significance of the left-hand idea is, especially if I have two hands to play it with, but there is no doubt a subtlety here that has escaped me. The piano part, at any rate, is fairly simple and the whole piece could join the haiku set without too much trouble, although *Night Piece* does not have that distinctive Japanese touch that Yu imparts to his settings of the haiku. But the approach to the piano is a unifying factor.

Prelude and Not-A-Fugue (1999), for piano trio, was written to commemorate the two hundred and fiftieth anniversary of Bach's death. As often with Bach's own Preludes, Yu's tends towards a motoric rhythm, with the patterns repeating and modulating whilst preserving the same gestures. The upward-thrusting figures in the violin reverse direction towards the end of the first movement, signalling that the end of the piece is approaching. The second movement uses the B-A-C-H motif throughout as thematic material, and is set out as a ground bass underpinning the whole movement. It is quite austere and dignified in expression. The *Quartet for Piano, Violin, Viola and Cello* as well as the *Trio for Piano, Violin and Cello Op. 26a* (1994) are essentially the same piece of music, which surprised me somewhat. If the trio came *after* the quartet, which is what the opus number suggests, it begs the question: what was unessential in the viola's presence? If the quartet came later then perhaps one could argue that a further elaboration or weight was felt necessary from the original trio. But, as it stands now, it looks like the same piece of music. Here the composer is challenged to expand his view of the world into a larger container, so the pieces are more expansive, building with similar materials to those used in the miniature pieces. Although in one movement, the works contain an introduction, an allegro, an andante and a finale allegro, thus conforming to a fairly conventional model.

The fast sections are especially exhilarating. Listeners will have to judge for themselves whether they prefer the more intimate and rhapsodic Yu to this more massive approach.

Example 8.9 J. Yu, *Quartet for Piano, Violin, Viola and Cello*, bars 1–5

Julian Yu's series of works called *Scintillation* is probably the best known from his output. *Scintillation II* is for piano, two vibraphones and glockenspiel (1987), although the percussion players have other metallophones to attend to besides their main instrument. The line-up of instruments, added to Yu's treatment of the piano, gives a good sense of what to expect. The piece is full of colour with extremes of dynamics from the most delicate to full-on.

Example 8.10 J. Yu, *Scintillation*, bars 57–9

Scintillation III (1987), for flute and piano, is much shorter, but treats similar materials, and in the same manner. This kind of writing seems to me to be the essence of Yu as a composer. His obvious affection for the flute manifests itself in yet another work for flute and piano: the *Sonata*, dating from 2004. The composer might easily have given this another *Scintillation* number, because the approach is very similar to both instruments, with the piano full of delicate tracery of arpeggios and the flute floating above it. The highly ornamented instrumental parts seem to form a language that most suits the composer, producing that typical rhapsodic/virtuosic effect.

I also looked at two earlier works by this composer: *Song of the Tajiks* (1978), for trombone and piano, and *Uygur Dance* (1976), for bassoon and piano. Both are surprisingly tonal and conventional settings of either real or quasi folk music from these two cultures; I do not think they represent Julian Yu, although they are charming enough.

Having met Julian recently, I can now also vouch for the fact that he has a most bubbly sense of humour, so I would now not only attest to this, but also show a musical demonstration of the fact. *Chaconnissima* (2004) is a work for four percussionists and piano. In his own program note, Julian writes:

> The chaconne…is an ancient Western form of music that was framed on a ground bass. But a distinguishing feature of the chaconne is its use of a unique repeated chordal progression. The greatest example of a chaconne is perhaps JS Bach's *Chaconne* from his *Partita II* in D minor for unaccompanied solo violin. The idea for my new piece came from traditional Chinese instrumental music. There, we can find a lot of music from different geographical areas, with different titles, all of which comes from the same 'mother piece'. When traditional Chinese musicians perform existing pieces, they always decorate them and add their own embellishments until the original work often becomes unrecognisable. But the original structure remains. I found this idea fascinating, and especially its similarity with the Western concept of the chaconne and passacaglia. The title *Chaconnissima* is my own humorous pseudo-Italian construction which is intended to mean 'extremely Chaconne'. In this new piece, I took JS Bach's *Chaconne* as my starting point or 'mother piece', and used ornamentation and elaboration to create an entirely new piece, complete with meditative and energetic passages and subtle Oriental touches.

The overlays of added material are thick and fast, but the original music does peep through, if you are listening carefully.

Example 8.11 J. Yu, *Chaconnissima*, bars 19–22

9. Maximalism

Chris Dench (1953–)

Opening the scores of Chris Dench's *Atsiluth* (1991) and *E(i)ther* (2003) confirmed that, for Dench, the heyday of this type of what I earlier termed 'maximalism' is not over. He has elected not to shift from his stated position of many years. The appearance of a Dench score is unmistakable in its exquisite calligraphy, with all the meticulously ruled stems, elegant numerals and thick bar lines. I find Chris's scores incredibly difficult to read, as the long stems seem far away from their note heads, and there is often a little of the stem line cutting through the note head itself. The time signatures (such as 17/32) do not make life any easier, nor do the brackets over groups of notes asking you to play something like 16:15. All this is further complicated by instructions from the composer:

> The entire score is notated at 3 centimetres = 1 second, irrespective of operating metronome marks…This scheme is reflected also in the parts… In the sections with superscribed accel./rall. The spatial distribution of note-heads does not attempt to render this small-scale modification visible, but retains the spacing appropriate to the *initial* (departure) metronomic tempo until contradicted when the new (goal) tempo is reached. The rhythmic life of this piece, as reflected in the notation, is to be understood as emancipated from any sense of unanimity. The individual barlines are to be understood as indicators for the players of the *relative* whereabouts of their fellows, but not as grids requiring scrupulous observance. Only at the double bars, and, particularly, the heavy double bars breaking up the larger sections, should the players actually agree on simultaneity…Such de-syncronised instrumental parts, which have no common simultaneities with the other voices, are to be understood as inhabiting a world dominated by interpretative rubato. The written detail is to be seen less as a 'philologically' exact notational equivalent of a precise executive outcome, than as a metaphorical representation of, indeed a symbolic trigger to, a particular expressive gesture. This understanding of the notation as a series of bracketed 'cartouches' capsules of information both technical and expressive which require *reading* (that is, decoding and digesting) rather than just reflex articulation, is central to the fluidity of the piece. The 'cartouches' are framed by barlines, and the contents if every one of these are to be understood as related: thus the performer's role is, in part, to seek and reveal these correspondences. In consequence of this highly 'imagised'

meaning ascribed to the notational detail, even simple rhythmic formulae should be read similarly empathically/metaphorically and be allowed to be distorted wherever the player deems appropriate.

The existence of notation at a number of levels (all with great detail and precision), coupled with the graphic basis of the score, and added to the apparent desire to create a world of rubato playing, all seem somewhat at odds. I have maintained personally to Chris that there must be a simpler way to communicate his desires to the performer, and thus alienate less of them. I do not wish to labour the points already made in my last book, but the fact is that, in the intervening few years, Australian musical culture has become even more conservative and timid than before; in the face of this, I would be the last person to discourage modernism and innovation. At issue here is dealing with the real world of the performer and finding a way to engage with it.

Riccardo Formosa (1954–)

Riccardo Formosa's scores date from the 1980s (*Durchfuerung*, for string trio and piano; *Vertigo*, for wind trio and piano), and there seems to be no music from a later time. His brand of maximalism is simpler in some ways than that of Dench. The rhythms are more straightforward, and blocks of sound often move together, in parallel articulation. It has its moments, but can be played without a conductor. The difficulty lies in the unanimous attacks required, but a strong leader as well as an incisive pianist would make it possible. The wind piece is marginally more difficult than the string one, and there is more sense of individual line here, too. The piano part has some bars of closely fingered chromatic passages that differ in the hands and—although background, and all over in seconds—would represent hours of practice to get right. It is an encapsulation of the problem of maximalism. Formosa writes usually in a simple four beats to the bar time signature, but that also creates obstacles given the style of writing; sometimes varying the bar length to coincide with the phrases might actually be simpler to read. The composer favours thirty-second and sixty-fourth notes, and one cannot help wondering if the scores would look less black if one doubled all the time values?

Michael Smetanin (1958–)

Michael Smetanin's output is briefly surveyed below, in the order in which I looked at the scores, rather than in any chronological way. This seemingly random approach actually allowed me to gradually unveil the style and perhaps gain a balanced view of the composer's output. *Kartenspiel* (1999) is for two pianos and two percussion players, and was written for ICTUS, the Belgian ensemble. It is a flashy, toccata-like piece, with the pianists in danger of repeated strain injury due to the incessant deluge of semiquavers in the piano parts. The work is quite colourful in an aggressive sort of way, and, at times, brilliantly plumaged, with a rich overlay of gestures. The gestures in themselves are often of the New York minimalist variety, but here they are pushed into an area of complexity not usually associated with the minimalist school. The work is representative of Smetanin's mature style, and is one of a number of similar chamber works, with an 'over-the-top' approach to fairly simple minimalist gestures, and a penchant for repeated notes and chords especially. *Triskelion (Piano Trio No. 1)* from 1978 is, on the other hand, a very early work, which the composer has now labelled as for study purposes only, not to be publicly performed. The trio is clumsily notated and would need considerable revision if it were to be seriously addressed by performers anyway. There is a quite expressive slow movement as well as a motoric last movement utilising asymmetric Bulgarian rhythms. The first movement clearly demonstrates that Smetanin is not a concert performer (certainly not a pianist), as notations appear that no seasoned performer would use. The composer himself has, no doubt, various reservations about this piece. And, I am assuming that 'Rubarto' is a misspelling, and not some exotic Italian term?

Next, I looked at *Sharp* (1992), for bass clarinet, piano, viola and cello. Again, there is a reliance on the repeated note and chord as well as scale runs. This is basically gesticulatory music (not necessarily a pejorative term). The piano part, as already noted, is rather ungrateful. Similarly, *Spray* (1990), for alto flute, bass clarinet and piano, yet again features overlays of scales and the by now familiar repeated notes/chords, suggesting a rather limited arsenal of expression. The wind instruments have to cope with extended playing techniques. The mature Smetanin has now come into full view, and we have also glimpsed the formative years and pieces. The two remaining works are early: *3 Songs for 3 Female Voices and Piano* (1989), in which the voices sing nonsense syllables, whilst the piano plays a very simple pattern almost unchanged throughout. The vocal parts, too, are quite simple and only at a particular moment tend to evolve into something a little more complex. Is this the composer experimenting with something closer to American East Coast minimalism? *Under-Tones* (1981), for amplified piano, bass clarinet (amplified) and percussion (amplified), another early piece, also shows the move towards gesture and repetition; but, this is also a gentler kind of minimalism, not yet fully developed into the more brutal Smetanin of later years.

Smetanin is a composer who knows what he is doing, and he pursues this inner vision without regard for the 'other guy's problems' (I mean the performer). Whether his evolution is going to continue or not is an open question.

10. Pluralism

Bruce Cale (1939–)

Bruce Cale, a well-known name in jazz circles, is present here due to a single work: his *Sonatina for Trumpet & Piano Op. 76* (1993). The composer says 'this piece was composed with the student musician in mind. This work is as demanding for a professional musician to perform excellently.' He is certainly not wrong there. Cale writes in what appears to be a quite *complex* style, partly, I suspect, because he attempts to notate the kind of offbeat rubato that is bread and butter to a jazz performer, but looks difficult on paper. The issue is further complicated by Cale's sometimes strange spelling of the notes in the piano part especially, which complicates the reading aspect of the score; there are many bars that would look much simpler with some little effort. It seems that Cale is aware that there is a problem, for he says '[e]nharmonics: the player may rewrite part for their own ease of reading'. The work is in five short movements, and deserves to be better known in the concert repertoire. The piano part is predominantly chordal, and since Cale's natural language veers towards bitonality, herein lies the root cause of his notational dilemma.

Moya Henderson (1941–)

There are a number of crosscurrents at play in Moya Henderson's music: folk elements, concerns with Aboriginal culture, feminism and the role of women in Australian life as well as environmental issues. When I last wrote about her, I thought she was nudging minimalism, but this was more a reflection of her pianistic skills than an aesthetic. Her works using piano in a chamber context are more numerous, so the picture that is presented is more complete.

G'day Africa II: Mbira ground and *G'day Africa III* (1995), both for clarinet/bass clarinet, viola, cello and piano, are bouncy, dance-like works, quite light in texture and substance, though not trite. The writing is transparent and linear and is marked by constant time change.

Australian Chamber Music with Piano

Example 10.1 M. Henderson, *G'day Africa III*, bars 245–8

Larrikin's Lot (for flute/piccolo, trombone, percussion and piano) is closer to home, dealing with episodes in early colonial life in Sydney. The titles and the varying scoring give some idea of the scope of colour in these seven pieces

1. 'Beantraps' (flute/piccolo, trombone, percussion, piano)
2. 'Donahs and Clinahs along the Argyle Cut' (flute, piano, percussion)
3. 'Chucking a Dummy on the Salvos' (amplified flute, trombone, percussion, piano)
4. 'Treadmill' (piano solo, with optional alemba)
5. 'Up the Scrub-End of Bourke Street' (flute, trombone, percussion, piano, optional alemba)
6. 'Sorry Little Giggler' (piano solo)
7. 'Drawing the Crow' (flute/alto flute, trombone, percussion, piano).

Additionally, the percussion is altered from movement to movement. The strange-sounding titles are from nineteenth-century criminal elements and activities in Sydney. Snippets of popular song and hymn make appearances in the score. Like the 'Africa' pieces, these are light and cheeky in scoring and texture.

Nembutal Rock, for tenor and piano, is in a different world altogether: unbarred and bleak, the whole song exists in a drug-induced, numb world. The piano interjects very sparsely in this highly atmospheric song. 'Tracker's Song' is not a song at all, but a transcription of a moment from Henderson's opera *Lindy* (Act III), for viola and piano. A somewhat tangential but pertinent comment: Henderson's opera, like just about every other opera by an Australian composer, has gone to that great opera house in the sky. It appears that we, on occasion, commission an opera and then forget about it, following a short run. But this is not the place for a diatribe on this painful subject, reflecting as it does lack of support from our government for Australian opera and, in any serious scope, for Australian music. Henderson, earlier in her career, seemed destined to be a music-theatre composer, but I suspect that lack of opportunity in this area has forced her into other fields of composition. She is drawn to settings of words by some of our best writers, including Gwen Harwood, Dorothy Hewett, Bruce Beaver and Patrick White.

Henderson's piano trio *Waking up the Flies* (1990) is 'in four movements, but the fourth movement which is independently titled *In and Off the Ground*, may be performed as a separate work. In all four movements I explore the inner reaches of suffering and loss but without ever abandoning hope and even optimism' (the composer writing in 1990). The word 'ground' in the trio refers both to the European tradition of ground bass, and variations built upon it, and to the closeness of the Aboriginal people to the ground, the Earth. The last movement moves from the lilting gaiety of an Irish jig to a lament. Henderson unifies the Irish and the Aboriginal by the tendency of both melodic lines to descend rather than ascend. A short analysis of this work appears in the study score issued by Grevillea Editions. Another trio, for bass clarinet, piano and viola, subtitled 'Glassbury Documents No. 3' (1984), with an optional tape part, uses what Moya Henderson calls 'cross-hatching' (a syncopated, hockett-like technique, referring to Aboriginal visual art). This is yet another example of the more serious side of the composer: lyrical and introspective. Finally, *Wilderness Pieces* (1995), for violin and piano, is a set of three, intended for student performers, bearing titles linked to bush scenery: 'Serenity Sound', 'Cushion Plants' and 'Stoppers'.

Simplicius Cheong (1942–)

Simplicius Cheong, another fine jazz musician, has a variety of approaches to the jazz/classical divide. His *Rhapsody for Violin and Piano* (1997) is actually a set of variations on the Gershwin tune *Embraceable You*, with the violin playing a sometimes elaborate line over the piano's basic harmonies of the song. Whether Cheong would choose to restrict himself to what is in the score would, I suppose, depend on the calibre of the solo violinist. In his *Sonata for Alto Flute & Piano* (1973), the composer allows the mellow wind instrument to often speak by itself, and the piano part tends to be discreet, with the composer preferring not to risk covering it with an overwritten piano part. It must be considered a welcome addition to the small repertoire for this instrument; an additional bonus is the interest inherent in the jazz idiom applied to a classical form. In the *Sonata for Flute & Piano* (1976), however, given a more piercing and powerful partner, the piano part is consequently lifted, and is often fierce and intense. The whole work, in fact, has an almost Schoenbergian complexity about it.

Example 10.2 S. Cheong, *Sonata for Flute & Piano*, bars 11–12

Most of the piano part is written on three staves. Both the flute and the alto flute sonatas are in three movements of moderate duration.

Ross Edwards (1943–)

In 1995 Ross Edwards wrote a short introduction to his *Maninya VI*. Since Edwards' *Maninya* series of pieces is amongst his best-known works, as well as being representative of his other compositions, I will let the composer speak for himself:

> In 1986 I completed a series of five instrumental and vocal pieces under the generic title *Maninya*. Two of the pieces (I and V), were later used in my violin concerto *Maninyas*. The title was extracted from the text of the first piece, *Maninya I*, for voice and cello, in which randomly chosen phonetic units are grouped together to form rhythmic cells. As I proceeded with the series the 'word' *maninya*, meaningless at first, began to connote, for me at least, certain characteristics of the *maninya* pieces [of] music I was writing: its chant-like quality, resulting from the subtly varied repetition of material within a narrow range of limitations; its static harmonic basis, the general liveliness of its tempi, and so on. The evolution of this 'maninya-style' may have been influenced by my sub-conscious absorption of a variety of non-western musics. African mbira music, for example, may be responsible to some extent for the characteristic terseness and angularity of the melodic shapes, while the manner in which these are woven together sometimes recalls the textures of Indonesian gamelan music. Some listeners have detected Japanese, Indian and Indonesian scales; others have considered the repetitive processes to be similar to those used to induce heightened awareness in much of the world's functional religious music, e.g. Australian Aboriginal chant, Sufi ritual music etc. Far more important

an influence than any music, however, was the natural environment, a timeless continuum from which much of the structural material was distilled. I've found the ecstatic and mysterious sound-tapestry of the insect chorus in the heat of the Australian summer to be a particularly fertile source of inspiration, and this is manifest in the somewhat quirkish periodicity of some of my early music. Although its presence is more abstract in the *maninya* pieces, it remains the supreme generative force behind everything I write.

So there you have it. The Aboriginal-sounding word 'maninya' is a made up word, contrary to many listeners' beliefs. The source of most of Edwards' repetitive but irregular patterns is the call of insects; and he obviously seeks to re-imbue so-called serious art music with a sense of dance and lightness. Here, my observation is that not much of the music is actually as fast as he perhaps would have us believe; neither is there much real difference between the 'maninya' pieces and others. Edwards' natural language seems to be a fairly simple and direct lyricism, modal or tonal by nature, but not always so. And the music is certainly easy on the ear; it presents little threat or challenge to the audience, and Australian audiences, especially at this time, are conservative. The repetitive patterns had, to my ears, in his earlier works, some affinity with the mantras of Messiaen—a favourite of Edwards' teacher, Richard Meale; however, that is one influence he does not acknowledge, so I might be off the mark. In his *Emerald Crossing* (1999), for piano quartet, the modal melodic line is floating over a constant and recurring pedal of B in the piano. But even in the much earlier *The Hermit of Green Light* (1979, four poems by Michael Dransfield), for voice and piano, the idea of repetition is already present, although the language is more chromatic and perhaps closer to Messiaen than the later music. Here I should declare my hand and say that I find the earlier music more interesting than the later, even though there is obviously more polish and surety in the mature pieces. Once I opened the score of *Maninya V*, for example, and played the piano opening, one could predict what was to follow.

Example 10.3 R. Edwards, *Maninya V*, bars 1–7

Not that Edwards' music is simple: it might sound and is in fact repetitive, but in notational terms it is quite complex to read accurately. The singer in the 'maninya' pieces has to virtually learn a new vocabulary of pronunciations and be able to read it fluently; the text is not conceptual at all, and makes no sense, except in the reiteration of certain syllables. If one surrenders one's ears, the result is like listening to a new language, which one does not know, and the meaning therefore is one imposed by the listener, not the composer. Edwards' piano writing is unadventurous, so one tends to hone in on the vocal line. In the three-movement *Piano Trio* (1998), one can play through the score and hardly encounter an accidental; the piece is all 'white' notes. Incidentally, in the introduction to the work, the composer uses the word 'maninya' as a legitimate word and even defines it as 'Australian dance/chant'. Clearly, the synthetic word has acquired a specific meaning for the composer, one that defines his own music. I looked at another early work, *The Tower of Remoteness*, for clarinet and piano, and once again found it more alluring than the later Edwards, recycling and quoting himself! Here, and in the last song of the Dransfield cycle, I found a Ross Edwards whom I regret having lost.

Alison Bauld (1944–)

Alison Bauld is a composer of the theatre and it is no surprise that her handful of chamber works is imbued with music theatre. *Banquo's Buried* (1982), for soprano and piano, is in fact a setting of Lady Macbeth's sleepwalking scene, and the composer acknowledges a 'powerful and idiosyncratic performance of the role by Dame Sybil Thorndike. The manner was operatic and perhaps, even then, unfashionable, but there was a "go-for-broke" spirit which made sense of the tragedy.' The setting is 'for all sopranos who enjoy a sense of theatre', which probably means most if not all sopranos. The piano acts as a miniature orchestra; although this particular setting has no stage directions, a theatrical performance is absolutely screaming at one from the page. The *Two Shakespeare Songs* (1989–90) certainly do contain stage directions: both 'Cry, Cock-A-Doodle-Doo' and 'The Witches Song' are powerful settings of Shakespeare's words, and the second song is actually linked to *Banquo's Buried*.

Example 10.4 A. Bauld, 'Cry, Cock-A-Doodle-Doo', from *Two Shakespeare Songs*, p. 3, bars 25–2

Copy Cats (1987) is a trio for violin, cello and piano. It was probably written in memory of a departed cat, for the score says 'in memory of Larry'; what spooked me a little was the date on the manuscript: 10 September, which is my birthday! Even this piano trio is heavily choreographed: all the movements of the players are indicated, and there is an addition of a 'ghetto blaster', pre-recorded by the cello. The composer writes 'lusciously, with apologies to Dotzaner' (a cultural reference that went over my head; it sounds like Bach to me!). The composer writes at the end of the piece that the trio 'may be performed as a concert piece, without staging, and without a "ghetto blaster"', but this is clearly not the full intent of this amusing and colourful piece.

Richard Hames (1945–)

Richard David Hames' *Dreamings* (1991) is really a work for solo violin. I include it here for the sake of completeness, as there is a piano obligato part in the last movement. The composition consists of the following short sections: 'Brolgas Dancing', 'Kaar—The White Cockatoo', 'The Morning Star' and 'Stringybark Creek' (with a heavily pedalled piano part as background). The string part is quite complex and requires a full command of the various effects and advanced techniques now expected from string players. The other score that we looked at was *A Solis Ortus Cardine* (1975), for what seems to be trombone and piano; I am uncertain because the score does not actually give the instruments! As well, it is the kind of calligraphy that makes a performer hastily put it away as soon after opening it as possible. The layout, barring and general overcrowded appearance of the score look almost deliberately designed to put one off. Much of the piano part is set out on three staves, and the composer insists that all the metronome marks be strictly adhered to. I freely admit that I would not trust myself to hit crotchet = 58, crotchet = 76 or crotchet = 168 on the button, out of the blue.

The chant given on the title page is imbedded in the score in some places, but it was very difficult to make out where precisely. I am happy to confess that the work might be worthwhile, but am certain that it would need to be reset to make it just a little more practical and friendly.

Martin Wesley-Smith (1945–)

Martin Wesley-Smith is a kind of Australian Theodorakis, using an often quasi-popular/light idiom to convey messages that are connected to a theatrical gesture of social commentary and satire. He and his twin brother, Peter, have jointly, and over many years, created a unique body of works that has tackled burning social issues of the day. This parallel to the Gershwin brothers intends to go beyond mere entertainment and sometimes in their work a savage political message is left to the end, doubling its impact. Many vocal/piano works were published as extracts from shows, and thus the piano part is quite often close in spirit to a vamp, or is a reduction of a pit orchestra. The principal shows have been *Boojum!*, a full-length piece of choral music-theatre based on the life, work and ideas of Lewis Carroll. *Songs for Snark-Hunters* also comes from *Boojum!*. Other well-known works are *Who Killed Cock Robin?*, savagely touching upon environmental pollution, as well as *Quito*, in which the target is East Timor. There is much music for children, and Martin is also well known for mixed-media and computer/electronic music—all outside the scope of this book.

Divorced from his brother's words, the music still maintains a quasi-popular lilt, but is more liable to shift metres and accents. A good example of Wesley-Smith's instrumental approach is *Oom Pah Pah*, for flute/alto flute and piano, in which the basic triple feel is never allowed to get comfortable and is constantly disrupted by other durations such as 5/16, 5/8, 7/8 and 4/4.

Example 10.5 M. Wesley-Smith, *Oom Pah Pah*, bars 29–32

So, even without words, irony and unexpectedness are achieved, using the simplest means.

Good examples of patter-songs taking the micky out of our political leaders past and present, with the piano once more employed in a vamping role, are *Recollections of a Foreign Minister* and *Second-Hand Sale* (2006). There are even songs such as *Tommy Tanna* and *Our Andy's Gone with Cattle* that approach a folk-song idiom. The 1984 *Snark-Hunting*, for flute, electronic keyboards, percussion, cello and pre-recorded tape, is heavily into electronics and, I decided, was outside the scope of this book.

Of all the composers who, for one reason or another, cross over into popular/jazz/dance rhythm, and so on, Martin Wesley-Smith seems to me to be the most accomplished and, more important still, has some burning issues to address.

Anne Boyd (1946–)

The oriental presence in the words of the song cycle *Poems from Telegraph Bay* (words by John Spencer and Jan Kemp) is probably the least overt in Anne Boyd's output; but of course it is there, and, more importantly, not just in the words but in the way the words are treated. Composed in 1984, the cycle of five songs is strong thematically and the piano is often used, by its sheer repetition, to coalesce the music. The words have a Zen-like quality and, superimposed on the fairly simple piano part, Boyd creates a result typical of her output. I began with this work, because in every other that I looked at, the oriental presence was obvious just from the title alone, without hearing a bar of the music. So, when one sees pieces named *Bali Moods* from the late 1980s, the result is not unexpected. Anne Boyd is a flute player, so many of her chamber works are for flute and piano, although I believe she abandoned the concert platform quite a long time ago. She has long professed a kinship with Asia and has even used the word 'Australasian' to try to describe the place her music holds. The Bali pieces use the piano to imitate the sound of a gamelan; she says herself that the music 'takes as its starting point traditional Balinese gamelan music and [is] written throughout in an equally tempered version of the pelog scale, one of the two predominant scale systems associated with Indonesian music. The "moods" of the title is also meant to imply "modes".' The repeated patterns of the piano=gamelan contain a hint of minimalist phasing between the hands and the flute. The flute is given unaccompanied cadenzas, and this gives an air of rondo form to the overall effect. *Cloudy Mountain* (1987) is also for flute and piano. This comes across more like a written-out improvisation than the more composed effect of the Bali pieces. The almost obsessive repetition of the piano arpeggios and scales is coupled with the endless crushed notes in the flute, creating an enticing work. The devices can be overworked of course and become mannered. Boyd, here and in other pieces, does skate close to the edge in this respect. Her *Cycle of Love*, for counter tenor, alto flute, cello and piano (five songs in Don'o Kim translations from the Korean), does pursue the same type of rhapsody in the writing. She tends to stay within her chosen mode, and there is little intrusion of 'outside' pitches—that is, once a key signature or mode is declared, there are few accidentals. The cycle has two interludes for cello and flute, with the cellist using a plectrum for oriental colour, and the vocal line repeating when possible the same pitch succession. The occasional exposed parallel octave movement, as well as portamenti, all assist to this same end. The music reaches its zenith in the fourth movement.

Example 10.6 A. Boyd, *Cycle of Love*, mvt 4, bars 22–4

Goldfish Through Summer Rain (1980) is another work for flute and piano. Once again, a feature of the music is the very restricted pitch material and a mesmerising atmosphere caused by a certain static element in the music. In *KaKan* (1984), for alto flute, marimba and piano, the flute part is almost folk-like in its directness, especially in the first two movements. 'Movement III' is more aggressive and contains many time changes. The marimba and the piano are treated in much the same fashion; the fourth movement is scored for flute and marimba alone. Finally, I looked at *Red Sun, Chill Wind* (1980), yet again for flute and piano. The keyboard part here uses the extremes more than in Boyd's other pieces, and, suddenly and surprisingly, there are a few clumsy and technically awkward bars for the pianist.

Robert Lloyd (1948–)

I have little to add to the brief mention of Robert Lloyd in my earlier book. Our search this time has thrown up only one piece. *Starting from Zero* is for vibraphone and two pianos, and treats all the instruments linearly, with single-note repeated patterns moving at a brisk pace. There are no pedal indications for the pianos, so one has to suppose that a dry flow is envisaged. There is an inbuilt ambiguity in the rhythm, dividing the given 6/4 bars into two groups of three as well as into duplets, all the while with quavers pattering away in a very typical minimalist perpetual motion. The dynamic and expressive range of this composition seems deliberately thwarted.

Margaret Brandman (1951–)

The composer is well known to me through her piano pieces, and here there were no surprises, as her style is consistent. Thus, *Antics* (1976), for flute and piano, is a set of three short pieces, which are light, frequently modal and of moderate difficulty. A song, *Find My Own Place* (1979), for voice and piano, apparently from a larger collection named *Original Songs* (a dangerous title for a composer, in one sense at least), is described as having lyrics by Cheryl Adlard. This immediately opens an expectation of a jazz-based song, and the expectation is borne out, with jazz chord symbols written into the piano accompaniment. This plugging into jazz practice further moves the song into the realm of cabaret and the popular-ballade genre. *Permutations* (1992), for clarinet and piano, is couched in a similar idiom, perhaps just a mite closer to the concert world. *Songs of Love and Desire* (2004, with words by Desiree Regina), for voice and piano, is the largest work by Brandman that I looked at. The composer now titles the work a 'song cycle' and the word 'lyrics' is not used. Labelling a work as a 'song cycle', however, does not automatically make it one! These are quite pleasantly melodic and harmonic, with predictable rhythms and chord progressions, though there are some nice tonal transitions. Since the composer's language seems circumscribed, there is not much contrast between the songs. Like the very first song we looked at, these are sentimental—redolent of a 1920s nightclub. All the songs tend to be slow or at best slowish. The last piece we examined was *When Spirits Soar* (1997), for saxophone or clarinet and piano. Though slight in musical content, it is a pleasant piece, inspired by a course of reiki taken by the composer and attempts to portray a kind of inner tranquillity. The composer writes:

> The work is…through-composed…in four sections. The beginning and ending…in the Dorian mode are thematically related. The second and third sections present varying melodic ideas moving away from the modal tonality. A feature of the second section is the four-bar long descant pedal, held by the saxophone. The soaring melody lines and relaxed approach created by moving away from fixed time signatures, entrains the listener to breathe deeply resulting in a feeling of wellbeing.

Gerard Brophy (1953–)

Gerard Brophy presents an image of a composer whose chamber music seems to divide into two distinct modes of attack, which he has pursued consistently and single-mindedly. His *Breathless* (1983), for three flutes and piano, uses the flutes to provide a wall of sound, with the flutes moving either in blocks or in quasi canons. The piano punctuates, but also participates in, the clouds of resonance. Characteristic of non-pianists, Brophy treats the keyboard as an extended xylophone, with little subtlety in the piano writing. Thus, in *Glove* (1995), for bass clarinet, cello and piano, the piano acts as drums on the whole. The texture of this piece is consistent: it is either loud and percussive or suddenly soft, with pedalled piano sound. The composer's approach in many of the chamber works that I looked at is relentless in its sound construction, with the beat duration variable, but not the sound itself. Given that most of the piano writing is in the bass register, the overall sound of the piece is quite dark, given low piano, bass clarinet and cello. This approach persists for 40 pages. Is the piece too long for its content? Probably, but as always there is the factor of the performer. Brophy's music requires a top level of performer, and they can make or break such a piece. All composers are vulnerable of course, but especially the ones who put all their eggs into one compositional basket, as this particular composer tends to do. *Head* (1988), for bass clarinet, piccolo and piano, is similarly violent, with a piano solo kicking off. Due to the choice of instruments, extreme textures are the inevitable result. *Head* is typical of the avant-garde of the time and its demand for top-level players if it is to succeed in performance. The piano is again favoured for short, sharp chords using quasi clusters as sound blocks, although here there is also the piano used in a softer fashion, with the wind now providing the staccato gestures. Like the last work described above, this one covers more than 40 pages of score. Like a dogged bloodhound, Brophy in these works will not let go until he has run what he feels is a full course with his combination. This characteristic might be either a compositional attitude or a trait of temperament—possibly the two combined.

With *mFm* (2002), for baritone/soprano saxophone, marimba, bass guitar and piano, a new sound emerges. There are some minimalist gestures as well as hints of jazz. The first movement, labelled 'Modinha', is an extended marimba solo, with much repetition redolent of minimalism, but pushing the material into fresh zones without mindless repetition, and even encouraging the performer to embellish the given material, although Brophy does not suggest how to embellish. The second movement, 'Funk', asks the performers to play 'always in the groove'. Here I came across for the first time a compositional trait clearly enthralling the composer: all the instruments moving in parallel motion in exactly the same durations, forcing the ear to listen to the resultant timbres as much as to the actual pitches. In the third movement of this work, 'Memoria', we are given reminiscences of the first movement with embellishment and commentary interrupting the flow of quotations. *Rubber* (1994), for piano, alto flute, bass clarinet and vibraphone, similarly requests a 'swing groove'. It is an earlier work than *mFm*, and less bloody-minded, with the parallelism broken up to some extent with interpolations: long notes and legato phrases. The piano and vibraphone often move together and this requires sensitivity and delicacy on the part of the pianist.

The last two works we collected reinforce the emerging view of Brophy. His *Sheer Nylon Dances* (2000) features prepared piano (Brophy calls it 'fetishised piano') with violin and violoncello. The previous work named *Rubber* now comes to full fruition; even the performance indications are suggestive: 'The piano is fetishised by the gentle but firm insertion of rubber wedges between the strings listed below.' The movement titles are indicative of a change in the composer's musical thinking

I.   '…Cakewalk avec carillons lointains'

II. '…Voiles tunisiennes'

III. '…La gymnopedie engloutie'

IV. '…Danse d'extase'.

This and the prior work indicate a shift by the composer away from the hardline Italian avant-garde of his earlier years. The score still bristles with knife-edge time changes and precision demanded of the players, and parallelism is still a very strong feature of the mix. The final work that we looked at, *Topolo—NRG* (2002), for baritone saxophone, double bass and piano, is indeed *wholly* in parallel movement ('allegretto, always in the groove').

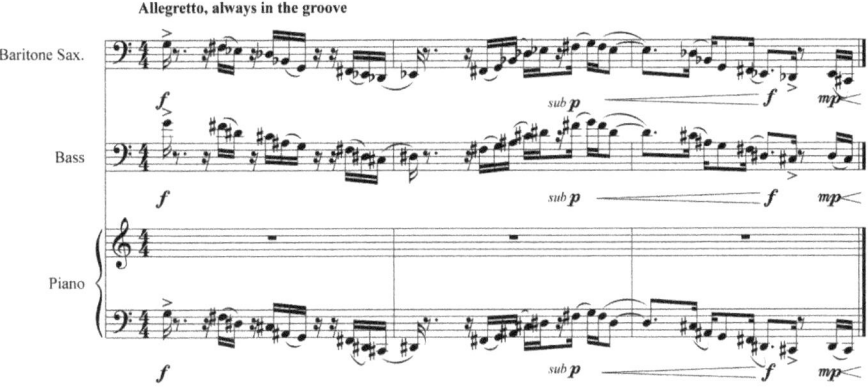

Example 10.7 G. Brophy, *Topolo—NRG*, bars 1–3

Brophy relishes the colour mix and match, rather than the possibility of counterpoint, of his instruments. We note—not for the first time—that the instrument choices tend to favour the lower register and thus darken the overall colour of his resultant scoring. Brophy is clearly a composer whose thinking has been gradually shifting over the years, and will no doubt continue to move.

Richard Vella (1954–)

Duo No. 1 for Cello and Piano: Sonata (1994) is the major work by Richard Vella that we selected. It appears to have been revised a few times, and in its present form is a major work for the combination, extending to 430 bars. It begins with the sound of all the open strings of the cello being plucked in a particular rhythmic pattern, which keeps returning as a reigning refrain. Between these open-string pizzicati, little melodic fragments are interposed. By the time the piano enters, the raw material of the whole piece has already been announced. The piece is initially given the key signature of G major, and although I cannot state that the piece is *in* G major, it is typical of Vella's music that some tendency towards a tonal centre is present. The opening sound featuring perfect fifths creeps its way into the piano part and then begins a slow and gradual process of evolution, with the open fifth ever present, but becoming less obvious as changes begin to occur. The composer had something akin to variations in mind, as the composition is signposted with double bars indicating a fresh 'variation' and a change of mood and tempo. One such variation has both instruments playing continuous semiquavers. Gradually, the density of the piece thins and the piano has the last say in a lyrical statement of the material. This level of remorseless control over the thematic material is also present in *Five Studies on a Trombone Melody* (1988), for flute/alto flute/piccolo, oboe/English horn, trombone, vibraphone/marimba/glockenspiel, piano and optional baritone voice. The six movements, which are titled and numbered, make the variation clear, in this fashion

1. 'Melody'
2. 'Layering'
3. 'Scherzo and Trio!!'
4. 'Chords'
5. 'Mosaic'
6. 'Unison Melody'.

The baritone appears only in the final movement, singing words by Georges Bataille, taken from his *Eroticism: Death and sensuality*. If no baritone is available, there is an instrumental option for the last movement, which is really a reprise of the opening melody. The titles give an idea of the process involved in each variation. I am uncertain why Vella added the exclamation marks to the scherzo and trio title: it is in strict ABA form, and perhaps the composer was stressing the unusualness of such a procedure in the late twentieth century?

Memory Pieces is a work written sporadically over a number of years. It is from a series named *Studies in Music Theatre*, and is suggested as suitable for a solo piano recital. The forces required are piano, pre-recorded tape and male speaker, and it would indeed break up the often-stifling formality of a piano recital. There are five movements

1. 'A piano reminisces (1979)…' (piano solo)
2. 'Czerny (1982)…' (piano and tape)
3. 'Mazurka Europa (1985)…' (piano and tape)
4. 'You Must Remember This (1982)…' (piano solo)
5. 'Beethoven (1985)…' (piano, male speaker, pre-recorded tape).

The composer's notes on the movements are instructive and amusing:

> The tape part for 'Czerny' is a recording of 'Dial-a-time' made from the Telecom service. The piano part is based on Czerny's Op. 299 No. 1. The tape part for 'Mazurka Europa' is a cut up/mix of four piano accordions playing a traditional folk song called 'The Firefly'. The tape part for 'Beethoven' is a mix and overlaying of three different recordings of Beethoven's 'Moonlight Sonata' (1st Movt.). The speaker in 'Beethoven' begins to speak after the pianist finishes 'You Must Remember This'. He should be seated amongst the audience as inconspicuous as possible as if he is an audience member. It may be necessary to have the speaker in 'Beethoven' talking through a microphone as if he is a stand up comic.

Tales of Love Suite (1990), for clarinet, cello and piano, consists of the following, all drawn from Vella's opera *Tales of Love*.

1. 'Tango'
2. 'Duet'
3. 'An Ecstatic Interlude'.

The tango also exists in a version for clarinet and piano; the wind player has to cope with some multiphonics, and the pianist needs to wear a glove with the fingers cut off due to some required loud glissandi. The pieces are quite attractive, but, out of context and without knowledge of the opera, they are less crafted than the other works we have described above. I should at least mention Vella's *Three Songs for Piano and Voice*: 1) 'Rain Poem' (1978); 2) 'Ryokan' (1977, both with words by Michael Dransfield); and 3) 'A Woman' (1983, words by Jane Berland). These are all very short and concentrated, with the piano providing a delicate and discreet backdrop to the vocal line.

Carl Vine (1954–)

Elegy (1985) is described by its composer, Carl Vine, as written 'for a friend who died unexpectedly in 1985'. The work is cast in a single movement with the following four sections

I. 'Reaction'

II. 'Reflection'

III. 'Rhythmic Explosion'

IV. 'Elegy Proper'.

It is a score that clearly shows Vine's compositional technique and preferences. The work is scored for flute/piccolo, violoncello, trombone, piano four-hands (first player doubling organ DX7) and percussion. The sound of two pianos or one piano four-hands makes sporadic appearances in Vine's output; it is clearly a sound he likes—perhaps a relic of the days when he was part of the Flederman Ensemble and there were two pianists available within the ensemble, or just an acoustic preference? Here, in the *Elegy*, as in many of his works, one can generalise by noting the importance of strong rhythmic beat, as well as the technique of overlapping ostinatos, sometimes of different cycle lengths, or else of using an ostinato to set up the beginning of a work or section of a work, and then beginning the procedure of overlaying the base ostinato. Thematically, there seems to be a preference for fourths and fifths, closely followed by sevenths and perhaps ninths, all comfortably sitting within the grasp of a pianist's hands. Vine was—and perhaps still is—a fine player, so his approach to the piano is a result of being an active practitioner for many years. If one adds to this mix his experience with dance theatre, you have the core influences on his musical style. Vine was not a romantic pianist, and approached the instrument in what I would perhaps dub a 'neo-classical' way, with a certain detached objectivity. The *Elegy* is a deeply felt work, and the sound of the DX7 organ adds an unexpected dash of colour. We were aware, too, of a piece called *Everyman's Troth*, for viola, violoncello and clavichord, but this is clearly not a piano part *per se*, although at a pinch it could be performed on one.

10. Pluralism

The suite from the ballet score *Hate* (1982) is for French horn, trombone, percussion and two pianos. Piano one lays down the ground ostinato built in fourths and the layering technique takes over again. The dry, punchy sound of two pianos playing cross-rhythms in staccato articulation is vintage Vine.

Example 10.8 C. Vine, *Suite from Hate*, bars 105–8

This two-piano figuration comes back with varying instrumental superimpositions. The sense of the work's dance origins is present for all to hear. I am not certain, personally, whether this translates totally successfully to the concert platform.

Miniature III (1983) is an important piece in Vine's output. I will let the composer speak for himself:

> The work is in three linked sections, each exploring a different principle of rhythmic organisation. In the first, continuous semiquavers are placed in a variety of groupings to create a constantly varying pulse. The second section is written as a constant 2/4 metre over which finger cymbals accentuate complex subdivisions of the beat, while the final section centres on a rhythmic ostinato of 3/4+3/16. Each section revolves around a series of cyclic harmonic patterns linked by bridge passages, most of which serve to change the tempo by metric modulation.

The fabulous trombonist in the Flederman Ensemble was Simone de Haan, and it was for him that Carl Vine wrote *Occasional Poetry* in 1979. Here the piano takes a somewhat subsidiary role, with widespread arpeggios over which de Haan is left free to play his melodic line. Yet another resultant work from Flederman was *Scene Shift*, with the favoured piano four-hands, trombone and double bass. Once again, the sound is dominated by both pianos playing fast staccato quavers, often repeating bars and patterns a number of times. This is another work transplanted from the dance theatre, this time a ballet by Micha Bergese.

Sonata for Flute and Piano (1992) uses the flute to set up the ground ostinato whilst the piano enters staccato against it. Much of the first movement is used to explore four against three rhythms. The flute part is effective and brilliant. The slow movement is framed by cadenzas at either end, with a more regular middle section. The last movement is very fast, and this time the piano sets up the ostinato. Again, we are in the world of perpetual rhythmic movement.

Finally, there are some miniatures. *Love Me Sweet* (1993), for voice and piano, is from the incidental music to the TV mini-series *The Battlers*, arranged for solo voice and piano. Similarly, from *Poppy* (Act 1, Scene 1) is a one-page song for soprano and piano: 'On s'Angoisse'. In 1976, Vine attended a summer school for choreographers, and as a result there survive two of 10 pieces composed during the school: *Slaughterhouse* (for two pianos and voice, another one-page piece employing aleatory techniques) and *Tempi*, for two violins, viola (or piano) and violoncello, in a similar vein, obviously dashed off under pressure. The composer says of this last piece that ideally a string quartet should be used. I include all these trifles merely for the sake of completeness.

Elena Kats-Chernin (1957–)

What does one say about a composer who is widely known and played, who must be deemed successful (at least on some levels), but whose music has been stuck in a rut for a good many years? Hints of all this were already present some years back when I last wrote about her, and I desperately hoped that something would alter and that, with a drastic shift, something bold and new would appear on the Australian music scene. Alas, that was not the way it went. When I picked up the fairly thick file of music by this composer and began to play through the pieces, my worst fears were realised: endless rags, endless arrangements of her hit, *Russian Rag*, followed by yet more rags, tangos, waltzes and countless occasional pieces. I happen to think that Elena is enormously gifted and a thoroughly trained composer, with huge reserves of technique, which she is squandering on trifles. Her hit rag is now 15 years old, and surely it is time to change something, and not fall for the easy applause that a lazy-eared public bestows upon her. Sometimes, her own titles betray what she must know is happening—thus, a set of violin and piano pieces is named *After Dinner Music*. Within the program descriptions of this collection, the composer refers to 'the harmonic language of the music of 1920s Russia', as well as to a 'palpable sense of nostalgia'—elements that I had already pointed out. The interminable patter of broken arpeggios, which is a Kats-Chernin hallmark, appears everywhere, often used to fill up space where there is a paucity of musical ideas, and that gives an illusion of substance and, at times, a sort of polyphony, whether in *Augusta's Garden Waltz* (2004), for bassoon and piano, or *Pink-Breasted Robin in Silvery Light* (2006), for clarinet, cello and piano. The songs from *Bombshells* (2004) (four songs published separately) are given with chord symbols, and obviously suggest improvisation and filling out. *Colours of the Sea* (2004), for alto flute, violoncello and piano, also pursues this tendency to make a busy texture without changing much, and in the middle of this piece one can watch the process build up and die down. There are glimpses of a more sombre and serious Elena at times in this trio; she is sporadically present as well in *Charmer's Apprentice* (2002), for oboe and piano—the finest of the pieces that I played through, and the most substantial, although there was also much that was facile and slick. I was left hoping, as I said at the start, that the glitzy façade would eventually wear out and expose something more profound underneath. For a start, she is a very gifted orchestrator—and that is a start that not many composers have naturally.

Mark Pollard (1957–)

If, in my last book, I expressed some doubt about grouping Mark Pollard with some other minimalists, a look at his chamber music was convincing proof that he never belonged there in the first place. There are reasons why he appeared in that company, and I will elaborate on them below. From 1997 comes the very successful *A Portrait of Elsie May (To the memory of Helen Wilkinson)*, for soprano or mezzo-soprano, oboe, clarinet, trumpet, trombone and piano. The composer was commissioned to write a work for the Port Fairy Spring Festival of that same year; he chose to find material for this solid 20-minute piece in the pages of the *Port Fairy Gazette* of 12 October 1887, thus ensuring that the first performance of this piece would occur 100 years after publication of material from the gazette. I will allow the composer to speak for himself:

> The work exists in five parts. The first is an instrumental prelude. The second is based on the text for the obituary of Elsie May Best who died of consumption at the age of twenty years. I found the text the most 'moving' and it thus became the source for the title. The third part is based on one of the many advertisements for herbal remedies that cover the Gazette. In this case the 'ad' for Beecham's Pills is used. The fourth is based on the report of the stockholders meeting for the local steamship company reflecting on the demise of the steamship business. The final movement is taken from the editorial concerning the elections and particular[ly] one of the candidates, Mr Thomas Bent. The sound for

> 'a portrait of elsie may' is inspired by the 'Gamelan' music of Java. This music has informed much of my recent composition and seemed highly appropriate for this composition.

The first movement is an instance of how Pollard might be taken for a minimalist: the gamelan-like semiquaver movement of the piano part is based on a small number of notes, and there is thus a superficial resemblance to what is normally labelled minimalism. But the notes, though limited, are not exactly repeated in the same manner, nor are they always predictable. Furthermore, their range evolves and expands. Over this, the composer gradually builds up a chorale-like movement from the other instruments; eventually, the motoric element ceases and the voice is superimposed over this quasi-chorale instrumental texture. The setting of the Beecham's Pills advertisement was probably irresistible given the later musical connections of this product to a famous conductor. The 'ad' is delivered in spoken rhythmic speech punctuated with dramatic chords, highlighting the totally outrageous claims made for this well-known product. The report to the stockholders is sung to a two-bar undulating piano part in A major. The final movement neatly returns to the opening gamelan figure as well as to the widely spaced chorale idea in the instruments. The movements are played non-stop.

Three other scores that we gathered are all earlier compositions: *Spirits of Innocence* (1990) is scored for flute doubling alto flute, piccolo, clarinet doubling bass clarinet, violin and percussion (one player: vibraphone, glockenspiel, marimba and piano); *Thrice Removed* (1985), for alto flute, piano and cello; and *To Cast a Shadow* (1986), for trombone and keyboards (celeste, harpsichord, piano—one player). These early works demonstrate that Pollard's beginnings were not in minimalism, but rather in a mainstream avant-garde, with strong theatrical elements built into the music, and a healthy dose of extended playing techniques woven into the score. The placement of instruments was important to the composer—sometimes asking for separation, sometimes the opposite. Complex counterpoint is a feature, but it rubs shoulders with seductive mormorando effects in the first piece, later fragmented in a dramatic fashion. The second piece demands extended techniques from the flute and cello, and some theatrical frozen movement after certain gestures. Continuous semiquavers occur in this work, and perhaps some of these morphed into gestures resembling minimalism in later works. The last piece is very demanding for trombone, once again pushing the limits. The keyboard player has to be adept at switching from one keyboard to another. Here, once more, a sense of perpetual motion is suggested in a swirl of regular semiquavers, which appears to be a signature gesture of the composer, at least in these works.

Colin Spiers (1957–)

Colin Spiers seems to be less of a minimalist in his chamber music than in his solo piano works, although much of the minimalist ethos remains obviously to the fore in these works too. We looked first at *The Day of Death and Dreams* (1989), for tenor and piano, setting words by Patrick White—a sort of concert aria or cantata in its scope; the work covers 35 pages. It begins with a passionate piano solo comprising grandiose chords requiring a massive stretch if they are meant to be played without arpeggiation. You can always tell whether a pianist is writing the piano part in any given piece, and Spiers is declaring here, loudly and boldly, that he is a pianist and that the piano is an integral part of his world. The words are set in varying ways, but there is a fair amount of parlando singing and recitative freedom; Spiers also enjoys melisma and here it is at times positively baroque in its application. As in his music for solo piano, the figures that Spiers uses come very much from the past: long stretches of quite conventional arpeggio patterns, as well as many scale runs, some quite difficult and sometimes in both hands, in both similar and contrary motion. There is some free notation but it is not applied as much here as in some other works. What are unusual are the sheer bulk and prominence of the piano part. A favourite texture of the composer is pulsing quaver chords—another habit derived from his minimalistic leanings. It is especially prominent in his *Elegy* (1993), for viola and piano, with the piano maintaining a constant throbbing A-flat or G-sharp, depending on the key signature, which, curiously, is in seven flats or seven sharps, for which I do not believe the viola player would have extended profuse thanks. That apart, this is a fresh take on the romantic elegy genre, of which there are so many examples in the piano repertoire.

Eulogy (1989), for tenor, cello and piano, is similar in scope to the Patrick White setting. The cello this time is given the honour of opening and closing the piece, which sets words by Thoreau. The piano part is quite like that of the White setting, and Spiers again demonstrates that he is not inclined to treat the cello and piano as mere accompanying instruments, but instead as equal partners in a concertante role. The patterns in the piano tend to stay fixed for long stretches, as we have come to expect from this composer, and the type of pattern is fairly consistent.

The largest chamber work to come our way is the innocuously titled *Fantasy*, for viola and piano, which now extends to 69 pages! It opens, again, with a big piano cadenza, gradually building to alternating hand octaves and fast scale runs. The viola does not make an appearance until page seven. The favoured quaver pulsing is there in the piano. Sometimes the roles are reversed in that at one time, the viola has a long section of reiterated semiquaver sextuplets, while the piano plays quite broadly and melodically under them. After this role reversal, there is another piano cadenza, which includes continuous right-hand runs in double thirds. The viola eventually is also allocated a massive cadenza. It slowly dawned on me that, in a way, Spiers is an Alkanesque composer: he works on a large scale, and will milk the material as long as he feels there is a drop left to be squeezed out of it. He thinks naturally on a larger than normal scale, and I do not believe that he sets out deliberately to write a 'big piece'. It seems natural to him. We find this again in his cello and piano sonata of 1999. There is nothing particularly new to discover in it, although the slow movement is largely cadenzas for the two instruments, so once again the angle of virtuosity is pushed beyond what one would expect in a duo sonata. The last movement is marked by asymmetrical rhythms and fast-changing bar durations in relentless semiquavers. But I must add that the technical demands, though of a high order, are not extreme, and everything is playable and clearly set out. The language is non-threatening, almost predictable. Given the scale of all these works, I found it difficult to give a music example that would convey the totality of the music.

There remain three shorter works with curious titles. *Nsj* (pronounced 'nistch', according to the composer) was written in 1995 and is for clarinet, basset-horn and piano. The composer grappled with a combination of free notation and strict traditional notational approaches. There are four dense pages of performance notes in which the composer struggles to make his intentions clear. This creates a complicated interplay and tension between the two systems. Spiers uses repeats of sections, indications of time in seconds and, sometimes, indefinite pitch against totally notated other parts, simultaneously. The wind instruments are amplified. In *Uwg* (pronounced 'oodge', 1993), for viola and piano, the point of the piece is repetitions of short bars and gestures. Although it seems short by Spiers' standards (39 pages), one has to take into account the fact that just about every bar is played a number of times, sometimes as many as four times. The tempo is fast. Here again, the viola is amplified, and I wondered whether this is a notion that could be entertained for the huge viola and piano piece, as the piano part is often huge, and the viola is so easily covered? The third of these oddly named pieces is *Zyj* (pronounced 'zidge', 1993), for trumpet and piano. This piece concerns itself with the sort of asymmetry that we already encountered in the last movement of the cello sonata. Spiers is an interesting example of a minimalist-inclined composer who is an unabashed romantic in language and instrumental writing, providing a sometimes-heady mix of old and new.

David Joseph (1954–)

Two instrumental works represent David Joseph here. *Fanciful Fancies* (1991) is scored for clarinet, viola, cello and piano. The piano part is difficult and

10. Pluralism

extravagant, and is possibly meant for the composer himself (or the composer identifies the piano with himself)—not that the other instruments are spared! This quartet is glittery and colourful; it contains absolute cascades of scales and arpeggios, and the overall sound is an exuberant impressionism. Whether more than 400 bars of this approach is too long is a question that can be answered only in performance. But this propensity in Joseph I had already mentioned before, writing about a work for solo piano. His *Piano Trio* (1987) is broken up into three movements, so the frenetic atmosphere of the outer movements is interrupted by the slow middle movement; *Fanciful Fancies* is in one continuous movement with little relief from the overdrive.

Graeme Koehne (1956–)

There was only one work by Graeme Koehne for me to look at that fitted this book's scope. It was a set of three songs of Byron for voice and piano. Like all of Koehne's mature music, this is backward looking and, though effective enough, would be comfortable at the end of the nineteenth century. I do not necessarily wish to open this particular can of worms, but there is an aesthetic question here concerning revisionist composition and whether it is desirable and has a place in the twenty-first century. I do not know definitively, but my heart says that the answer is 'no'. It might be something for the reader to ponder!

Mark Isaacs (1958–)

Isaacs is a very fine jazz pianist whose 'art music' shows unmistakable signs of his activity in the jazz world. I looked at the following pieces: *Cantilena*, for bass clarinet and piano; *Elegy* (1987), for cello and piano; *Memoirs* (1986), for vibraphone, percussion, piano and bass marimba; *Mirage*, for flute and piano (originally named *Interlude*: three pieces for viola and piano called 'Night Song', 'Lullaby' and 'Dream Chant'); and finally, *Songs of the Universal* (1995), for clarinet, viola, violoncello and piano. The short pieces especially are prone to be very similar: sophisticated jazz harmony permeates them all, with a lazy, even indolent beat lurking among the slower pieces. The larger works do, naturally, contain faster music. *Memoirs* is an example of Isaacs tackling a larger form. Although only eight minutes long, the work demands quite an array of colourful percussion (including a police whistle!), and its subtitles suggest an attempt at contrast by the composer—thus

Australian Chamber Music with Piano

I. 'Extension'

II. 'Rumination'

III. 'Projection'

IV. 'Direction'.

Isaacs writes a first movement in a fairly flowing moderato. The second, from its very heading, is the slow movement of the work. The third, almost inevitably, is the scherzo, and is fast and boisterous with many time changes; and the last is a brief but energetic wind-up of the whole piece. The work for flute and piano is an exception in that, though short, it is energetic and brilliantly projected throughout. The manuscript date is unclear, but looks like 1975, which would make this an early piece by the composer; the piano part is busy and showy and is obviously meant for the composer himself. The work has not been published and deserves to be better known. The most substantial work we found by Isaacs was written for the Perihelion Ensemble. It was inspired by Walt Whitman's *Song of the Universal*, and each movement has a short quotation from Whitman as its motto.

1. 'Come said the Muse, Sing me a song no poet yet has chanted, Sing me the universe.'

2. 'Soothing each lull a strain is heard, just heard, From some far shore the final chorus sounding.'

3. 'Over the mountain-growths disease and sorrow, An uncaught bird is hovering, hovering, High in the purer, happier air.'

4. 'From imperfection's murkiest cloud, Darts always forth one ray of perfect light, One flash of heaven's glory.'

5. 'And all the world a dream.'

Like most of Isaac's music, here the textures are uncluttered and the chord progressions suave. The opening of the third movement is a piano solo and neatly encapsulates the essence of the composer's compositional and pianistic approaches.

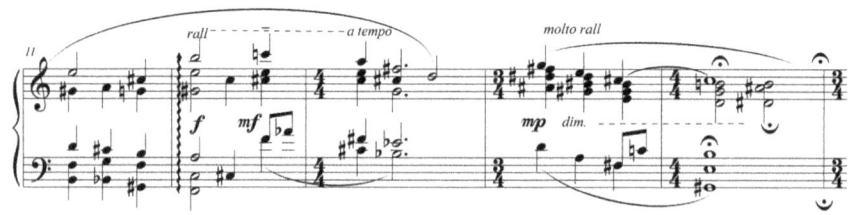

Example 10.9 M. Isaacs, *Song of the Universal*, mvt 3, bars 11–15

Nigel Westlake (1958–)

It is little wonder that Nigel Westlake is so much in demand as a film composer: he has the ability to evoke an appropriate atmosphere and colour within a few bars. Take for instance his *Jovian Moons* (2001) in four movements, each named after one of the moons of Jupiter

1. 'Ganymede'
2. 'Europa'
3. 'Callisto'
4. 'Io'.

The work is written for the strange and dangerous combination of guitar and piano, and poses various traps for the composer, unless the guitar is amplified beyond sounding like an acoustic instrument, which I am certain was not the intention, as Westlake has been ultra-cautious—and with good reason—with the balance of the duo. It is, by its very nature, a limited possibility acoustically, but here, in the first movement, with the piano slowly descending, Westlake creates a feeling of mysterious space without becoming overly conventional and corny, as the topic has been tackled in so many hundreds of films, with varying success. The piano plays mostly single notes, pianissimo, with the pedal kept down to create a resonant space; it is treated in a most circumspect manner, with due regard for the tessitura question constantly kept in mind. A Messiaen-like mantra holds much of this first movement together, ending with a long pedal on the note E slowly moving like a pendulum in octaves. The second movement is a little more active, with some contrapuntal and quasi-canonic imitation in evidence; the piano is still moving in single notes. By the third movement, the writing for piano has moved to soft chords. Here the guitar combines with the piano in this very still combination of chords, and a lovely sound is achieved. Mind you, the 'space' music colouration does become a wee bit tiresome after a while, with the pedal constantly down, and either the wide spacing or the close ostinato unremittingly present. But in the last movement, with the guitar playing loud chords, a climactic moment does occur. It is a fascinating attempt at a combination that will be attempted very rarely, at least with acoustic guitar.

Westlake's trio for violin, cello and piano comes from 2003. It begins in close canon, and then shifts to the more usual melody with accompaniment. But some powerful passages using unusual octave doublings lift the music out of the ordinary.

Example 10.10 N. Westlake, *Trio*, for piano, violin and cello, mvt 1, bars 57–8

The piano is treated linearly. In the very slow second movement, Nigel again invokes the spirit of Messiaen, with the softly reiterated throbbing chords in the piano, like the end movement of the Frenchman's *Quartet for the End of Time*. A climactic mantra, written in 5/16 and memorable, is gradually arrived at.

Example 10.11 N. Westlake, *Trio*, for piano, violin and cello, mvt 2, bars 46–8

As to be expected, the last movement is more brilliant. For pianists, Westlake has an irritating habit, making it plain enough that he is not a keyboard player. Single notes on the piano are usually distributed between the hands by the composer, even if the player alters it here and there; similarly, there is no point in bracing semiquavers moving a long way apart on the same stem. It is both annoying and confusing to the eye. Westlake is a brilliant clarinetist, and a virtuoso on the bass clarinet, so we partly forgive him, but it is an unnecessary trait. There is an exciting passage in fast semiquavers in the strings, punctuated by piano chords at the peak of this movement.

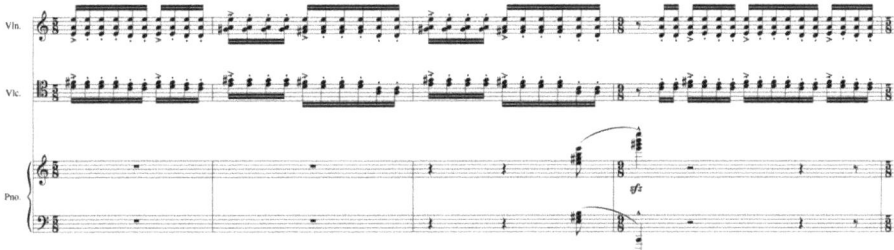

Example 10.12 N. Westlake, *Trio*, for piano, violin and cello, mvt 3, bars 23–6

The trio ends softly and slowly in a moving farewell coda. I was interested to scan another work for piano trio entitled *Urban Myths* (2001). Unfortunately, this is the first movement of the piano trio, apparently first published separately.

Phillip Wilcher (1958–)

We gathered a number of this composer's chamber works. It would be easier to comment on them as a group, as Wilcher's style and output tend to be homogeneous.

I looked at: *Ave Maria* (1995), for voice and piano; *Blue Glaze*, five short pieces for flute and piano; *Brouhaha* (2000), for cello and piano; *Down by the Salley Gardens* (1998, Yeats), for voice and piano; *Elegy* (2007), for bassoon or cello and piano; *Incantation* (1998), for violin and piano; and *Pavane* (2004), for flute, cello and piano.

Wilcher is essentially a composer of light music who appears to have strayed a little into the concert milieu we are exploring in this book. His music is consistently diatonic: once the key signature is put in place, there is hardly an accidental to be seen. There is almost no change of rhythm or bar duration, or, indeed, even of tempo. His music therefore is easy on the ear and, even when it moves quickly, as in the cello and piano piece, the harmony remains static. Nor is there much feeling for drama. In the setting from Yeats, when there is clearly an emotional time bomb imbedded in the final lines, neither the vocal line nor the accompaniment shifts, but continues their tranquil way to the end. It is only in the violin and piano piece that something new appears to stir.

Example 10.13 P. Wilcher, *Incantation*, bars 41–8

This is, however, an aspect of Wilcher that is unusual. I am only drawing attention to it as a possibility that the composer might yet move away from his thus far well-trodden path.

Nigel Sabin (1960–)

Nigel Sabin's minimalism is close to the New York school, which seems to have spawned adherents all over the world. *Points of Departure* (1991), for clarinet/bass clarinet, violin, viola and piano, is characteristic of his music. Since a journey is depicted, the movement titles are: I) 'Embarkation'; II) 'Resting Point'; and III) 'Arrival'. The first movement begins with an instantly rapid groundwork of semiquavers from the piano, with a gradual superimposition occurring from the other instruments, which then settle into their own obsessively repeated ostinatos, creating essentially a thick web of F-sharp major triadic sounds with extra notes. The patterns change a few times, with the piano usually initiating the changes by lapsing from a tight tremolo-like figure to a repeated arpeggio figure. The role of the other instruments also changes somewhat, taking on a more melodic and polyphonic role; a few such shifts occur. The second movement is very slow and is cast for viola and piano, subtitled 'In Memoriam Peter George'; but with the third movement we are back into the more expected minimalist world, although the composer does explore some less rigid methods of notation. The Sabin thick mass of sound is a signature technique.

Example 10.14 N. Sabin, *Points of Departure*, mvt III, figure 17, p. 16

Incidentally, it appears that the middle movement can be performed separately as a viola/piano solo.

I also looked at *Inner-City Counterpoints*, for clarinet, viola, cello and piano. Also in three movements (fast-slow-fast), this work did not reveal anything new compared with the prior score.

Barry McKimm (1941–); Ian Farr (1941–2006); Penelope Thwaites (1944–); Martin Friedel (1945–); Ian Cugley (1945–); Andre Oosterbaan (1947–); Claudio Pompili (1949–); Michael Barkl (1958–); Stephen Benfall (1957–); Warren Burt (1949–); Michael Whiticker (1954–)

Collecting hundreds of scores and sifting through them, it is inevitable that one comes across separate works by composers that need to be at least mentioned and listed, even if there is no other music by the same composer for this book. I include of few such pieces at this juncture.

Barry McKimm writes in a tonal, late-romantic idiom, although not overly chromatic. The piano parts can be quite ornate, but not difficult to read, as their harmonic basis is always clear. We have seen an *Andante Tranquillo* that exists in versions for either tuba or viola and piano (1997), a *Concert Piece* (1983), for viola or flute and piano, and a *Rhapsody* (1981), for tenor trombone and piano; this last was, for me, the most absorbing of the works gathered. He knows his instruments and there is always a sense of colour present.

Ian Farr's *Four Rimbaud Songs*, for voice and piano, on the other hand, are at the opposite end of the spectrum. The songs—1) 'Jeune Goinfre', 2) 'Sensation', 3) 'Fete Galante', and 4) 'Lys'—are vintage avant-garde post–World War II, now sounding mannered and a bit weary. The piano writing is characteristically pointillist.

Penelope Thwaites' *A Lambeth Garland (To honour the restoration of Lambeth Palace garden)* (1986), for soprano, alto, tenor, baritone and piano duet, would not have been out of place if it had been written 100 years earlier. Set out as a cycle of short songs, it is redolent of Victoriana

1. 'The Lambeth Waltz'
2. 'A Gardener's Song'
3. 'Song of a Scotsman'
4. 'An English Rose'
5. 'The Wildlife Garden'
6. 'Reprise: The Lambeth Waltz'.

Various voices and soprano, alto, tenor, bass (SATB) are mixed within the songs. This cycle, as well as Thwaites' *Psalm 19* (1973), for voice and piano or organ, does make one wonder about relevancy, without meaning to be unkind. *Vijay's Fable* (1994), for piano trio, does little to dispel these impressions, although at least a free-flowing sense of rubato is created by the violin often playing quintuplets against the 4/4 D drone in the piano.

Martin Friedel's *Fragment from Sonata for Clarinet and Piano* (1979) made me wish that he had completed the work!

Ian Cugley, who was well known to me in the old days in Hobart, has left for us, as a portion of his small compositional legacy, *Three Little Pieces for Clarinet and Piano* (1971). As with all of Ian's music, these are delicately crafted tiny pieces, perhaps inspired by the Berg pieces. They have subtitles—I) 'Leaps', II) 'Little Fingers', III) 'Counting'—which demonstrate the essence of each piece.

In a similar vein, 10 years later (1981), we have Andre Oosterbaan's *Three Haiku for Flute and Piano*. Like Cugley, Oosterbaan puts an actual haiku text in front of the respective pieces. I have two copies of the work: one typeset and the other probably the earlier original manuscript version. On the manuscript, the title is different. It says *Sonata for Flute and Piano*, but the music is the same. The haikus are present in both versions. These are a little more muscular and wider in scope than the Cugley pieces. The language of both composers is related: a free-flowing chromatic modernist flow, with widespread gestures in the Oosterbaan pieces. Wind players should really rediscover both of these sets.

The only music that we could locate by Claudio Pompili dates from 1991, and consists of two songs, entitled *Wandrers Nachtlied I & II* for high female voice and piano. The words are by Goethe. The settings emulate German lieder, are highly tonal and are written in a way that would currently be described as 'postmodern'. I cannot quite understand the tag, since most pieces so described seem to be looking back rather than forward. Perhaps they should be called 'pre-modern'?

Michael Barkl is another modernist (in a more correct sense), this time with a penchant for perpetual motion—an incessant movement of music with few rests. Witness as an example *Fuellstimme* (1981), for vibraphone, marimba and piano, wherein the parts move in rhythmic parallel, the piano right hand blending with the other two percussion instruments, whilst the piano left hand acts as a punctuating part, with jabbed, well-spaced chords; it is only in the last few bars that the texture suddenly thins and the piece is over. *Night Words: The ravishing* (for voice and piano), on the other hand, is closer in spirit to cabaret, with the voice at times employing *Sprechstimme*, and the piano supplying a dreamy, lazy background of smoky nightclub atmosphere. This also exists in a version for viola and piano as well as other instruments/piano. This is somewhat curious, as I would have thought that the meaning of the words is central to the impact of the piece; however, composers are constantly tinkering with their own music as well as with music by other composers. We have done this for centuries, and who am I to quibble over such a long tradition? Barkl's *Romance for Piano with Clarinet, Bassoon, Violin & Cello* (1977) combines elements of both of these worlds, with the composer using the effect of keeping the third pedal down through dry figuration. The other instruments sometimes have approximate notation only; at other times they double the melodic piano line, or interject. *Rota* (1981), for violin, cello and piano, is in the traditional fast-slow-fast, three-movement format. It begins in a pointillist style, but much of the work returns to the world of *Fuellstimme*, with massive parallel motion in all parts. An encore piece for flute and piano, *Twenty-Five Felicitations for the AMC*, has the piano playing a quasi-boogie bass with sharp interjecting chords in the mid-range of the instrument, with the flute strutting its stuff above all this. The piece is 25 bars long and presumably was written for the twenty-fifth anniversary of the Australian Music Centre.

Barkl has fulfilled roles as community composer-in-residence as well as the more conventional commissioned composer writing for established ensembles. In 1986 he was in Orange, NSW, in his first capacity, and one of the results was a work called *An Orange Blitz*, for unison voices, keyboard, bass and drums. Most of this is merely the simple vocal line, with the rest only hinted at via chord symbols. The numbers making up this set of songs are amusing: 'Out of Nowhere', 'Mechanical Chant', '303 Rifles', 'Mixed Cocktail', 'Davo's Diner' and 'Gold!'. A work still using chord indications, but with much more actually written out, is *Blue Music*, for electric guitar, bass guitar and electric piano. I do not know anything about the history of the piece, but suspect that Barkl is a pragmatic composer and wrote for an available ensemble, with certain reading skills; the work is crafted accordingly. It exhibits a restless counterpoint interspersed with standard chords from the jazz world. The players would need special competencies, with a foot in both worlds, so to speak, to play this piece convincingly. In 1984 Barkl was commissioned by the Seymour Group, for which he composed *Ballade*. The scoring is for flute, clarinet, vibraphone, piano, violin and cello. The instruments are listed here as given by the composer, moreover, this is the order in which they appear in the score itself. Playing through it, it is at once apparent that the sextet consists of three groups of two, and that the instruments work in pairs—that is, the two wind, the vibraphone and piano, and the two strings. The Seymour Group often worked with a conductor, and maybe that is how this piece was realised; however, given a good ensemble it should have been possible to play it without a baton, but it would need more rehearsal. The writing is ceaselessly polyphonic and complex, with entries on upbeat semiquavers and the like. Barkl extracts much colour from the group, and frames the entire work with an opening and ending by piano solo. I would expect that the seating of the ensemble would mirror the pairing of instruments, as it would certainly make life easier for everyone. Since Barkl obviously enjoys the odd pun, it should not surprise us that there is a tiny (perhaps encore?) piece named *See More Music*. This is for a similar ensemble and is set out in a similar fashion: flute, clarinet, horn, percussion, piano, viola and cello.

Speaking of encore pieces allows me to neatly segue to *Blues at Eleven* (1996) by Stephen Benfall. As the title suggests, this piece is

> in slow blues style and in 11/8 time. The original version for viola and piano was written for Helen Tuckey, violist with the West Australian Symphony Orchestra, who asked me for a blues piece for her students. I have since prepared other editions of the work for flute, clarinet. Eb and Bb saxophones, and violin—all equally suitable for the private studio and concert platform.

This piece was a surprise for me, having looked at the composer's music for solo piano; it does not represent the composer in a broad sense. Much closer to my expectations is the *Sonata for Oboe and Piano* (1987). This is a complex work— bristling with difficulties for both players—in five short movements. The main problems have to do with coordinating the rhythmic groupings between the instruments. This is not for everyone, but a good performance of this work will leave an exciting impression!

Warren Burt, as usual, provided some of the most thought-provoking and often diverting scores during the writing of this book. *63 Whispers in Memoriam Morton Feldman* (1989), for clarinet, drums, viola, bass and piano, is, as one would expect, a series of short, soft events, mostly disconnected—a real tribute to what we now instantly recognise, rightly or wrongly, as 'the Feldman style'. The composer gives us no clue as to how the music was put together, but quite often Warren is involved with technology to a greater or lesser degree. Another piece with a Feldman-like approach is *From the Dreambooks: November eighteenth* (1980), for trombone and piano. In *A Vassar Piece for the Bardic Tradition* (1983), Burt insists that the program note be read aloud to the audience before the piece is played, 'in order to establish a context'. The note says:

> This piece is another spin-off from my ongoing investigation into creating programs that compose. A process was set up on a very large analog synthesizer system. This process selected pitches and rhythms according to certain instructions I programmed into it. Note that although I set up the process, the machine itself made actual decisions as to which pitches and rhythms it played. Large-scale decisions controlling the form of the piece were made by me interacting with the synthesizer program while the tape was being made.
>
> The piano part was generated by a computer program that selected pitches using the same process as the synthesizer, but applied them to different gestures. The program printed out information that was transcribed into score form. While the printout was occurring I interacted with the program, changing values to shape its output, just as I had done with the synthesizer while it was being recorded.
>
> What this piece is 'about' is setting two extremely similar processes in motion on two different machines and seeing how their results compare. Will chords generated by the synthesizer appear in the computer-composed piano part? Over the course of the piece, will the two parts, piano and tape, appear as united or separate? I wrote this piece because I was curious to see if any interactions would occur between the two programs. As a listener, then, the question is *not* 'Is the musical output of these two systems interesting?', but rather, 'Do the *unique* outputs of these two systems exhibit (show) any hearable relationships, and if so, what are they?'

I have chosen to quote Burt's note in full since it is provocative and challenges some basic assumptions about the compositional process. *Six Political Piano Miniatures* (1990–92), for piano and speaking voice, is a kind of chamber music in that the pianist also speaks. The pieces are essentially political protest and a demand for change. The titles speak for themselves, as it were

1. 'War is a Dumb Idea'
2. '1492–1992: 500 years of genocide and colonialism'
3. 'All Nations—hallucinations'
4. 'Fact'
5. 'Yuppie Feeding Frenzy—a portrait of the 80s'
6. 'Act up!'.

The piano part is often violent and deliberately verging on the unplayable in one instance.

In comparison, Michael Whiticker, in his song cycle *Love's Blazing Fire* (1991), for mezzo-soprano, baritone and piano, with available versions for soprano and tenor, treats the keyboard in a much kinder way. The cycle, with text taken from the Song of Solomon in the Old Testament, consists of six songs

1. 'Black as the Raven', for mezzo-soprano and piano
2. 'You have Ravished My Heart', for baritone and piano
3. 'Behind Your Veil', for mezzo-soprano, baritone and piano
4. 'With the Moisture of the Night', for mezzo-soprano and piano
5. 'My Beauty, Do Come', for mezzo-soprano, baritone and piano
6. 'Love's Blazing Fire', for mezzo-soprano and baritone.

The use of available forces is not just for colouristic contrast, as it also provides the composer with thematic references between songs. The piano parts are quasi minimalist—that is, they restrict themselves to groups of notes and patterns, and the changes that occur with repetition are not huge. The vocal part is treated in a similar way, although a little less mechanistically. Long arches of melody are not Whiticker's choice of vocal writing; the voice is treated in short bursts of phrases, aping the brusque gestures of the piano (though there are exceptions to this treatment). A similar technique is applied in his 1988 trio *Min-Ame*. Here, the accent is on beats of uneven length; there is much rhythmically parallel writing and doubling. The patterns reiterate themselves as a kind of mantra, except that the repetitions are never totally predictable. This short trio does succeed in producing a hypnotic spell upon the listener. In an earlier work,

Korokon (1983), for violin and piano, Whiticker works in a more organic fashion, so that the instrumental parts become more and more heavily decorated with *fioratura* upbeats as the piece progresses.

Part 4: The Fourth Generation

Ten years have passed since the cut-off point of my last book. So now it is possible to speak of the fourth generation of composers. Writing about living composers still emerging in their careers, and still forming their musical personalities, is not only fraught with danger and the strong possibility of error; it is also most probably premature. We certainly need time to look back on an era and be able to ponder on it with some objectivity and distance. For this reason, this section of the book will be the shortest of all, as it is dealing with unknown territory in many ways. I have noticed in my teaching career that the crop of students that surfaced at the end of the twentieth century and the first decade of the twenty-first is conservative and unadventurous, at least to someone who has been a modernist all his life. The postmodern (whatever that might mean) has reverted to tonality—not functional tonality, true, more the sound of the triad as an event in itself. On the positive side, the current composer seems more easily to engage with popular music and various multimedia available in the digital age. Australia itself is at present a very conservative society, too. When we elected a Labor government four years ago, I expected some apparent change in the tertiary sector; unfortunately, little seems to have changed: it is business as usual, with the various arts still taking a back seat in the eyes of government. Subsidies and various support systems are still scarce so composers must find it tempting to please at all costs, as a means of survival, perhaps. The real composer will have to show more backbone than usual, I suspect! Our orchestras are now free-floating entities and have to put bums on seats to be able to continue, so there is little incentive there for anything even remotely 'dangerous'. Long live revisionism!

11. The Fourth Generation

Stephen Leek (1959–)

This book does not include 'educational' music, so named. This is not out of a sense of feeling superior to it, nor is there any implied suggestion that music written for children need be in any artistic way inferior to concert music; not at all. The decision was made simply to make the volume of material to be processed for this book a manageable size. But, some of the music falls into the cracks, as it were. Stephen Leek (who studied with me) is an example of one such composer. He clearly does not write specifically for the concert platform, but neither is it purely teaching-studio material. I have included him in the book because he has produced a sizeable amount of middle-difficulty chamber music with piano of demonstrable quality. One set of 12 pieces is designed to be useful for performance, with or without dance, and aims to introduce the sound of new music to dance students—a group that probably misses out generally on exposure to such sound. This project, named *New Music–New Dance*, has a number of pieces utilising the piano in a chamber music setting. I list the relevant numbers

1. 'Promotion', for clarinet, percussion and piano
2. 'Suspension', for clarinet and piano
3. 'Ruined', for flute, clarinet, cello, percussion and piano
4. 'Long Distance', for flute, clarinet, cello, percussion and piano
5. 'Colourwheel', for flute, clarinet and piano.

'Colourwheel' is representative of the whole set. Within six pages of score, the players are introduced to various new music devices in an accessible and non-confrontational manner, without artistic compromise or a sense of writing down to the performers. Other similar pieces by Stephen of similar proportion and intent are: *Goombungee*, for violin or cello and piano, as well as *Plateau*, for cello and piano, dedicated to his cello teacher, Nelson Cooke, and comprising five movements, which are in fact placenames

1. 'Hammersley'
2. 'Katajuta'
3. 'Kanangra'

4. 'Port Campbell'

5. 'Nambung'.

Various cello special effects are explored in this work. Stephen has also self-published some instrumental music: I have seen *Rookery*, for clarinet and piano, as well as *Ross Roy*, for the same combination.

Brigid Burke (1960–)

It was good to come across some music by Brigid Burke. I remember her as a student here in Canberra, playing the clarinet and producing both paintings (I have a few examples of her work at home and in my studio) and compositions, with which I hope I helped her a little. Most of the scores I have in front of me involve her own instrument and were probably written primarily for her own performance. The first piece I played through was *Another Mode* (2001), for flute, clarinet and piano: a light-textured piece, in which the piano is treated very linearly, all in an energetic and bustling 4/4, reminding me somehow of Milhaud. The piano often doubles, and eventually becomes prominent, with an insistent low C staccato towards the end of the piece. It is all slightly boppy and quite attractive. I then opened the pages of *Come for Tea* (2001), for clarinet and piano, and realised that it was very familiar indeed. Actually, it is exactly the same as the previous piece, minus the flute part. I then surmised that perhaps the composer wanted a busier result than she arrived at here with just the clarinet, so superimposed the flute part over an already existent piece; fair enough, one would think. I then happened to open the score of *In a Frenzy* (1997), for clarinet and piano, and, yet again, found myself on familiar ground! This time, however, there were only some elements of the prior two pieces, and this work is much shorter than the other two, which were exactly the same length. *In a Frenzy* is labelled by the composer as a gesticulatory piece, always in a 'panic mode'. Brigid writes: 'It contains a recurring theme with variations...irrational rhythmic pulses (especially in the piano)...accentuated by interruptions of quarter-tone rhythmic patterns in the clarinet part.' It appears that I viewed these works in reverse order, so for those who are interested in how composers' minds tick over, here are three pieces based on the same material, but gradually evolving.

Burke's other works are all for clarinet and piano. *A Breathing Stone* (1997–98) is very thin and transparent. The composer writes: 'The clarinet material is based on a series of eleven quarter tones within the range of a perfect fifth. The rhythmic pulse and dynamic range accentuate this transparent sound world, while the piano, in a quiet and sparse manner underpins the microtonal structures.' Burke always gives the fingerings for any microtones and multiphonics that appear in her pieces. *Heart Dances* (1997–98) pushes the boundaries further and here the clarinet 'uses vocal gestures and inflections to suggest children at play. The musico-linguistic sounds of high shrieks, buzzes, sibilants and simultaneous pitches, whispered phonetic sounds, tongue clicks, quarter tones and multiphonics vocatively convey this mood.' The piano part here acts as a mere backdrop of continuous quintuplets. Finally, there is a slowly unfolding and slow piece named *Once Removed* (1997), which 'investigates gesture and pitch manipulation'. All these short clarinet/piano pieces would make attractive recital additions.

Stephen Cronin (1960–)

Stephen Cronin's folio exhibits a wide range of approaches and techniques. The earliest piece we have by him is a *Duo for Horn and Piano* from 1982. It begins with a rather traditional first section with triads in the right hand and octaves in the left hand of the piano punching out a march-like piece, with the horn playing conventional fanfares against it. I was feeling disappointed as I played, but then something quite madcap occurred—still very spare and almost skeletal, but with a savage irony that reminded me of Shostakovich from his early days. Buoyed by the experience, I moved on to the next work, a display piece for xylophone and piano named *Gesta* (1987). Surprisingly, the piano was treated as though it was another xylophone (which it is, if no pedal is applied!), so we had a super-dry piece as a result. The piano part is not of advanced difficulty, but the xylophone has at least two cadenzas and much of it requires considerable dexterity. *Angel* (1999), for voice, cello and piano, is another quite demanding piece for the instruments, setting up a background of continuous semiquavers, with the voice given mostly triplets against this (text is by Leon Waller). *Sample Only! Not for Sale* is a short, 4.5-minute piece with a touch of the blues about it, for flute, oboe cello and piano—perhaps composed as an encore? But it gave me a taste for yet another facet of Cronin, hinting at contrapuntal skills underneath the main argument of the little piece, carried by the flute.

I discovered this skill finally in *The Snake-Pit* (1990), for clarinet, viola, cello and piano/harpsichord. This is a major work, requiring amplification, multiphonics, reverberation facilities and foot switches for the players to control the amplification. The piece is full of effects and colours, including key effects and air sounds such as respiration, tongue slap and throat effect, and would not be easy to set up or to bring off. I have not heard a recording, but it looks fascinating. I wonder if it can be done without a conductor? Probably not, so, as in the case of some other works, this is not a real example of chamber music. The harpsichord is most effectively and imaginatively used combined with the amplified wind instruments doing their special effects.

The year 2004 saw the production of *Music for Calming and Healing*, for cello and piano. This is a very still, meditative piece; the piano part hardly alters and the atmosphere is not unlike a Brian Eno piece. Cronin demonstrates his versatility yet again!

Three Brief Insinuations (2005), for bassoon and piano, is witty and to the point. The first piece has a constant rhythm from the piano, with the bassoon asked to play its chromatic gestures 'with a snide and nasty attitude'. The second movement is very soft and asks the piano to provide a high-pitched smokescreen, with the bassoon playing long notes underneath. The last movement is like a fast and busy waltz—the players instructed to play 'energetically as if gossiping'.

Finally, there are two very traditional vocal pieces. *Golden Boy* (2001, text by Pat McCahey), for soprano and piano, could have come from a Broadway show. *Three Old English Poems*, for voice and piano, consists of

1. 'The Ploughman's Song' (words by Nicholas Breton)
2. 'Gipsy Joys' from *More Dissemblers Besides Women* (words by Thomas Middleton)
3. 'Weep No More, Sad Fountains' (words anon.).

These settings are completely traditional, almost like an exercise in pastiche.

Andrew Schultz (1960–)

When I last wrote about Andrew Schultz, there was little raw material to go on, as he does not essentially treat the piano as a solo instrument. With this tome, however, a wealth of scores was revealed and it was with great pleasure and excitement that I waded into the task of reading through Schultz's chamber music output. There are some slender pieces, and we might as well mention them first. *Christmas Song* is for horn and piano and is really a teaching piece. The composer even assigns a particular examination grade level for the work. *As* (2006) is a tiny but atmospheric piece for bass clarinet and piano. Here one immediately senses that we are in the presence of a composer whose music grows logically and organically. There is another piece for clarinet and piano, named *Everlasting Arms*, which, contrary to the slow and mysterious *As*, is fast and spiky. It is a good piece to witness the Schultz technique and observe the gradual evolution of the opening figure on the clarinet, its growth and reiteration lending a strong cohesion to this piece. With *Master Mariner—Lost at Sea*, for oboe and piano, we again enter a slow and mysterious world, but the composer demands both rubato and a sense of tempo going forward and back in this three-page work; we also meet for the first time the device of preparing two of the strings of the piano using masking tape. Schultz seems to enjoy the sound of the piano transformed, and it is present not just in these small works but in the large-scale chamber pieces, too. The oboe part is like some distant sea shanty growing and waning in intensity. *Suspended Preludes* is a set of tiny pieces for double bass and piano, gathered together to make a substantial larger work. The titles of the preludes give clues to their content. Prepared piano is present here, too. This set is meant to be heard as a cycle, rather than as just simply a collection of short pieces

1. 'Resonate'
2. 'To Sleep'
3. 'Piano Drum'
4. 'Rocks in Slow Flight'
5. 'Ground'
6. 'Gravity'
7. 'Trans'.

The preludes are mostly tiny, but now and then one senses the composer trying to contain himself from bursting out with a development of an interesting idea. The set is a worthy addition to the double bass repertoire.

We are now entering the realm of the medium-proportioned pieces. *After Nina* (2007) has the piano playing mostly in the bass clef; this does give a rather gloomy air to the work with clarinet and cello. Schultz is a freely chromatic composer, with a rich palette of expression, but he is not afraid to use simple triads when it suits him. The low tessitura gives the simple chords a powerful expression.

Example 11.1 A. Schultz, *After Nina*, p. 4, bars 44–7

Australian Chamber Music with Piano

And so we arrive at the large works. *Barren Grounds* (1988), for clarinet, viola, cello and piano, is a massive piece covering 82 pages of score, in two movements: '…This ground' and 'The Twittering Machine'.

The first movement accrues very slowly, with controlled growth giving birth to plaintive bird calls, trills, arpeggios and an imitation of electronic reverberation. It is not until page 25 that we arrive at the climactic moment of this movement.

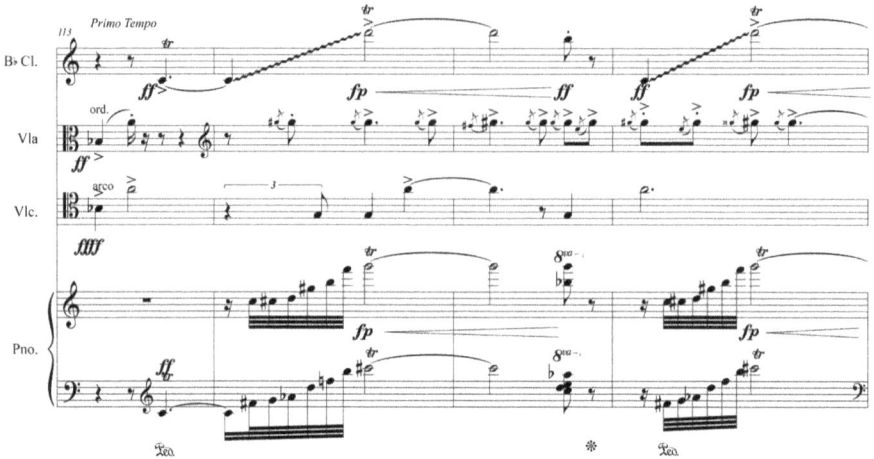

Example 11.2 A. Schultz, *Barren Grounds*, p. 25, bars 113–16

The second movement is a diametrically opposite sound-scape. It is full of repeated chords and jerky short runs, like some malfunctioning robot stuck in one command. It would be difficult to perform, since the whole is peppered with time changes, and much of it requires total coordination in the chordal attacks. Like other Schultz in full flight, this requires virtuoso players, and could sound really laboured if performed sluggishly. There is a piano cadenza in the second movement.

A composition from 1990, *Duo Variations*, for viola and piano, is perhaps even more relentless than *Barren Grounds*, and is structured as theme followed by 12 variations played without a break. Most of it is breathlessly virtuosic and pushes both players to full concentration over its 700-plus bars. In passing, I should list here a *Stick Dance* from 1987, for clarinet, marimba and piano, which incorporates, in a relatively short piece, some of the character and quality of the longer works.

Three ambitious works remain: *L'Oiseau Fantastique* (1984) is scored for clarinet, violin, cello and piano (with some prepared notes), and an ad lib organ part. The two movements titles are 'Crescendo' and 'Toccata'.

Beginning with a simple F-sharp–G-sharp bird call on the clarinet, the movement, by degrees, gains in complexity and polyphony, until, in a quasi-aleatory notation, there is an outburst from all the instruments. The movement begins with sustained sounds, which gradually take on life and join the opening clarinet in a very dense layering of voices. The organ (if one is used) provides a 30-second link named 'Trope' to the second half of the composition. The toccata moves using a combination of free and strict notation to a section of tutti chords before it winds up. Having completed this work, the composer must have felt that not all the ideas had been fully explored; in the same year (1984), Schultz composed *L'Oiseau Fantastique II*, this time scored for two violins, viola, cello and piano. This time the two movements are 'Prelude' and 'Passacaglia'.

'Prelude' is a short, whispered introduction to the very substantial and exciting 'Passacaglia', in which the piano is the main protagonist, giving out the theme against a blanket of held strings. A reference to the 'Prelude' signals a new section, and the bird polyphony begins again, with the piano still playing its passacaglia arpeggios uninterruptedly. Finally, it surrenders to the prevailing instruments, and becomes two more birds in the chorus. These two *L'Oiseau* pieces are an important addition to the repertoire.

With a View to Infinity (1982), for flute/piccolo, percussion and piano (prepared and played on the strings as well as normally), does not add substantially to our knowledge of this composer. The work is in three movements: a 'Sostenuto', centred on the note B; a set of un-numbered variations with a theme similar to the robot idea from *Barren Grounds*; and a short 'Lacrimosa', with some recollection from the first movement.

With this collection of chamber works, Andrew Schultz proves himself to be a composer of the first rank, unafraid to ignore popularism and leaving himself free to evolve further on his chosen path.

Brett Dean (1961–)

We have three scores by this well-known composer. Certain common traits were exhibited. *Huntington Eulogy* (2001), for cello and piano, is in three movements

1. 'Nightsky'
2. 'Swarming'
3. 'Elegy (for Jason)'.

Dean's scores are extremely detailed in their instructions to the performers, especially when he writes for strings, since he is a viola virtuoso—a fairly rare breed. So, in this piece, just looking at the slow cello opening, which is rhapsodic, one immediately detects excursions into microtones, strings chosen for the player, and so on. The piano writing is another matter. I thought we had been there and done that, so to speak: I am referring to the business of reaching inside the piano, plucking strings, using various mallets to strike the strings, and brushing the strings with the fingers. It is a pretty enough sound, but we now have other ways of getting it, and I conjectured that we had left these gimmicky approaches to the piano well behind us by now (I have been as guilty as others in using them, incidentally). Anyway, Dean certainly likes these effects and they appear constantly in his piano parts. He is a composer who certainly knows what he wants and his knowledge of instrumental effects and possibilities is there for all to see. The scores are really highly crafted and calculated with great precision as to the overall effect. The piano parts on the keyboard are not as idiomatic as the string writing; indeed, the keyboard writing is quite often awkward and ungainly. That said, Dean is a composer who has a strong sense of the thematic combined with the organic, so events happen in a developing way, with a strong sense of logic combined with a flair for the rhapsodic, which is admirable. Certain pitches are singled out as important, and the return to these pitches acquires musical significance, both in slow and in fast passages. At times, the piano signals an almost romantic progression of harmony with its descending bass notes. Dean often writes passionately—a quality often absent from much contemporary Australian music.

Example 11.3 B. Dean, *Huntington Eulogy*, bars 25–7

The fast middle movement here, and in other works, has some affinity with Bartók and especially with Bulgarian-style rhythms, which permeate the whole movement. High virtuosity is demanded of both players, and the piano part has a feel to it that happens only when non-pianists write for the keyboard. Patterns do not lie within the hand and much of the writing is just plain hard work, as against difficult writing that is nevertheless pianistic. I hope the distinction is clear. In Dean's more dreamy moments, such as we found in *Night Window* (1993, revised 2004), for clarinet, viola and piano, there is some affinity with

George Crumb in his own particular night pieces. Much of this trio (Dean's brother is an expert clarinetist) explores a very mysterious nocturnal world. The work consists of an introduction followed by a theme and variations. Much of the introduction is once again that spiky, dry, angular music that we already experienced in the middle of the previous work. The variations move more and more into what the composer describes as a 'world of whispers'. The clarinet should give so little air pressure that the notes are more breath and key-mechanic sounds than tone. The viola now concentrates on *ponticello* sounds here, and again *col legno tratto*. Both instruments use the given phrases as merely an indication of the main harmonic sphere of a particular bar. This soft world does give way to the more barbaric sound that seems to be the other side of Dean's imagination. Thus, in *Voices of Angels* (1996), for violin, viola, cello, double bass and piano, the movement titles of 'Evocation' and 'Different Realms' are in fact these two extremely contrasting sides of the coin to be heard in well-defined fashion. The first is slow and dreamy, and we are back inside the piano yet again (with a fast section in the middle of the movement), while the second is mostly fast and rhythmically irregular, finally settling down to the mood of the opening of the whole piece.

Gordon Kerry (1961–)

Gordon Kerry writes in a highly rhapsodic style, at times drifting towards the Felix Werder ideal of 'discontinuity', although it never quite arrives there, because there are cohesive elements of repetition—sometimes literal repetition—thematic ideas, even if at times they represent a single interval, and occasional signposting of either a strong triadic presence or open octaves and fifths at some important instance in the composition. We assembled a good collection of Kerry scores, from the miniature *A Colder Music* (2001), for piano trio, and *Dream* (1987), for violin and piano, to larger-scale works such as *Piano Trio #2* (2000), and some others to be mentioned below. The composer has certain favoured characteristics. The growing of a small cellular idea into a longer, but still recognisable shape is one: sometimes this is achieved by singling out a note within the gesture and giving it some prominence by reason of dynamics or tessitura. If the process gets away from the composer, the music rapidly becomes gesticulatory, and the actual pitches begin to matter less than the shape itself. The second piano trio has a kind of recapitulation, which no doubt helps the composer to impose structure. The songs that we saw, such as *Moonrise* (1983, for soprano and piano), or *Night after Bushfire* (2003, also for soprano and piano, from the cantata *Through the Fire*), succeed through atmosphere and tight intervallic control. At its best, Kerry's music has a strong sense of improvisation, the music springing to life right before the listener. Another trio—this one for violin, horn and piano, named *No Abiding City* (2001)—uses a minor third as a predominant interval. Within this work, the piano uses the octave and fifth widespread chord as a milestone, and there is an outburst of loud G-major triads (a little like Alfred Schnittke, for shock value), which acts as a paradoxical dissonance in Kerry's particular idiom. The song about bushfire had, effectively, C-minor and A-minor passages towards the end of the song, maybe for a similar reason.

Another trio we examined, *No Orphean Lute* (1994, marked 'Deo Gratis' at the end of the piece), is a bigger work in three movements, also for piano trio; perhaps this is number one? By now, I had noted two further stylistic habits of Kerry. The first is the habitual piano writing, which is overwhelmingly in the high register, in single notes distributed between the hands. This is done so much and so often that in the end it becomes an irritant, especially to a pianist! The second habit is the rather complex method of notation, heading towards what I call the 'maximalist' school, although it is, thankfully, never as dense. But it does leave one wondering: would there be a simpler way to notate the music and still get the same desired effect? Composers of necessity work 'in slow motion', and complex details seem vital at that stage of composition; however, when the performance tempo happens, some of what is carefully notated disappears. It is a simple, unavoidable, acoustic fact.

Kerry certainly has a sense of instrumental colour, and when he has a number of instruments racing around in continuous semiquavers, there is a splash of excitement generated. Overall, the music is not without passion, although I would not quite classify it as red-hot passion—it is too objective for that.

Two other works for solo instrument and piano, *On the Summer Map of Stars* (2000, for bassoon and piano) and *Paradi* (1996, for viola and piano), are a contrast in effect in that the simpler piece, the one for viola, speaks more eloquently and directly to the listener; the bassoon piece might very well be overwritten, though carefully crafted.

The two most ambitious pieces we examined were *Rasa, Piano Quartet No. 2* (2000, dedicated to that fine composer and pianist Roger Smalley) and *Sonata* (1990), for flute/piccolo, percussion, piano and cello. The piano and percussion work in the gap between the piccolo and the cello, with the piano really used as a percussion instrument (which it is). In the piano quartet, Kerry writes passages of complex counterpoint in the string instruments, which cause a fuzziness in the rhythmic outlines and forward propulsion of the work. But Kerry is a composer of undoubtedly high craftsmanship and seriousness of purpose, and it will be interesting to observe his future development.

Stephen Lalor (1962–)

We were more fortunate with locating a number of scores by Stephen Lalor. *Apropos Flying* (1997), for tenor saxophone or trumpet or clarinet, bass guitar and piano, is, like Lloyd, in minimalist technique to begin with, but with a more interesting rhythmic sense and unexpected shifts of triadic chords. The density of this piece, laid on a quirky piano foundation, gradually grows and then wanes. The sense of quirky humour continues with the *Austrada Waltz* (1998), for clarinet and piano. There is a what must be a deliberate reference to Satie at the start, and this little piece continues from there, with an appealing melodic eccentricity and abrupt modulations. The technical demands are very moderate. *Bright Gulfs in the Distance* was composed in 1992; the settings are from the Russian poet Nina Gagen-Torn, translated by Michael Molnar. This is an altogether darker piece, as the author, in her lifetime, had to deal with imprisonment and oppression. The piano plays arpeggio patterns, with the vocal part almost folk-like in its simplicity. *Childhood Friend* has a similar texture; it was written in 1989 and is for medium voice and piano. Curiously, the arpeggiated chords of the piano part are identified, as though it is a chord chart. Is this an invitation to elaborate, or for a guitarist to play? There is no explanation in the score. Two further songs are of a similar ilk: *The Blue Dress* (words again by Libby Hathorn), for female voice and piano—a simple but quite effective piece; and another Hathorn setting, *Stories Grandmothers Tell* (1990), with a middle section that the composer describes as 'funk'.

Six Angels (1997) comprises four settings for male voice from James Joyce's *Portrait of the Artist as a Young Man*. The excerpts chosen are short but telling. The vocal line is still folkish, but now there is parlando as well, and the piano part is no longer a simple and flowing accompaniment. There are drama and rhetoric in the writing, and it seems to me that this cycle is well worth doing. A similar departure from what I came to expect from this composer is his *Prelude and Dance* (1988), for violin and piano. The composer says of this work:

> Prelude: this is a prelude in the true sense of the word—intended to create a very calm, languid atmosphere as a prelude to the highly-charged Dance. A simple, repeated 4-bar motif is the basis of a short movement of continuity and dream-like regularity. Dance: in complete contrast to the Prelude, this movement is energetic, often frantically wild and probably inspired by the composer's association with, and study of, folk music—particularly that of Eastern Europe.

The 'Dance' has some quasi-aleatory sections and quite irregular bar lengths, in contrast with most of the output we surveyed.

Mary Finsterer (1962–)

Mary Finsterer is generally associated with electronic/computer music. We did find a single work for voice, oboe, cello and piano. It appears to have been originally a radiophonic work, and the words appear to have some connection with Samuel Beckett (I am hesitant to say this definitively since Beckett rarely if ever allowed composers to set his words), or else this piece was used in a program based on Beckett. At any rate, the voice and cello seem to be the star performers in this piece, with the composer taking great care with her vowel and consonant placements, and the atomisation of the words themselves. It is a characteristic Finsterer score in its attention to detail and its meticulous notation. Though meant for radio, this would work quite well in a music-theatre situation. It might need a conductor, as the rhythms are not simple and the lines generally independent of each other.

Ian Shanahan (1962–)

Both works by which Ian Shanahan is represented here were composed as memorial pieces. The first of these is *153 Infinities* (1996), for solo piano and percussion. The composer has provided copious notes to the piece, explaining the metaphysics driving the piece, the mathematical symbolism, the optional nature of the percussion parts, the religious significance of the groupings of the percussion, the method of notation of the score, and so on. There is no room for me to go into all this here. The piano part was inspired by Roger Woodward's playing, and, added to all this, there are strong music-theatre elements in the way the piece is choreographed and the percussion is arranged on stage: a large space is required for mounting this work, and the composer wishes that the grand piano be amplified. Ian is a recorder virtuoso, so the approach is from a virtuoso's standpoint. There is nothing timid about the piece! Quite long silences are built into the score, and carefully notated. The piano part tends to explode into these silences (whether loud or soft) with thick chords and brilliant gestures. After all the setting up and no doubt intense preparation required, it is all over in about 11 minutes! The piano part is drawn from two previous works for solo piano.

The second work, *Harmonia (in pp)* (2001), was written as a memorial to the late Peter Platt (hence 'pp' in the title), Professor of Music at the University of Sydney, and beloved by many. The composition is for tenor recorder and piano, with the recorder part obviously written by Ian for himself. Once again, there are copious performance notes preceding the score. Like the previous work, this is in time-space notation, and an inevitable freedom will result at each performance. The piano writing is similar, too, but somewhat less explosive and virtuosic. The overall timing is somewhere about five to six minutes. The recorder part contains advanced playing techniques.

Sophie Lacaze (1963–)

Sophie Lacaze is here due to two works. The first is *Histoire sans paroles*, for violin, cello and piano. It is written in a sparse idiom, with the piano initiating events with soft, well-spaced staccato quavers, centred on middle G, and gradually increasing in density and with the other instruments creeping in with some mixed articulation and longer notes. Everything proceeds in this fashion until bar 153, when a form of slow movement seems to happen, with sustained sounds; finally, patterns are given to the keyboard to repeat ad lib as long as indicated, until everything sinks into silence. The whole is notated in 4/4. The second piece is *Sons—Jeux*, for clarinet and piano, and is similarly terse, this time G sharp being the pivot note. This is a little busier than the first piece, but is similarly economical and also written in 4/4.

Wendy Hiscocks (1963–)

Some years ago, writing about Wendy Hiscocks' music for solo piano, I had already noted a tendency towards programmatic content, as well as an attraction to modality. After her early vigorous *Toccata*, for solo piano, I suppose I was somewhat disappointed. These tendencies are now strongly confirmed in the chamber music that we have gathered—a sizeable amount of material that must be considered representative of her output. There is a remarkable uniformity about all of these works

- *Bush Christmas* (soprano and piano), words by David Martin
- *Coral Fantasy* (violin, cello and piano), descriptive words by the composer embedded in the score
- *The Day of the Singing Birds* (soprano and piano), words by Dennis Stoll; also, a version of the same song for flute, soprano and piano or harp
- *Elegy* (soprano and piano), traditional words from the American Makah tribe
- *The Flame* (violin and piano)
- *I Look Out and See* (four songs for bass and piano), words by David Martin, Walt Whitman and Rabidranath Tagore
- *Libretto of the Eight Year Old* (soprano and piano, or soprano and string trio), words by the composer

- *Mother and Child* (clarinet, voice and piano, or clarinet, voice and strings), words by Rabidranath Tagore
- *Poem* (cello and piano), programmatic titles by composer within the score
- *The Twenty-Ninth Bather* (soprano and piano), words by Walt Whitman
- *Two Shakespeare Songs* (soprano and piano), words by William Shakespeare
- *Winter* (voice and piano), words by Nefra Canning
- *Friendship* (voice and piano), words by Nefra Canning.

As a composer myself, often inspired by the printed word, I can obviously have nothing against a composer whose chamber music output is almost exclusively word setting. Neither could I find any fault whatsoever with her choice of poets and poetry for setting. I could not help feeling, however, some concerns upon opening the purely instrumental scores.

The *Coral Fantasy* is replete with subtitles: 'Sunlight Dancing on the Surface of the Water'; 'Under the Sea'; 'The Coral Reef'; 'Coral Anemone'; 'Jellyfish'; 'Fish'; 'Clownfish'; 'Rising to the Surface of the Water'; 'Sunset'. This, essentially, is no different to those programmatic Victorian pieces depicting various historical or romantic events, with a printed little running commentary on what the music 'means'. We regard these pieces now as amusing examples of high kitsch, and yet here we are faced with a similar aesthetic from a contemporary composer.

The cello *Poem* is even more explicit in its programmatic depiction: 'Lullaby'; 'Snow'; 'Autumn Turns to Winter'; 'Summer Turning to Autumn'; 'Spring Turning to Summer'; 'Spring. Pas de deux'. There is obviously a hidden program here. That in itself is hardly a criminal offence, despite lurking suspicions of a naivety on the part of the composer.

Further, the plethora of performing instructions is curious: some are direct and helpful to the performer, but many others actually do not assist in the music making, because they attempt to tell you what you need to *feel* rather than what you need to *do*. Once more, the often-sentimental instructions add to a forming picture of this composer.

The textures tend to be very similar in all these pieces, with a preference towards a rather busy piano part, often with running scale patterns and tonal arpeggio figures filling the space—a space that is rhythmically rather static and predictable, and with triadic signposts ever present. The use of the piano is traditional and even timid; I found moments that seemed to me to be 'pretty' or even 'cute'. I hate to write this way about another composer; in the end it is a matter of personal taste and personal aesthetic, and I simply found this music too close to kitsch for comfort.

Raffaele Marcellino (1964–)

More than 10 years ago, I received a phone call from the composer Raffaele Marcellino, who wanted to meet me and discuss some aspects of the art of transcription, based on my studies and performances of the great Ferruccio Busoni's achievements in this field of composition. I of course agreed to do this, but somehow the meeting never happened. Over the years, I sometimes wondered what the phone call was all about, but now I know, having certain scores of Marcellino open in front of me: he was headed into related territory. In his introduction to the score of *Amorality: The art of love and death. I. Zerfliesse, mein Herze, for cello, guitar, marimba and piano* (1999), he says:

> The musical material for this…is derived from the last aria of Bach's *St. John Passion*. The lyrics of the Bach aria speak of a profound sadness of the death of the Saviour, sadness so deep that the heart will *dissolve*. In writing this work material from the Bach was treated as musical artifacts—imagine the original music dissolved and then distilled into a new work, reminiscent of the old but intensified as an object of contemplation. Structurally the music seeks to create a mosaic in the same manner of Sufi sacred mosaics that used the elegance of design as an entry point to contemplation.

The work is given the key signature of two sharps, although the bulk of the work is in E minor. The mosaic construction is certainly clearly there, with repeats and elaborations of materials, and with the inevitable steady pulse so prevalent in Bach's music dominating the score. The chosen scoring contains brittleness, and the cello carries much of the melodic and sustained material, although all manner of combinations occurs regarding the line. Marcellino is not a pianist, so, if he was after the sumptuousness of Busoni's Bach settings, he did not achieve it—but I cannot jump to such a conclusion. There is a mantra of syncopated quavers that must surely represent the point of meditation, and much of the florid embellishment that is in the score has baroque sources. A deeply felt work of 239 bars, this seems to have marked a serious turning point in Marcellino's style and aesthetic.

The mantra idea was already present in an earlier piece from 1984, *Credo in Them*, for flute, horn, trombone and piano, where the whole 105 bars of 4/4 contain a single-bar idea, with some variations and new material superimposed. The raw 'mantra', consisting of four pitches, is given at the very opening of the work.

Example 11.4 R. Marcellino, *Credo in Them*, bars 1–5

The idea of transcription is also present in *Songs from A Strange Kind of Paradise*. The cycle of three songs (2008, voice with piano) was inspired by the Monteverdi aria 'Lasciatemi morire'—apparently the only surviving fragment from his opera *Arianna*. The composer tells us what he has done: 'The first song takes the original melody and reorchestrates and reharmonizes the accompaniment. The second song takes the melody and original harmonic framework translated into a tango-like dance. The third song uses the harmonic structure of the original with a new melody and text.' The complete program note is worth reading in full, and illuminates not just this work, but the contemporary concept of 'appropriation', which seems to be a part of the so-called postmodernist movement. This amuses me, as the art of transcription (another name for much the same thing) is hundreds of years old. The piano part of the Monteverdi transcription (if I might be so bold) is often interesting and elaborate, although clearly not written by a pianist, as there is some awkwardness and possible misjudgment of sonority. But it is effective enough, and the low octaves in the third song do have a Busonian ring about them.

There is a related short work, titled *Mangia, Alimentary aria with continuo for 2 voices and keyboard, by Reg. Calabria (16?-17?), trans. Raff. Marcellino 1998*. Not surprisingly, there is no Reg Calabria in Grove's! The climax of this baroque aria about eating is 'Yum, Yum…'.

We are left with *The Lottery in Babylon* (1994), for flute, clarinet, violin, cello and piano. I have left this to the end because, although not based on ancient sources, title apart, the elements of a baroque suite and continuo technique are ever present. It consists of eight movements.

I. Strings and piano provide a continuo; wind is separate and act in parallel and separate motion. The movement is quite long and builds to an ending in quavers in all instruments.

II. No wind instruments, the continuo set-up is similar, but now the movement is dance-like and in irregular beats.

III. Back to crotchets and quavers, but in a more complex distribution of parts and counterpoint.

IV. No piano, flute and violin acting as solo instruments, cello becomes the only continuo instrument.

V. Quavers distributed through all parts, on the beat, and in syncopation; piano interpolations finally lead to a big climax.

VI. [This is incorrectly numbered IV in my copy] Linked to movement II, a very full and intense dance rhythm yet again.

VII. Florid, mostly scale patterns.

VIII. Dance again, fast.

The various alternations of speed, extraction of colour via the use of different solo instruments and the changing continuo colour all make for an exciting whole. It will be interesting to see whether Marcellino pursues this line of work.

Robert Davidson (1965–)

When I last wrote a few words about Robert Davidson, there was little material available for solo piano, and consequently, there was not much to say. The material, moreover, gave an impression of the composer that was not quite right; the ensemble pieces reveal a more complete picture and unveil a composer who provides an interesting mix of tendencies. For example, *Junction Road* (1994), for clarinet, violin, viola, cello and piano, certainly contains traits of what we label as minimalist, but it is not the mindless minimalist variety: repetition is there, but it is not mechanical, and some rhythmic unpredictability adds piquancy to the music. Davidson's music is tonal and often employs key signatures; the melodic lines are skirting the edge of a popular idiom, but never quite enter the territory. His music is inventive, with a real grasp of formal structure. I found the work attractive, especially in the manner in which it combines different worlds within the one piece.

We looked at a series of solo works with piano. *Lento* (1997), for viola and piano, is an extended song wherein the opening chords of the piano part gradually expand and develop into more elaborate versions of themselves. Other solo pieces include *Mabo Tango: The lizard of Oz* (2000), a witty one-page piece for clarinet, with the piano playing elbow clusters beneath it in a kind of ersatz drum fashion. *Melody*, for cor anglais and piano, *Passage*, for clarinet and piano, and *Refrains*, for double bass and piano, are all direct and quite tonal works, with the solo line floating over an essentially repetitive piano part. The double bass solo is more extended, running to 32 pages of score, allowing the composer to execute a rise and fall back to the opening via the idea of a refrain. I cannot help wondering if these solo pieces were preparatory studies for some larger project, or for a technical exploration.

Squaring the Circle (1998), for clarinet, cello and piano, was composed for the Perihelion Ensemble, which performed an enormous amount of new Australian music in its time. Regarding this composition, Davidson explains that the title is taken

> from a preoccupation of classical and renaissance theorists with the problem of making a square with the same area as a circle—essentially with trying to capture something infinite in a finite representation. The work is concerned rather indirectly with the notion of capturing timelessness in a medium of linear time.

The composer achieves this via an open, floating quality. The letters in the score mark a series of modulations and boundaries of discrete episodes, still linked thematically. Hints of minimalist phasing appear at letter 'N', for example, with engaging time shifts, giving way to a scalar episode and finally an ecstatic, almost Scriabinesque trill and repeated chord section before fading into the distance.

Tapestry (1989), for clarinet, viola, cello and piano, is another work written for Perihelion, this time with a strong Canberra connection, which naturally attracted my attention. It was inspired by the tapestry art on display in Parliament House, and Davidson here attempted to make a 'musical analogy' of this visual art. The work was indeed performed in front of the very tapestry that inspired it, in the Great Hall of Parliament House. Davidson has written a very clear explanation of how he tackled this compositional problem:

> *Tapestry* is structured in eight distinct panels, each of which is clearly defined and self-contained, employing its own independent process. Movement is achieved, therefore, not by development, but by variation. The opening panel introduces the ensemble members one by one, as clarinet, viola and cello are featured in turn, within the context of a repeating cycle which grows progressively shorter. The piano is featured in the second panel, performing an improvisatory melody over an alberti-like left hand. A three part canon is the basis of the third panel, which is constructed over the background of static, overlapping functional triads. Another canon forms the fourth panel, this one structured by

augmentation—the bass part is twice as long as the treble part, which is in turn twice as long as the middle part. Panel five is built around the repeating pattern from the first panel, executed here in virtuosic, rapid hocket, accompanying a comical clarinet melody. Material from the first panel also forms the foundation of the sixth panel's bass line, counterpointing pentatonic melodies using additive rhythm. A rhythmic pattern is played in a three part repeating canon in the seventh panel, moving through several harmonic areas, while the clarinet and piano hold a conversation of progressively shortening melodic statements. The final panel is a study in harmony, consisting of a series of chords which change gradually, one note at a time, finally settling on the sonority and bass motive which opened the piece.

Davidson's mature works show a composer who is evolving and who has acquired control over the larger-scale aspects of composition, as well as the minutiae of bar-by-bar compositional technique.

Tyalgum (for baritone saxophone, violin, viola, double bass and piano) in three movements exhibits kinship with the above larger works. The second movement is an extended piano solo, which seems to encapsulate much of the Davidson ethos.

Example 11.5 R. Davidson, *Tyalgum*, bars 411–14

This solo concludes in the same way as the first movement. The third movement, on the other hand, begins with a figure from the first. The piano solo that makes up the middle movement is in itself often canonic and quite difficult. Incidentally, the basic pattern of the piano part also appears in *Tapestry*, but is here treated differently and more extensively.

Barton Staggs (1969–)

Hindenburg Mix III (2001) by Barton Staggs is really a form of minimalism. The piano plays mostly single notes. The pitches are a fixed selection, but they rotate in a quasi-improvisatory order, moving mostly in quavers, semiquavers and triplet quavers at a moderato pace. The pitches form a harmonic complex that is mostly C-sharp minor. The tape part is notated and is predominantly a drone type of accompaniment. The string instruments, too, gradually creep in to form a background to the piano activity. Staggs wrote a similar piece in 1998 called *Other Voices Other Rooms*, but this was purely for piano and tape, so the piano patter was broken off a few times to play some soft chords; otherwise, the same basic idea was in operation.

Stuart Greenbaum (1966–)

The title of Stuart Greenbaum's two-page miniature for clarinet and piano is almost longer than the piece itself: *Waiting for the Green Man. Traffic lights at a Narre-Warren intersection (a meeting of the UFO sightings club). A brief study in the rhythmic ratio 7:8*. The composer's note states:

> The title is partially in jest, but who knows—maybe there really are 'green men' out there! In any event, it would seem that Narre Warren (in Melbourne's outer East) has had more than its fair share of UFO sightings and it seemed as good a place as any in which to set this miniature. The music depicts the phasing of independent pedestrian crossing signals (a study in the rhythmic ratio 7:8) set in a harmonic world that might just conceivably conjure an extra-terrestrial vibe. If you sense anything during the performance look out of the windows. If you see anything strange, call the Australian UFO research network hotline on 1800 772288 (but only after the conclusion of the performance).

Elliott Gyger (1968–)

We have three shortish compositions by Elliott Gyger to mention. *Shards* (1988), for flute, oboe, clarinet and piano four-hands, is a three-minute piece in which a series of chords seems to gradually reveal itself, finally stated as a progression at the very end of the piece. The four-hand piano use is unusual in a chamber work, but not unique; here it appears necessary to give the harmonic underpinning its full flow—not possible with two hands. Like all of the Gyger scores I have seen, *Shards* is clear in intent and notation, and well crafted in balance and tessitura. The free sections also work very well, and the composer only partly relinquishes his reins over the work. *Strands*, written in the same year and possibly a related work, is for violin, cello and piano (two hands this time!). The title suggests a polyphonic approach as the basis of the composition, so here even the piano is treated as a two-voiced instrument, with not a chord in sight. Like its companion piece, this is equally short, and the two programmed together would make an interesting unveiling of the composer's language. His *Trio Sonata* (1994), for alto flute, clarinet and piano, combines some elements of both the above works, although the piano is still mostly treated as a single-line instrument. The sostenuto pedal is employed to good effect in one section. The trio is somewhat more polished and developed than the other two works; Gyger writes in a chromatically saturated idiom, and the works are not easy to put together.

Matthew Hindson (1968–)

Hindson seems to be a busy and prolific composer—judging by the list of works available and the fact that most of them come from the past two decades only. Some are meant for student use, such as the *Prelude and Estampie* (1986), for viola and piano, and are early works in his own output, too. I took a look at *Teddy Bear* (1989), for bass clarinet, piano, percussion and cello—a busy, motoric piece with plenty of time changes, which, like *Unnatural Bondage: Sonata for violin and piano* (1992), seemed to me overwritten and overly fussy, a kind of laboured avant-garde, with all its attendant signatures. Perhaps the composer felt this as well because the later works are considerably simpler and have moved away from the world of 'art music' into a much simpler and straightforward sphere. This seems to have occurred somewhere about the mid-1990s, as evidenced by *Lament* (1996), for cello and piano, and is most obvious in the piano part with its triadic-based chords combined with a strongly tonal cello part. From the same year comes a piece for student saxophone player with piano, *In Search of Ecstasy*, and a preface in which the composer writes: 'This work is influenced by popular music, in particular the aspects of the *techno* genre.' From there on, the path seemed more or less fixed. The music seems to have a slow introduction, and then launches into techno beat, with the piano providing the obvious machine sound. The rest of the scores that I looked at tended to follow this pattern. The techno is a kind of extension of what was once minimalism, except that now it is cruder and more raucous. Hindson's melodic lines might be linked to popular music, but they are not quite as memorable as some popular music can be. *Night Pieces* (1998), for saxophone and piano, has a popular feel in the first movement and more of a dance feel in the second; there is more rhythmic variety here than in other more recent pieces. Even in *Pi*, for SATB and piano, once we get going into the *ritmico* section, it is predictably techno behind the vocal lines. In 2000, Hindson received a very negative review from someone on the *Sydney Morning Herald* staff. He wrote *Plastic Jubilation*, for piano and CD, as a kind of rebuttal. This is always a dangerous thing to do for a composer, since the music critic will inevitably have the last say, sharpening his pencils and waiting for the next opportunity. I am really uncertain what Hindson accomplished by writing the piece. He might very well have confirmed the critic's views. And so we go on—on a now fairly predictable path: *Ignition: Positive* (2002), for saxophone and piano, with the usual vamping piano part in coarse triadic shifts; and *Nintendo Music* (2005), for clarinet and piano, using the idea of different game levels as an inspiration for sudden changes of beat—and banality of both melodic line and harmony. *Violin Concertino: Summer stories* (2009), for violin and piano, is once again aimed at the examinations market, but apart from the naive programmatic notes supplied with the piece (another Hindson trait), the piano writing generally in his output is ungainly and uncomfortable. Here a figure, which is fairly simple on the violin, is actually very difficult on the keyboard, and the chordal progressions in the piano are, well, corny. Likewise, the double trills on the first page of *Siegfried Interlude No. 2* (1999) are very difficult for most pianists. Finally, I looked at *Love Serenade* (1998, if it is the same piece as for cello and piano), for bassoon and piano. By this time, I confess that I was looking for a piece about which I could say something positive about this composer; I did not find it here either! It will be interesting to see how this is played out: whether the composer is at a dead end, and has written himself out, or whether something will alter and produce an incarnation more vitally engaging.

Paul Stanhope (1969–)

Paul Stanhope's *Phospheric Variations* (1998) exist in versions for either saxophone or clarinet and piano. Stanhope writes that this work

> extracts and expands a series of variations from the original piece which is structured around the repetition of a simple ground bass. The term 'Variations' is used somewhat loosely and does not conform to the strict connotations of the classical 'Theme and Variations' form. Rather, it is used in the sense that the presented themes are decorated and varied over a repeated ground bass and is thus more like a contemporary version of a Chaconne.

These variations are impressive in the manner in which the original idea is allowed to grow to a brilliant end gesture. Musically, events occur with logic and the decoration is palpable to the ear, not just on paper. The many time changes can be clearly perceived, as they, too, happen in a highly structured manner.

Matthew Shlomowitz (1975–)

Matthew Shlomowitz's *Deidre's Threat* (2000), for violin and piano, contains the full panoply of the maximalist footprint: the usual 5:7, 5:4, 7:8 and others, dense and constant mixtures of dynamics, jungles of grace figures, special notations for microtones, and so on. But in this piece we also have an abundance of somewhat strange performance instructions. I list just a few of them and wonder what the violinist and pianist are to make of them: aloof, engaging, urbane, assured, carelessly, carefully, eccentric, rigid, inward, content... Are the performers expected to 'act out' these moods, or is this to come out through the sound, whilst one is desperately holding on to one's place in the score? There is even a bar where the violinist is asked to be 'moronic'. Needless to say, I have no idea what this means. Perhaps one needs a brilliant mime to play and convey these moods simultaneously? A slightly earlier piece, from 1998, *Remembering Beginning*, for flute/bass flute, piano and harp, is 'the final piece of *My Museum*, a fifty minute six piece series'. The composer then lists all the pieces and their scoring, which alters from piece to piece, but uses the same three players. *Remembering Beginning* is a less extreme example of Shlomowitz's style, the flute tending to wear the brunt of the problems, with all the quarter-tone fingerings required. No wonder the flautist is at one point asked to be 'claustrophobic, anxious'. But the piano and harp do not escape unscathed. There is a direction more than once to be 'vulgar, offensive'. I do not know how you do that playing some innocuous staccato single notes. For some reason, many of the flute glissandi are marked 'slippery'. The ensemble problems are still formidable in this piece as well.

Roxanne Della-Bosca (1977–)

Two pieces by Roxanne Della-Bosca are *Duo for Viola and Piano* (1997) and *Microscope Cross-Sections: Three small pieces* (1998), for flute and piano. These are aphoristic, both in length and in gesture. The piano is treated most sparingly but sensitively, as are the viola and flute lines. The duo is a rather more expansive piece, and there is room for some development, given its larger scope.

Tim Dargaville (1962–); Ross Hazeldine (1961–); Andrew Harrison (1971–); Stephen Adams (1963–)

A small group of fourth-generation composers is represented here by single or a small number of pieces, so we have grouped them together, not insinuating any commonality, or any ranking by their order of appearance.

Tim Dargaville is represented in this section by two short pieces: *Invisible Dance for Cello and Piano* (2006) and *Night Song for Oboe and Piano* (1997/2004). Both pieces feature a slow, hypnotic, soft ostinato-type piano part, with the lyrical solo line floating over it. Unlike the difficulty of the composer's piano writing, these are only moderately demanding. The cellist is asked to whistle along while he plays, at the same pitch.

Then, we have Ross Hazeldine's *Movements for Guitar and Piano*. These constitute a number of titled pieces.

1. 'Essay of 3 Janes'. This has a curious appearance for a start, as the piano part is written on one stave, and consists of single notes. The guitar and piano move in exactly the same rhythm (and not simple rhythm, either), but not the same pitches. Eventually, the parallelism falls apart, but this does not make life any easier! Nevertheless, coordination is not easy. This is quite a lengthy piece and would present a study in concentration for all concerned.

2. 'Andantino'. This is a foray into chords for the guitar and two-note chords for the piano (still written on one line).

3. 'Temperance Songs'. The piano finally earns the usual two-stave appearance. This movement, like the others and like most of Hazeltine's music, is highly motoric, complex and driven.

4. This begins like the previous movement, but then is interrupted with a short series of piano fragments marked 'Song #2', 'Song #3', 'Song #4' and 'Song #5', presumably while the guitar line continues unabated as in the prior movement.

5. 'Paralysis', with the guitar predominating and having the final say.

Example 11.6 R. Hazeldine, *Movements*, p. 8, system 1

The mixture of the two instruments might appear problematic and is certainly not a choice most composers would make, but Hazeldine presents himself with an interesting compositional nut to crack.

Andrew Harrison (who studied with me for a while) has a composite work here: *Four Compositions for Small Jazz Ensemble*. The compositions come from different times and are not thematically related or cyclical. Their notation, with chord symbols, allows for the flexibility that jazz musicians enjoy. This same flexibility combined with Andrew's curiosity and study of 'art music' practices placed him in a no man's land as a student and might still be a source of bother to him, since we love to pigeonhole composers by style. The four pieces are: 1) 'Silly Billy'; 2) 'Don't Nudge Me Over A Hill'; 3) 'Cut and Run'; and 4) 'Blues for Skep'.

Stephen Adams also exhibits varied influences in his music, judging by the short *SirenS*, for alto saxophone and piano, with pulsing jazzy chords, not quite regular in durations, and a melodic line that has connection with jazz but is not quite jazz.

Concluding Remarks

This is my second book on an aspect of Australian music. The previous book stopped at the end of the twentieth century, and concentrated on music for solo piano. The present book pushes the chronology up to the year 2010 and focuses on the piano as a member of a chamber music ensemble. In both cases, I have drawn upon my personal career and interests as a composer and pianist, as well as somebody who cares passionately about the future of what we might loosely label 'art music' produced in this country. My perspective, therefore, is of one who has actively participated in the making of music in Australia ever since my family brought me here in 1951. This is not theoretical pontificating: I have lived my subject for the past 60 years!

Both books attempt to trace the imprint of modernity on Australian music since the serious beginnings of our art music—somewhere about the time we began our historical journey as a nation. Pre-Federation music has not engaged my attention, not because I do not know about it, but largely because I have so little of it that is of any intrinsic merit. The graph of music that pushes the envelope, attempts to say something profound, tries to lift the human spirit, and avoids lazy conventions, slothful thinking and comfortable conformism has fluctuated over the years, naturally. It probably reached its peak somewhere approximately two-thirds of the way through the twentieth century, and then went into a slow but steady decline. At the same time, even though the thread of modernity has been slender, it is important to note that it was always present, which gives me heart, because currently it has dipped yet again.

Support for the arts has always been necessary: our history is not long enough to trace patronage by the church or by aristocrats, but we have instead experienced support from various government sources, and that, needless to say, varies with the political climate and the predominant ideology. It is currently under siege, and, in general, composition has been lurching towards pop, rock, techno, rap, and so on—whatever is popular and is earning brownie points for the composer.

We have experienced periods of political correctness, political incorrectness, jingoism, playing the patriotic card, playing the multicultural card, playing the populist card, various 'isms', flirting with Asian culture…have I missed any? These things come and go by their very nature, but what is more serious is that the trends are mirrored in our educational institutions and particularly in our tertiary educational institutions. There was a time—seemingly eons ago—when our tertiary training of musicians was unashamedly elitist and exclusive, looking for the highest talents and then creating an environment for that level of talent to go as far as possible. At least now it is no longer necessary to go abroad to 'finish' one's musical education, but something more disturbing is happening.

The word 'elite' has one letter too many to be a dirty word, but otherwise it is certainly a forbidden word. Our music education at tertiary level has now drifted more and more towards generalist rather than specialised degrees, and we are in danger, therefore, of losing the cream on top when we produce the bottle of milk. Training high-level musicians is expensive, and has always been the case, since so much depends on one-to-one teaching, and that is precisely what is under fire. Most tertiary institutions have teaching weeks numbering about 26 out of 52—that is, we are pretending that we can train musicians by teaching them for only six months of the year. This, as any good teacher will tell you, is manifestly impossible and untrue. Those same good teachers have found ways to subvert the system, but technically they are breaking the rules; others just shrug and give in to the rules. The culture of the country is the loser in the end.

As I write this, the Australian Music Centre, which was founded when the graph I wrote about was at its highest, is now fighting a rearguard action for its very survival, and is being amalgamated or absorbed into the Australasian Performing Right Association (APRA). I am certain that the reasons behind the move are financial, but it is also a symptom of the very serious illness that I am writing about, and would have been unthinkable only some years ago. There was also a move, very recently, to close down the Australian Academy of Music—the Government backed away only because of the hue and cry that followed this announcement—but my feeling is that it is now only a question of time; the crime of this institution was no doubt that it was too elite.

The performance record of government-funded bodies such as our symphony orchestras is, as far as Australian content is concerned, on the downward slippery slide. The orchestras are now independent and have to make money. 'Putting bums on seats' is the colloquial way of putting it. Australian music that does get programmed is short, easy on the ear, requires minimum rehearsal and is calculated to please as many people as possible. Intellectual challenge and confrontation are not on the agenda, because they do not pay. With other institutions, lip-service to Australian music is the order of the day. You slip in a piece between the approved canon pieces; hopefully it will not cause any measurable waves, and if you are really lucky, it will be pink and fluffy as well. I predict that in future, music historians will see our present as a kind of Dark Age.

Writing this book—and therefore being aware of who is out there and producing—I have noticed a tendency that is disturbing. It seems to me that the number of active composers in this country is declining. I am not speaking of natural attrition here, but rather of promising composers of only some years back who have dropped out of the profession, completely or in part, for obvious reasons. They have to pay the rent, like anyone else, and the amount of work out there has noticeably dwindled. This needs statistical surveying to be proved, but it seems clear to me, observing the comings and goings in the profession over approximately the past decade and a half. As I write this, we are in the middle of an election campaign, voting day being only two weeks hence. When the current Labor Government won power three years ago, the arts community expected a change to occur for the better. Actually, what occurred was nothing. Nothing altered in any dramatic way. My feeling is that it does not matter who wins in two weeks. For the arts, and for music and music education, not much difference will be experienced either way.

One of the referees for this book wrote in his/her concluding remarks: 'The encyclopedic format distorts the hard reality that only some works have gained and maintained currency', and later: 'we will see whether posterity got it right after all.' The first statement might well be correct, but it is absolutely necessary to have a broad survey to be able to arrive at some conclusions about the overall tendencies. As for posterity (depending on what time span you mean by such a term), it is now manifestly clear that our immediate posterity certainly got it wrong as far as Australian music of the early and middle twentieth century were concerned. The big names of that era are now but footnotes in our history. Personally, I expect a similar fate for some of our current media darlings. The same referee also complained that 'more could have been written about' certain composers. I agree: more could have been written about almost every composer in the book, but in this kind of effort a line needs to be drawn somewhere, sometime. The book is intended as but a beginning, a spur to further study and analysis of the genre.

Since I am a hopeless romantic, and a product of a system that taught music as a high calling and the province of only a few privileged and gifted individuals, my belief system stays in place. I still firmly hold to the view that music has a high spiritual function and that what the good fight is about is recognising the power of music to accomplish that very objective. It is far beyond music as a mere entertainment. It can change the world.

Canberra, 8 August 2010

Appendix

Database of works considered

This is a list of the scores that were perused in the initial stage of gathering data. Eventually, decisions were made to either discuss or not discuss a particular work. Decisions were governed by various considerations including the space available, and were not made exclusively on grounds of interest. Various online sources were extensively consulted, including the National Library of Australia, the Australian Music Centre, all the State libraries, a number of university libraries and archives, and private collections.

Keys Press and Wirripang should also be mentioned for their significant roles in publishing both recent and historically significant Australian music referred to in the database.

Relevant web-links are as follows.

- Australian Music Centre: <http://www.australianmusiccentre.com.au/>
- Currency Press: <http://www.currency.com.au/default.aspx>
- Keys Press: <http://www.keyspress.com.au/index.php>
- National Library of Australia: <http://www.nla.gov.au/>
- Wirripang: <http://www.australiancomposers.com.au/>

Australian Chamber Music with Piano

Last name	First name	Birth year	Title	Ensemble	Date	Location	Publisher
Adams	Stephen	1963	Sirens	Alto saxophone & piano	1998	NLA	AMC
Allen	Harold	1930	Sonata for CL and PF	Clarinet & piano	1974	NLA	J. Albert & Son, c1975 - Updated ensemble
Bainton	Edgar	1880	Sonata for Violoncello and Piano	Cello & piano	c1953	NLA	
Bainton	Edgar	1880	Dawn	Voice & piano	c1924	Online	<http://catalogue.nla.gov.au/Record/274968?lookfor=edgar%20bainton&offset=4&max=60>
Bainton	Edgar	1880	Ring Out, Wild Bells	Voice & piano	1924	Online	<http://catalogue.nla.gov.au/Record/3995000?lookfor=edgar%20bainton&offset=34&max=60>
Bainton	Edgar	1880	A Red, Red Rose	Voice & piano	c1951	NLA	
Bainton	Edgar	1880	Valley Moonlight	Voice & piano	c1920	Online	<http://catalogue.nla.gov.au/Record/2121238?lookfor=edgar%20bainton&offset=24&max=60>
Bainton	Edgar	1880	Young Love Lies Dreaming	Voice & piano	c1928	Online	<http://catalogue.nla.gov.au/Record/4230797?lookfor=edgar%20bainton%20young%20love&offset=1&max=81658>
Bainton	Edgar	1880	All Night Under the Moon	Voice & piano	c1920	Online	<http://catalogue.nla.gov.au/Record/598850?lookfor=edgar%20bainton%20all%20night&offset=1&max=221101>
Bainton	Edgar	1880	Slow, Slow, Fresh Fount	Voice & piano	c1920	Online	<http://catalogue.nla.gov.au/Record/2295013?lookfor=edgar%20bainton%20slow&offset=1&max=1>
Bainton	Edgar	1880	To the Children	Voice & piano	c1923	Online	<http://catalogue.nla.gov.au/Record/1493231?lookfor=edgar%20bainton&offset=17&max=60>

Last name	First name	Birth year	Title	Ensemble	Date	Location	Publisher
Bainton	Edgar	1880	The Nightingale Near the House	Voice & piano	c1920	Online	<http://catalogue.nla.gov.au/Record/100282?lookfor=edgar%20bainton&offset=29&max=60>
Bainton	Edgar	1880	The Little Waves of Breffny	Voice & piano	c1927	Online	<http://catalogue.nla.gov.au/Record/157137?lookfor=edgar%20bainton%20waves&offset=1&max=1>
Bainton	Edgar	1880	Spring Comes	Voice & piano	c.1924	NLA	
Bainton	Edgar	1880	Frolic	Voice & piano	c1920	NLA	
Banks	Don	1923	Commentary	Piano & 2-channel tape	1971	NLA	Schott & Co., 1971?
Banks	Don	1923	Trio for Horn, Violin and Piano	Horn, violin and piano	1962	ANU	Schott & Co., 1966 - Updated title and ensemble in database (5/2/10)
Banks	Don	1923	Prologue, Night Piece and Blues for Two	Clarinet & piano	1968	ANU	Schott & Co., 1970
Banks	Don	1923	Sonata for Violin and Piano	Violin & piano	1954		Schott & Co., 1954
Banks	Don	1923	Three Studies for VC and Piano	Cello, Piano	c1954	ANU	Schott & Co., 1954
Banks	Don	1923	4/5/7 for Septet	Flute, clarinet, 2 percussion, piano, violin, viola		AMC	AMC? - Updated ensemble in database (5/2/10) - Suggest checking AMC score or Papers of Don Banks at NLA MS for more information
Barkl	Michael	1959	Fullstimme	Vibraphone, marimba and piano	1981	NLA	AMC
Barkl	Michael	1959	Night Words	All sorts of arrangements plus piano	1977	NLA	AMC
Barkl	Michael	1959	Night Words: The ravishing	Mezzo-soprano and piano	1977	NLA	AMC

Australian Chamber Music with Piano

Last name	First name	Birth year	Title	Ensemble	Date	Location	Publisher
Barkl	Michael	1959	Romance	Piano with clarinet, bassoon, violin and violoncello	1977	NLA	AMC
Barkl	Michael	1959	Rota	Violin, cello, piano	1981	NLA	AMC
Barkl	Michael	1959	Twenty-Five Felicitations for the AMC	Flute & piano	1999	NLA	AMC
Bauld	Alison	1944	Banquo's Buried: A song for soprano and piano	Soprano & piano	1989	NLA	Novello, 1989?
Bauld	Alison	1944	Two Shakespeare Songs: 'Cry, Cock-A-Doodle-Do', for voice and piano, 'The Witches' Song', for solo female voice	Voice & piano	1995	NLA	Novello, 1995?
Bauld	Alison	1944	Copy Cats: A trio for violin, cello and piano	Violin, violoncello, piano	1987	ANU	AMC
Beath	Betty	1932	From A Bridge of Dreams	Flute & piano	2001	NLA	Self-published, 2001
Beath	Betty	1932	From A Quiet Place	Viola & piano	1997	NLA	Keys Press, 1999
Beath	Betty	1932	Lagu Lagu Manis	Cello & piano	1993	NLA	AMC, 1993
Beath	Betty	1932	Lament of Ovid	Oboe, clarinet, bassoon, horn, voice, piano	2004	NLA	Beath-Cox, 2004
Beath	Betty	1932	Moon Flowers, Man	Voice, flute, piano	1972–90	NLA	Wirrapang, 2006
Beath	Betty	1932	Nawang Wulan – Guardian of earth and of rice	Alto flute & piano	1980	NLA	Wirrapang, 2006

Appendix

Last name	First name	Birth year	Title	Ensemble	Date	Location	Publisher
Beath	Betty	1932	*Nawang Wulan — Poems by Subagio Sastrowardojo*	Voice & piano	1980	NLA	Self-published, 1980
Beath	Betty	1932	*Points in a Journey*	Voice, flute, piano	1987	NLA	AMC, 1987
Benfall	Stephen	1957	*Blues at Eleven*	Solo instrument & piano	1991	NLA	Hovea Music Press, 1995
Benfall	Stephen	1957	*Sonata for Oboe and Piano*	Oboe & piano	1987	NLA	AMC
Benjamin	Arthur	1895	*Before Dawn*	Voice & piano	c1924	Online	<http://catalogue.nla.gov.au/Record/726828?lookfor=arthur%20dawn&offset=2&max=44>
Benjamin	Arthur	1893	*Five Negro Spirituals*	Violin & piano	c1929	NLA	Oxford University Press
Benjamin	Arthur	1893	*From San Domingo*	Violin & piano	c1945	NLA	Boosey & Hawkes
Benjamin	Arthur	1893	*Le Tombeau de Ravel: Valse-caprices for viola and piano or clarinet and piano*	Viola/clarinet and piano	c1958	ANU	Boosey & Hawkes
Benjamin	Arthur	1893	*Linstead Market: Jamaican folk song*	Voice & piano		ANU	Boosey & Hawkes
Benjamin	Arthur	1893	*Sonata for viola and piano*	Viola & piano		ANU	Boosey & Hawkes
Benjamin	Arthur	1893	*Sonatina for Violin and Piano*	Violin & piano		NLA	AMC, 1999
Benjamin	Arthur	1893	*Sonatina for Violoncello and piano*	Cello & piano	c1939	NLA	Hawkes & Son
Benjamin	Arthur	1893	*Song of the Banana Carriers: Jamaican folk song*	Voice & piano	c1957	ANU	Boosey & Hawkes
Benjamin	Arthur	1894	*Three songs. III, Wind's work*	Voice & piano	c1935	NLA	Winthrop Rogers

Australian Chamber Music with Piano

Last name	First name	Birth year	Title	Ensemble	Date	Location	Publisher
Benjamin	Arthur	1893	Tune and Variations for Little People	Violin & piano	c1939	NLA	Hawkes & Son
Bertram	Michael	1935	The Green Castle: Five songs for soprano	Soprano with pf or sq or st + pf	1994	NLA	AMC
Bertram	Michael	1935	I Will Write to You, Opus 11: Three love songs for soprano	Soprano & piano	1992	NLA	Keys Press, 1998
Bertram	Michael	1935	Variations for Flute and Piano, Opus 10	Flute & piano	1991	NLA	Keys Press, 1998
Beutler	Adolphe	1882	NIL			n/a	
Bourne	Una	1882	A Cloudless Night (barcarolle)	Song & piano	c1925	NLA	Allan & Co.
Boyd	Anne	1946	At Telegraph Bay: Five songs	Baritone with piano	1984	NLA	AMC
Boyd	Anne	1946	Bali Moods No. 1	Flute & piano	1987	NLA	Faber, 1994
Boyd	Anne	1946	Bali Moods No. 2	Flute & piano	1988	NLA/ANU	AMC
Boyd	Anne	1946	Cloudy Mountain	Flute & piano	1981	NLA	Faber, 1995
Boyd	Anne	1946	Cycle of Love	Counter tenor, alto flute, cello and piano	1981	NLA	Faberprint, 1981?
Boyd	Anne	1946	Goldfish through Summer Rain	Flute & piano	1978	NLA/ANU	Faber, 1980
Boyd	Anne	1946	Kakan	Alto flute, marimba & piano	1984	NLA	AMC
Boyd	Anne	1946	Red sun, Chill Wind	Flute & piano	1980	NLA	Faber, 1995
Boyle	George	1886	NIL			n/a	
Bracanin	Philip	1942	Eternal Image	Soprano voice, clarinet in B flat, horn in F, piano.	1998	NLA	Maecenas Music, 2004?

260

Appendix

Last name	First name	Birth year	Title	Ensemble	Date	Location	Publisher
Bracanin	Philip	1942	*Three Bagatelles*	2 treble instruments & piano		NLA	AMC
Brandman	Margaret	1951	*Antics*	Flute & piano	1976?	NLA	AMC
Brandman	Margaret	1951	*Original Songs*	Voice, piano or guitar	1931	NLA	AMC
Brandman	Margaret	1951	*Permutations*	Clarinet & piano	1935	NLA	Jazzem Music, 1992
Brandman	Margaret	1951	*Songs of Love and Desire: Song cycle*	Voice & piano	2003	NLA	Jazzem Music, 2004
Brandman	Margaret	1951	*When Spirits Roar*	Piano, alto saxophone or clarinet	1996	NLA	Furore Music, 1997?
Brewster-Jones	Hooper	1887	*Song of the 10th Battalion*	Voice & piano		Online	<http://nla.gov.au/nla.mus-an12849064>
Brewster-Jones	Hooper	1887	*Song of the Australian Flying Corps*	Voice & piano		Online	<http://catalogue.nla.gov.au/Record/3575599?lookfor=brewster-jones%20flying&offset=1&max=2>
Brewster-Jones	Hooper	1887	*The Song of Wandering Aengus*	Voice & piano		Online	<http://catalogue.nla.gov.au/Record/1712672?lookfor=brewster-jones%20aengus&offset=1&max=1>
Brewster-Jones	Hooper	1887	*Night in the Desert*	Voice & piano	1917	Online	<http://catalogue.nla.gov.au/Record/3256851?lookfor=brewster-jones%20night&offset=1&max=1>
Brewster-Jones	Hooper	1887	*Various songs in manuscript*	Voice & piano		Online	<http://catalogue.nla.gov.au/Record/1712662?lookfor=brewster-jones%20songs&offset=1&max=8>
Broadstock	Brenton	1952	*All That is Solid Melts into Air*	Alto flute, bass clarinet, piano	1992	NLA	AMC

Australian Chamber Music with Piano

Last name	First name	Birth year	Title	Ensemble	Date	Location	Publisher
Broadstock	Brenton	1952	And No Birds Sing	Flute/alto flute/piccolo, Bb clarinet/bass clarinet, violin, piano, percussion	1986	NLA	AMC
Broadstock	Brenton	1952	Boolee: For two pianos	2 pianos	1984	NLA	AMC
Broadstock	Brenton	1952	I Touched Your Glistening Tears	Soprano saxophone, piano	1998	NLA	Reed Music, 2006
Broadstock	Brenton	1952	I Touched Your Glistening Tears	Oboe, piano	1998	NLA	Reed Music, 1998?
Broadstock	Brenton	1952	Nearer and Farther: For horn and piano	Horn, piano	1991	NLA	AMC
Broadstock	Brenton	1952	Not Too Near, Not Too Far	Alto saxophone, piano	2006	NLA	Reed Music, 2006?
Broadstock	Brenton	1952	Clear Flame Within	Cello & piano	1996	amc	AMC
Brophy	Gerard	1953	Breathless	3 flutes, piano	1983	NLA	AMC
Brophy	Gerard	1953	Glove	Bass clarinet, violoncello and piano	1995	NLA	AMC
Brophy	Gerard	1953	Head	piccolo, B-flat bass clarinet and pianoforte	1988	NLA	AMC
Brophy	Gerard	1953	mFm	Baritone/soprano saxophone, marimba, bass guitar and piano	2002	NLA	AMC
Brophy	Gerard	1953	Rubber	Piano, alto flute, bass clarinet and vibraphone	1994	NLA	AMC
Brophy	Gerard	1953	Sheer Nylon Dances	Violin, violoncello and fetishised piano	2000	NLA	AMC

Last name	First name	Birth year	Title	Ensemble	Date	Location	Publisher
Brophy	Gerard	1953	Topolo-NRG	Baritone saxophone, double bass and piano	2002	NLA	AMC
Brumby	Colin	1934	Aria	Violin, piano	1996	NLA	AMC
Brumby	Colin	1934	Bassoon Sonata	Bassoon, piano	1984	NLA	AMC
Brumby	Colin	1934	Chiaroscuro	Clarinet, violoncello, piano	1977	NLA	AMC
Brumby	Colin	1934	A Little Romance	Alto saxophone and piano	1998	NLA	AMC
Brumby	Colin	1934	Little Waltz	Violin, piano	1996	NLA	AMC
Brumby	Colin	1934	Menteith	Flute, Piano	1997	NLA	Wirripang, 2009
Brumby	Colin	1934	Mundoolun	Cor anglais, piano	1989	NLA	AMC
Brumby	Colin	1934	Piano Quartet	Violin, viola, cello, piano	1984	NLA	AMC
Brumby	Colin	1934	Malinconia, Ninfa Gentile	Voice, piano	1998	NLA	AMC
Brumby	Colin	1934	A Poor Young Shepherd (words, Paul Verlaine)	Voice, piano	2007	NLA	Part of 'Two French Songs: For medium voice and piano'; AMC
Brumby	Colin	1934	Serenade (words by Aubrey de Vere)	Voice, piano		NLA	AMC
Brumby	Colin	1934	Sospiri	Clarinet, Piano	1975	NLA	AMC
Burke	Brigid	1960	Another Mode: For flute, clarinet and piano	Flute, clarinet, piano	2001	NLA	AMC
Burke	Brigid	1960	A Breathing Stone: For B flat clarinet and piano	Clarinet in B flat, piano	1998	NLA	AMC
Burke	Brigid	1960	Come for Tea: For clarinet and piano	Clarinet in B flat, piano	2001	NLA	AMC
Burke	Brigid	1960	In a Frenzy: For B flat clarinet and piano	Clarinet in B flat, piano	1997	NLA	AMC

Australian Chamber Music with Piano

Last name	First name	Birth year	Title	Ensemble	Date	Location	Publisher
Burke	Brigid	1960	Heart Dances: For B flat clarinet and piano	Clarinet, piano	1998	NLA	AMC
Burke	Brigid	1960	Once Removed: For B flat clarinet and piano	Clarinet in B flat, piano	1997	NLA	AMC
Burnard	Alex	1900	Suite Op. 25	Violin, piano	1940	Newcastle	ms
Burnard	Alex	1900	The City Child Op. 1, No. 1	Voice & piano	1924–25	Newcastle	ms
Burnard	Alex	1900	Birdie and Baby Op. 1, No. 2	Voice & piano	1925	Newcastle	ms
Burnard	Alex	1900	Rapsody Op. 2	2 cellos, piano	1926	Newcastle	ms
Burnard	Alex	1900	Three Sometset Folksongs Op.3	Voice & piano	1926	Newcastle	ms
Burnard	Alex	1900	Three Songs of Farewell Op.50	Voice & piano	1970	Newcastle	ms
Burnard	Alex	1900	Four Australian Songs Op.27	Voice & piano	1943	Newcastle	ms
Burnard	Alex	1900	Three Songs Op.17	Voice & piano	1929	Newcastle	ms
Burnard	Alex	1900	Australian Songs of Festival Op.22	Voice & piano	1937	Newcastle	ms
Burnard	Alex	1900	A Cycle of Six Songs	Baritone and piano	1952	Keys Press	
Burnard	Alex	1900	The Answer	Soprano & piano		Keys Press	
Burt	Warren	1949	63 Whispers in Memorium Morton Feldman	Clarinet, 5 drums, viola, bass, piano	1989	NLA	AMC
Burt	Warren	1949	A Vassarpiece of the Bardic Tradition	Piano & tape	1983	NLA	AMC
Burt	Warren	1949	November Eighteenth: From the Dreambooks	Trombone and piano	1998	NLA	AMC

Last name	First name	Birth year	Title	Ensemble	Date	Location	Publisher
Burt	Warren	1949	Six Political Piano Miniatures	Piano (spoken voice by performer)	1992	AMC	AMC
Butterley	Nigel	1935	Child in Nature	Voice, piano	1957	NLA	Wirrapang, 2008
Butterley	Nigel	1935	Conversation Pieces	Flute, piano	1982	NLA	Allans, c1989
Butterley	Nigel	1935	Evanston Song	Flute, piano	1978	ANU/NLA	Wirrapang, 2006
Butterley	Nigel	1935	Forest 1	Viola, piano	1990	NLA	AMC
Butterley	Nigel	1935	Forest 2	Trumpet, piano	1993	NLA	AMC ('Copyright University of Newcastle')
Butterley	Nigel	1935	Frogs	Voice & piano	1995	NLA	Wirrapang, 2006
Butterley	Nigel	1935	The Owl	Voice & piano	1983	NLA	AMC
Cale	Bruce	1939	Sonatina	Trumpet & piano	1993	NLA	AMC
Carr	Edwin	1926	Five Wolfskehl Songs	Baritone, piano		NLA	Waiteata Press, Wellington, NZ, c1991
Carr	Edwin	1926	Two Dances: For viola and piano	Viola, piano	1963	NLA	AMC, 1999
Carr-Boyd	Ann	1938	Ann and Del in Oz	Flute, piano	2004	NLA	Wirripang, 2006
Carr-Boyd	Ann	1938	Beneath the Yellow Moon	Cello, piano	2005	NLA	Carlisle Print, 2005/2006
Carr-Boyd	Ann	1939	Billabong	Voice, piano	2005	AMC	Carlisle Print, 2005
Carr-Boyd	Ann	1938	Brown Pansies	Mezzo, piano	1997	NLA	Carlisle Print, 1997, 2005, 2006
Carr-Boyd	Ann	1938	Combinations	Violin, cello, piano	1973	NLA	AMC
Carr-Boyd	Ann	1938	Dance for Strings	Violins, cello, piano	1978	NLA	AMC
Carr-Boyd	Ann	1938	Fabia's Fantasy	Horn, piano	2003	NLA	Carlisle Print, c2006
Carr-Boyd	Ann	1938	Folk Songs '76	Voice, recorder/flute, guitar, harpsichord/piano, cello, percussion	1976	NLA	AMC

Australian Chamber Music with Piano

Last name	First name	Birth year	Title	Ensemble	Date	Location	Publisher
Carr-Boyd	Ann	1938	Julian Turns Night into Day	Flute, clarinet, piano	2005	NLA	Wirripang, 2005, 2006
Carr-Boyd	Ann	1938	Moonscape Remembered	Violin, cello, piano	1991	NLA	AMC
Carr-Boyd	Ann	1938	Moreton Bay	Flute, violin, cello, piano	1983	NLA	AMC
Carr-Boyd	Ann	1938	Museum Garden	Voice, piano	2001	NLA	Wirripang, 2005
Carr-Boyd	Ann	1938	On the Shores of Aswan	Clarinet, piano	1996	NLA	Carlisle Print, 2006
Carr-Boyd	Ann	1938	Railroad Gallop	Flute, violin, cello, piano		NLA	AMC
Carr-Boyd	Ann	1938	Song of the Women of the Menero Tribe	Flute, cello, piano		NLA	AMC
Cary	Tristram	1925	Earth Hold Songs	Soprano, piano	1993	NLA	The Southern Dot Factory, 1994
Cary	Tristram	1925	Songs for Maid Marian	Songs (medium voice) with piano	1961	NLA	The Southern Dot Factory, c1998
Cheong	Simplicius	1942	Sonata for Alto Flute	Alto flute and piano	1973	NLA	AMC
Cheong	Simplicius	1942	Sonata (No.2) for Flute	Flute and piano	1976	NLA	AMC
Cheong	Simplicius	1942	Rhapsody for Violina and Piano	Violin and piano	1997	NLA	AMC
Cronin	Stephen	1960	Three Brief Insinuations: For bassoon and piano	Bassoon, piano	2005	NLA	AMC
Cronin	Stephen	1960	The Snake Pit: For clarinet, viola, cello, piano/harpsichord	Clarinet, viola, violoncello, piano/harpsichord	1990	NLA	AMC
Cronin	Stephen	1960	Sample Only, Not for Sale!	Flute, oboe, violoncello, piano	1988	NLA	AMC
Cronin	Stephen	1960	Duo for Horn and Piano, No. 1	Horn, piano	1982	NLA	AMC
Cronin	Stephen	1960	Golden Boy	Soprano, piano	2001	NLA	AMC

Last name	First name	Birth year	Title	Ensemble	Date	Location	Publisher
Cronin	Stephen	1960	*Angel*	Soprano, violoncello, piano	1985	NLA	AMC
Cronin	Stephen	1960	*Music for Calming and Healing: For cello and piano*	Violoncello, piano	2004	NLA	AMC
Cronin	Stephen	1960	*Gesta: For xylophone and piano*	Xylophone, piano	1987	ANU	AMC
Cronin	Stephen	1960	*Three Old English Poems*	Baritone voice, piano	1980	ANU	AMC
Cronin	Stephen	1960	*The Perihelion Rag*	Clarinet, viola, violoncello, piano	1988	NLA	AMC
Cugley	Ian	1945	*Three Little Pieces*	Clarinet, piano	1971	NLA	J. Albert & Son, 1971
Dargaville	Tim	1962	*Invisible Dance*	Cello and piano	2006	NLA	AMC
Dargaville	Tim	1962	*Night Song*	Oboe and piano	1997 (ob + pno version 2004)	NLA	AMC
Davidson	Robert	1965	*Junction Road*	Quintets (piano, clarinet, violin, viola, violoncello)	1994	NLA	AMC
Davidson	Robert	1965	*Lento*	Viola and piano	1997	NLA	AMC
Davidson	Robert	1965	*Mabo Tango*	B-flat clarinet and piano	1997	NLA	AMC
Davidson	Robert	1965	*Melody*	Cor anglais and piano	1988	NLA	AMC
Davidson	Robert	1965	*Passage*	Clarinet and piano	1988	NLA	AMC
Davidson	Robert	1965	*Refrains*	Double bass and piano	1989	NLA	AMC
Davidson	Robert	1965	*Squaring the Circle*	Alto saxophone, viola, double bass and piano	1998	NLA	AMC

Australian Chamber Music with Piano

Last name	First name	Birth year	Title	Ensemble	Date	Location	Publisher
Davidson	Robert	1965	Tapestry	Clarinet, viola, violoncello and piano	1989	NLA	AMC
Davidson	Robert	1965	Tyalgum	Baritone saxophone, violin, viola, double bass and piano	1997	NLA	AMC
de Beaupuis	Emanuel	1860	NIL			n/a	
De Cairos Rego	Iris	1894	Trio in A Minor	Piano trio	194_?	NLA MS	
De Cairos Rego	Iris	1894	The Forest Shall Conquer	Song SSA, piano	c1959	NLA—n/a	
De Cairos Rego	Iris	1894	A Frolic*	Song, piano	1928	Online	<http://catalogue.nla.gov.au/Record/7722203?lookfor=De%20Cairos%20Rego%20frolic&offset=1&max=347920>
De Cairos Rego	Iris	1894	The Masque of Iris (manuscript)	Voice, chorus, piano	194_?	NLA	
de Cairos-Rego	Rex	1894	Love's Recompense	Song with piano	c1913	Online	<http://catalogue.nla.gov.au/Record/1718846?lookfor=De%20Cairos%20Rego%20recompense&offset=1&max=347800>
de Cairos-Rego	Rex	1894	When Over the Hills	Song with piano	c1913	Online	<http://catalogue.nla.gov.au/Record/2180850?lookfor=De%20Cairos%20Rego%20hills&offset=2&max=571257>
de Cairos-Rego	Rex	1894	Grief and Joy	Song with piano	c1911	Online	<http://catalogue.nla.gov.au/Record/1566242?lookfor=De%20Cairos%20Rego%20grief&offset=1&max=348887>

Last name	First name	Birth year	Title	Ensemble	Date	Location	Publisher
de Cairos-Rego	Rex	1894	O Mistress Mine	Song with piano	c. 911	Online	<http://catalogue.nla.gov.au/Record/4558801?lookfor=De%20Cairos%20Rego%20mistress&offset=1&max=349029>
de Cairos-Rego	Rex	1894	Phyllis can be Kind and Sweet	Song with piano	c. 912	Online	<http://catalogue.nla.gov.au/Record/4558795?lookfor=De%20Cairos%20Rego%20phyllis&offset=1&max=349330>
de Cairos-Rego	Rex	1894	She is a Maid of Artless Grace	Song with piano	c. 911	NLA	
de Cairos-Rego	George	1894	Vive la France!	Song with piano	1917	Online	<http://catalogue.nla.gov.au/Record/496400?lookfor=De%20Cairos%20Rego%20vive&offset=1&max=347905>
de Cairos-Rego	George	1894	God Bless Our Commonwealth	Song with piano	1901	Online	<http://catalogue.nla.gov.au/Record/3069581?lookfor=De%20Cairos%20Rego%20commonwealth&offset=1&max=409502>
Dean	Brett	1961	Huntington Eulogy	Piano, violoncello	2001	NLA	Boosey & Hawkes – Bote & Bock, 2001?
Dean	Brett	1961	Night Window	Piano, clarinet, viola	1993	NLA	Boosey & Hawkes – Bote & Bock, 2000?
Dean	Brett	1961	Voices of Angels	Piano, violin, viola, violoncello, double bass	1996	NLA	Boosey & Hawkes – Bote & Block, 1996?
Della-Bosca	Roxanne		Arc: Over those who love me, duo for viola and piano	Viola, Piano	1997	NLA	AMC
Della-Bosca	Roxanne		Microscope Cross-Sections: Three small pieces for piano and flute	Flute, piano	1998	NLA	AMC

Australian Chamber Music with Piano

Last name	First name	Birth year	Title	Ensemble	Date	Location	Publisher
Dench	Chris	1953	Atsiluth	Flute/bass flute, bass clarinet and piano	1991	NLA	AMC
Dench	Chris	1953	E(i)ther	Violin and piano	2005	NLA	AMC
Douglas	Clive	1903	Pastorale and Ritual Dance: For violin and pianoforte, from the symphonic suite 'Namatjira'	Violin, piano	1957	NLA	Allan & Co., Melbourne, c1957
Douglas	Clive	1903	The Road: Song for mezzo-soprano	Mezzo-soprano, piano		NLA	AMC, 1999
Douglas	Clive	1903	Ballads of the Outback, Nos 2 and 3 ('Drover's Greed' and 'Opals')	Voice, piano	1957	NLA	
Douglas	Clive	1903	Reflections	Voice, piano		NLA	
Douglas	Clive	1903	Song Landscape, Nos 1 and 2 ('Blue Mountains' and 'Toorbul Lullaby')	Voice, piano	1957	NLA	
Dreyfus	George	1922	Tender Mercies: For French horn in F and piano	French horn, piano	1983	NLA	Allans Publishing, Melbourne, [199-]
Dreyfus	George	1922	Carboni	Male voice, piano	1979	NLA	AMC
Dreyfus	George	1922	Grand Aurora Australis	Piano, oboe, percussion	1973	NLA	Allans Publishing, Melbourne, 1973
Dreyfus	George	1922	Larino, Safe Haven	Piano, trumpet	1992	NLA	Allans Publishing, Melbourne, 1992
Dreyfus	George	1922	Alcoa Aluminium	Piano, voice	1966	NLA	Paton's Advertising Service, 1966/ George Dreyfus
Dreyfus	George	1922	Songs for Manning Clark's 'History of Australia, the musical'	Voice, keyboard	1987	NLA	NLA MS?

Appendix

Last name	First name	Birth year	Title	Ensemble	Date	Location	Publisher
Dreyfus	George	1922	7 Songs for Bruce Knappett	Voice, piano	1987	NLA	AMC
Dreyfus	George	1922	In Memoriam, Raoul Wallenberg: Suite in variation form for clarinet and piano	Clarinet in B flat, piano	1984 (1989-NLA?)	ANU	Allans Publishing, Melbourne, c1989
Dreyfus	George	1922	Ein kaffeekonzert: mit klaviertrio und sopran	Soprano voice, piano, violin, violoncello	1977	ANU	Allans Publishing, Melbourne, c1977
Eagles	Moneta	1924	Conversation	Clarinet, piano	2000	NLA	
Eagles	Moneta	1924	I Love All Beauteous Things	Voice, piano	c1950	NLA	
Eagles	Moneta	1924	Lullaby	Clarinet, piano	c1957	NLA	
Eagles	Moneta	1924	Night's Thoughts	Children's voices (2 parts), piano	c1969	NLA	
Eagles	Moneta	1924	The Dreamer	Part song for mezzo, piano	1954	NLA	
Eagles	Moneta	1924	Two Sketches	Clarinet, piano	1964	NLA	
Edwards	Ross	1943	Emerald Crossing	Piano quartet	1999	NLA/ANU	AMC
Edwards	Ross	1943	Hermit of Green Light	Voice (counter-tenor or contralto), piano	1979	NLA	Universal Edition, 1984
Edwards	Ross	1943	Maninya V	Voice & piano	1986	NLA	Universal Edition, 1987, 1992
Edwards	Ross	1943	Maninya VI	Voice & piano	1995	NLA	AMC
Edwards	Ross	1943	Piano Trio	Piano, violin and violoncello	1998	NLA	Ricordi, 2004
Edwards	Ross	1943	Tower of Remoteness	Clarinet and piano	1978	NLA	Faber, 1980
Evans	Lindley	1895	Australia, Happy Isle	Piano, 2 voices	c1937	NLA	Allan & Co., Melbourne, c1937
Evans	Lindley	1895	The North has my Heart	Piano, voice		NLA	Allan & Co., Melbourne, c1925
Evans	Lindley	1895	The Tale of a Fairy	Piano, voice		NLA	Allan & Co., Melbourne, c1956

Australian Chamber Music with Piano

Last name	First name	Birth year	Title	Ensemble	Date	Location	Publisher
Evans	Lindley	1895	Waltz for Two Pianos	2 pianos		NLA	Chappell, London & Sydney, c1954
Farr	Ian	1941	Four Rimbaud Songs	Voice, piano	1999?	NLA	AMC
Finsterer	Mary	1962	Madam He	Soprano voice, oboe, violoncello, piano	1988	NLA	AMC
Ford	Andrew	1957	And Now	High voice, piano	1998	NLA	AMC
Ford	Andrew	1957	Chimney-Sweepers	Voice and piano	2006	NLA	AMC
Ford	Andrew	1957	Domestic Advice	Soprano, piano	2007	NLA	AMC
Ford	Andrew	1957	Foolish Fires	Clarinet/bass clarinet, piano	1985	ANU	AMC
Ford	Andrew	1957	Golden Slumbers	Voice and piano	2008	NLA	AMC
Ford	Andrew	1957	Martian Sends a Postcard Home	Tenor, horn and piano	1986	NLA	AMC
Ford	Andrew	1957	Parabola	Two voices, bass clarinet, percussion & piano	1989	NLA	AMC
Ford	Andrew	1957	Pit	Bassoon, double bass, piano; double bass and piano also play some percussion	1981 (rev. 1999)	NLA	AMC
Ford	Andrew	1957	Ringing the Changes	Piccolo, bass clarinet, piano	1990	NLA	AMC
Ford	Andrew	1957	Salt Girl	High voice and piano	1994	ANU	AMC
Ford	Andrew	1957	Sonata for Four Instruments	Flute, oboe, clarinet, piano	1978	NLA	AMC
Ford	Andrew	1957	Terrible Whiteness	Mezzo-soprano and piano	1984	NLA/ANU	AMC
Ford	Andrew	1957	Very End of Harvest	Viola and piano	2000	NLA/ANU	AMC

Last name	First name	Birth year	Title	Ensemble	Date	Location	Publisher
Ford	Andrew	1957	Whole Lot of Shaking	Cello & piano	1988 (rev. 1999)	NLA/ANU	AMC
Ford	C.Edgar	1881	Echo and Narcissus	Clarinet, piano		NLA	
Ford	C.Edgar	1881	Thalia	Violin, piano		NLA	
Ford	C.Edgar	1881	I'm Just in the Mood To-night	Voice, piano (with ukulele)	1929	NLA	
Ford	C.Edgar	1881	Petunia	Violin, piano	c˜956	Online	<http://catalogue.nla.gov.au/Record/1593300?lookfor=edgar%20ford%20petunia&offset=1&max=2>
Ford	C.Edgar	1881	Song of the Wattle	Part song with piano	c˜953	NLA	
Formosa	Riccardo	1954	Durchfuhrung	String trio and piano	1984	NLA	AMC
Formosa	Riccardo	1954	Vertigo	Flute/piccolo, oboe, clarinet, piano	1986	NLA	AMC
Fowler	Jennifer	1939	And Ever Shall Be	Mezzo, plus 8	1989	NLA	AMC
Fowler	Jennifer	1939	Invocations to the Veilev Mysteries	Flute, clarinet, bassoon (+cbsn), violin, violoncello, piano	1982	NLA	Echoes Music, 1982/AMC
Fowler	Jennifer	1939	Letter from Haworth	Mezzo, clarinet, violoncello, piano	1984	NLA	Echoes Music, 2005/AMC
Fowler	Jennifer	1939	Line Spun with Stars	Flute, cello, piano	1982	NLA	Universal Edition, c1982
Fox	Malcolm	1946	Ten Thousand Years Goodbye: Three frog poems for soprano, clarinet and piano	Soprano, clarinet, piano	1992	NLA	AMC
Fox	Malcolm	1946	Six Miniatures: For violin and piano	Violin, piano	1977	ANU	AMC

Australian Chamber Music with Piano

Last name	First name	Birth year	Title	Ensemble	Date	Location	Publisher
Friedel	Martin	1945	Fragment from Sonata for Clarinet and Piano	Clarinet and piano	1979	NLA	AMC
Ghandar	Ann	1943	Sonata for Cl and Pf	Clarinet, piano	2005?	NLA	Keys Press, 2005
Ghandar	Ann	1943	Autumn Chimes	Flute, oboe, violin, cello and piano	1995	NLA	Grevillea Editions, 1996
Ghandar	Ann	1943	Birds in Light Rain	Flute and piano	1998	NLA	Keys Press, 1998
Gifford	Helen	1935	Fantasy	Flute and piano	1958	ANU	In Contemporary Australian flute. Volume 2, edited by Mardi McSullea and Lawrence Whiffin, Currency Press, 1997
Gifford	Helen	1935	Time and Time Again	Flute, B-flat clarinet, large suspended cymbal, maracas, vibraphone, piano and 'cello	1981	NLA	AMC
Glynn	Gerald	1943	Interplay	Cello, piano	1980	NLA/ANU	AMC
Glynn	Gerald	1943	Love's Coming	Medium voice, piano	1986	AMC	AMC
Glynn	Gerald	1943	Music for Clarinet and Piano	Clarinet, piano	1971	ANU	AMC
Glynn	Gerald	1943	Rose of Amherst	Medium voice, piano	1991	AMC	AMC
Glynn	Gerald	1943	Strata	Violin, piano	1994	NLA	AMC
Greenbaum	Stuart	1966	Waiting for the Green Man	Clarinet and piano	1998	NLA	AMC
Gross	Eric	1926	3 Interventions	Clarinet, piano	c1997	NLA	AMC – Updated ensemble
Gross	Eric	1926	Euphonics II	Bassoon, piano	2002	NLA	AMC
Gross	Eric	1926	Clamorosa	Clarinet, piano	2002	NLA	AMC

Last name	First name	Birth year	Title	Ensemble	Date	Location	Publisher
Gyger	Elliott	1968	Shards	Flute, oboe, clarinet, piano (4 hands)	1988	NLA	AMC
Gyger	Elliott	1968	Strands	Violin, violoncello, piano	1988	NLA	AMC
Gyger	Elliott	1968	Trio Sonata	Alto flute, clarinet in A and piano	1994	NLA	AMC
Hall	Frederick	1878	Various popular songs			Online	Numerous popular songs available online at <http://www.nla.gov.au/>
Hames	Richard	1945	Dreamings	Piano, violin	1977? / 1989 (AMC RECORD)	ANU	AMC
Hanson	Raymond	1913	Fallen Veils	Voice, piano		ANU	AMC, 1999
Hanson	Raymond	1913	Landing Barge	Voice, piano		ANU	AMC
Hanson	Raymond	1913	Romance	Tuba, piano		NLA	AMC, 1998
Hanson	Raymond	1913	Sonata for Flute and Piano	Flute, piano		NLA	AMC
Hanson	Raymond	1913	Sonatina for Viola and Piano	Violin, piano		NLA	AMC
Hanson	Raymond	1913	Songs Op.16, Nos 1–3	Voice, piano		ANU	AMC
Hanson	Raymond	1913	The Cyclone	Voice, piano		NLA	AMC, 1999
Hanson	Raymond	1913	This is My Delight, Op. 15	Soprano, Piano		NLA	AMC, 1999
Hanson	Raymond	1913	Two Songs, Op. 7	Voice, Piano	1939	NLA	AMC
Hanson	Raymond	1913	Two Songs, Op. 8	Voice, Piano		ANU	AMC
Hanson	Raymond	1913	War! Op. 13	Voice, Piano		NLA	AMC, 1999
Hanson	Raymond	1913	Three Songs, Op. 4	Voice, Piano		ANU	Keys Press

Australian Chamber Music with Piano

Last name	First name	Birth year	Title	Ensemble	Date	Location	Publisher
Harrison	Andrew	1971	*Four Compositions for Small Jazz Ensemble*	Piano, bass, drums, trumpet - instrumentation can be altered if required, eg. saxophone instead of trumpet, or guitar instead of piano	2006	NLA	AMC
Hart	Fritz Bennicke	1874	*10 Songs, Op. 64 and 124*	Voice, piano		NLA	
Hart	Fritz Bennicke	1874	*Orpheus*	Voice, piano	c1952	Online	<http://catalogue.nla.gov.au/Record/1903531?lookfor=fritz%20hart%20songs&offset=8&max=29>
Hart	Fritz Bennicke	1874	*If You Have Nought to Say to Me*	Voice, piano	c1920	NLA	G. Schirmer
Hart	Fritz Bennicke	1874	*Herrick Songs*	Voice, piano		NLA	Centre for Studies in Australian Music, c2000
Hart	Fritz Bennicke	1874	*Seven Songs. Set 1*	Voice, piano	c1923	NLA	Stainer & Bell
Hart	Fritz Bennicke	1874	*Whalin' up the Lachlan*	Voice, piano	c1923	Online	<http://catalogue.nla.gov.au/Record/2928214?lookfor=fritz%20hart%20lachlan&offset=1&max=1>
Hart	Fritz Bennicke	1874	*Carol*	Oboe, piano		NLA	
Hart	Fritz Bennicke	1874	*AE Songs*	Voice, piano	2005	NLA	University of Melbourne Centre for Studies in Australian Music
Hart	Fritz Bennicke	1874	*Love and Sleep*	Voice, piano	c1923	Online	<http://catalogue.nla.gov.au/Record/671573?lookfor=fritz%20hart%20love&offset=3&max=5>
Hart	Fritz Bennicke	1874	*Upon Love*	Voice, piano	c1920	Online	<http://catalogue.nla.gov.au/Record/128495?lookfor=fritz%20hart%20love&offset=2&max=5>

Last name	First name	Birth year	Title	Ensemble	Date	Location	Publisher
Hart	Fritz Bennicke	1874	Three Choral Preludes	Violin, piano	c1925	Online	<http://catalogue.nla.gov.au/Record/2866008?lookfor=fritz%20hart%20chorale&offset=1&max=7>
Hazeldine	Ross	1961	Movements	Guitar & piano	1993	NLA	AMC
Henderson	Moya	1941	6 Urban Songs	Mezzo-soprano and piano	1983	NLA	AMC
Henderson	Moya	1941	G'day Africa II: Mbira ground	Clarinet/bass clarinet, viola, violoncello, piano	1995	NLA	AMC
Henderson	Moya	1941	G'day Africa III	Piano, clarinet, viola, violoncello	1995	NLA	AMC
Henderson	Moya	1941	Larrikin's Lot	Flute, trombone, percussion, piano	1982	NLA	AMC
Henderson	Moya	1941	Nembutal Rock	Tenor voice and piano	1973	NLA	AMC
Henderson	Moya	1941	Tracker's Song	Viola and piano	1997	NLA	AMC
Henderson	Moya	1941	Waking up the Flies	Piano trio	1990(AMC list)/1988(NLA list)	NLA	Grevillea Editions, 1995
Henderson	Moya	1941	Who'd-a-Thought-It?	Bass clarinet, piano, viola, optional tape (tape available from composer)	1984	NLA	AMC
Henderson	Moya	1941	Wild Card: The Dorothy Hewett song cycle	Soprano, cello & piano	1991	NLA	AMC
Henderson	Moya	1941	Wilderness Pieces	Violin and piano	1988	NLA	Grevillea Editions, 1995
Hesse	Marjorie	1911	An Irish Croon	Violin, piano		NLA	Augner Ltd, c1939
Hesse	Marjorie	1911	7 Songs for Children	Voice, piano		NLA	Leeds Music, c1962
Hesse	Marjorie	1911	Two Australian Songs	Voice, piano		NLA	Chappell & Co., 1948

Last name	First name	Birth year	Title	Ensemble	Date	Location	Publisher
Hill	Alfred	1870	Alfred Hill's Very First Violin School for Beginners	Violin and piano	c1921	NLA	Nicholson & Co., c1921
Hill	Alfred	1870	I Saw a Tui	Voice, piano		NLA	Chappell & Co., Melbourne, c1966
Hill	Alfred	1870	Little Songster	Voice, piano		NLA	Chappell & Co., Melbourne, c1966
Hill	Alfred	1870	Mazurka	Violin and piano		NLA	Alan & Co., c1936
Hill	Alfred	1870	Poor Fellow Me: Wanderer's song	Voice, piano		NLA	Chappell, Sydney, c1950
Hill	Alfred	1870	Selected Songs by Australian Composers. Volume 2	Voice, piano			Allans Publishing, Melbourne, c1987
Hill	Alfred	1870	Songs of the Maori	Voice, piano			John McIndoe, Dunedin, NZ, c1926
Hill	Alfred	1870	The Young Dancer	Violin and piano		NLA	Southern Music Publishing, c1956
Hill	Alfred	1870	Wood-Nymph's Dance	violin and piano		NLA	Southern Music Publishing, c1956
Hill	Alfred	1870	A Brigand Am I': Song from A Moorish Maid	Voice, Piano		NLA	A. Eady & Co., [190-?]
Hill	Alfred	1870	Album of Violin Pieces	Violin and piano		NLA	Nicholson's, Sydney, c1919
Hill	Alfred	1870	Alfred Hill's Maori Album	Voice, piano		NLA	Southern Music Publishing, c1951
Hill	Alfred	1870	Alfred Hill's New Guinea Songs	Voice, piano		NLA	Southern Music Publishing, Sydney, c1953
Hill	Alfred	1870	An Old Remembered Song	Voice, violin, piano		NLA	Chappell & Co., Sydney, c1952
Hill	Alfred	1870	Berceuse	Two violins, violoncello and pianoforte		NLA	Stiles Music Publications, London, c2002
Hill	Alfred	1870	Black Baby	Violin and piano	1958	NLA	
Hill	Alfred	1870	Blue Evening	Violin and piano	1936	NLA	Allan, c1936
Hill	Alfred	1870	Carina (also titled Little Darling)	Violin and piano	1934	NLA	Allan, c1934

Last name	First name	Birth year	Title	Ensemble	Date	Location	Publisher
Hill	Alfred	1870	Dolci Manine = O dainty hands	Voice, piano		NLA	Chappell & Co., London, c1956
Hill	Alfred	1870	Hinemoa's Song': from Hinemoa	Voice, piano		NLA	Allan, c1936
Hill	Alfred	1870	Home is Calling	Voice, Piano		NLA	Chappell & Co. Ltd, Sydney, 1924
Hill	Alfred	1870	Humoreske	Violin and piano		NLA	W. H. Paling, Sydney, 1911
Hill	Alfred	1870	In Fairyland: A Maori legend	Voice, piano		NLA	John McIndoe, c1921
Hill	Alfred	1870	In Such a Night	Violin and piano	1935	NLA	Allan & Co., 1935
Hill	Alfred	1870	Land of Promise	Voice, piano		NLA	
Hill	Alfred	1870	Little Saint	Voice, piano		NLA	Chappell & Co., Sydney, c1952
Hill	Alfred	1870	Love is a Flow'r	Voice, piano		NLA	Southern Music Publishing, Sydney, c1951
Hill	Alfred	1870	Loverland	Voice, piano		NLA	A. Eady & Co., Auckland, [1911?]
Hill	Alfred	1870	Melody	Violin or cello and piano		NLA	Allan & Co., 1949
Hill	Alfred	1870	Miniature Trio No. 1 in F	Piano, violin or clarinet and violoncello		NLA	Stiles Music Publications, c2008
Hill	Alfred	1870	Miniature Trio No. 2 in C Major	Violin, cello, piano		NLA	Stiles Music Publications, c2008
Hill	Alfred	1870	My Fairest Child	Voice, piano		NLA	Frederick Jones & Co., Wellington, NZ, c1895
Hill	Alfred	1870	My First Sonata: And how to make one like it	Violin and piano		NLA	Nicholson & Co., Sydney, 1921
Hill	Alfred	1870	Oh leave me not	Voice, piano		NLA	Sydney: Boosey & Hawkes, 1946
Hill	Alfred	1870	Pokarehare	Voice, piano		NLA	Allans Music, 1969
Hill	Alfred	1870	Romance	Cello and piano		NLA	Stiles Music Publications, c2002
Hill	Alfred	1870	Sonata for Cornet and Pianoforte	Cornet and piano		NLA	Stiles Music Publications, c2004

Australian Chamber Music with Piano

Last name	First name	Birth year	Title	Ensemble	Date	Location	Publisher
Hill	Alfred	1870	Sonata in A Minor for Clarinet and Piano	Clarinet in A and piano		NLA	Stiles Music Publications, c2008
Hill	Alfred	1870	Sonata in F	Violin and pianoforte		NLA	Stiles Music Publications, c2003
Hill	Alfred	1870	Sonata Movement in B Minor	Violincello and piano		NLA	Stiles Music Publications, c2002
Hill	Alfred	1870	Sonatine	Violin and pianoforte		NLA	Paling and Co., [between 1900 and 1920]
Hill	Alfred	1870	Song from the Bush	Voice, piano		NLA	Allan & Co., Melbourne, 1957
Hill	Alfred	1870	St Mary's	Voice, piano		NLA	Nicholson & Co., Sydney, c1921
Hill	Alfred	1870	Sweet, So Sweet	Voice, piano		NLA	D.Davis & Co., c1938
Hill	Alfred	1870	Tangi: A Maori lament	Voice, piano		NLA	Boosey & Co., c1905
Hill	Alfred	1870	The Debut: Waltz	Violin and piano		NLA	Allan & Co., 1936
Hill	Alfred	1870	The Fairy Bridge	Voice, piano		NLA	Chappell & Co., Sydney, c1949
Hill	Alfred	1870	The Guerdon of Love	Voice, piano		NLA	W. H. Glen & Co., Sydney, c1901
Hill	Alfred	1870	The Organist	Voice, piano		NLA	Elkin & Co., London, c1926
Hill	Alfred	1870	Thou Art Mine	Voice, piano		NLA	W. H. Paling & Co., Sydney, c1897
Hill	Alfred	1870	Two Songs with Words by Robert Burns	Voice, piano		NLA	Chappell & Co., London & Sydney, c1959
Hill	Alfred	1870	Valse Lente	Violin and piano	1936	NLA	Allan & Co., 1936
Hill	Alfred	1870	Waiata Poi	Voice, piano		NLA	Chappell & Co. Ltd, Melbourne, 1908
Hill	Alfred	1870	Wake, My Tender Thrilling Flute	Voice, piano		NLA	Allan & Co., Melbourne, c1936
Hill	Alfred	1870	Waltz	Violin and piano	1934	NLA	Allan & Co., Melbourne, 1934
Hill	Alfred	1870	Waltz Caprice	Violin and piano	1934	NLA	Allan & Co., Melbourne, 1934
Hill	Alfred	1870	We All Want to Go [music]: Hail children of the Empire	Voice, piano		NLA	Albert & Son, Sydney, 1914

Last name	First name	Birth year	Title	Ensemble	Date	Location	Publisher
Hill	Alfred	1870	When the Empire Calls	Voice, piano		NLA	W. H. Paling & Co., Sydney, [between 1911 and 1923]
Hill	Alfred	1870	Zephyrs	Violin and piano		NLA	Chappell & Co., Sydney, c1932
Hill	Mirrie	1892	Abinu Malkenu: Ashkenazic ancient melody	Violin, piano	1974	ANU	J. Albert & Songs, Sydney, c1977
Hill	Mirrie	1892	In a Moonlit Garden	Violin, piano		NLA	Allan & Co., Melbourne, 1949
Hill	Mirrie	1892	The Dancing Fawn	Flute, piano		NLA	Boosey & Hawkes, Sydney, 1969
Hill	Mirrie	1892	Bourree and Sarabande	Flute, piano	1971	NLA	Castle Music, Sydney, c1971
Hill	Mirrie	1892	Come Summer	Clarinet, piano	1969	NLA	Boosey & Hawkes, Sydney, c1969
Hill	Mirrie	1892	Four Songs for Medium Voice	Voice, piano	c1912	NLA	Nicholson's, Sydney, 1954
Hill	Mirrie	1892	Two Pieces for Flute with Piano Accompaniament	Flute, piano		NLA	Castle Music, Sydney, 1971
Hill	Mirrie	1892	Dream Cloud	Voice, piano		NLA	Allan & Co., Melbourne, 1959
Hill	Mirrie	1892	Mother's Day	Voice, piano		NLA	Nicholson's, Sydney, 1957
Hill	Mirrie	1892	A Garden is a Lovesome Thing	Voice, piano		NLA	Allan & Co., Melbourne, 1934
Hill	Mirrie	1892	The Loving Word	Voice, piano		NLA	Allan & Co., Melbourne, c1944
Hill	Mirrie	1892	My Bird Singing': In Selected Australian Songs	Voice, piano		NLA	Castle Music, Sydney, c1973
Hill	Mirrie	1892	In Spite of All	Voice, piano		NLA	Chappell, Sydney, c1947
Hill	Mirrie	1892	Little Babe of Arnhem Land	Voice, piano		NLA	Chappell, London, c1954
Hill	Mirrie	1892	Down Sunlit Glades	Voice, piano		NLA	Chappell, London, c1937
Hill	Mirrie	1892	Viking Song	Voice, piano		NLA	Southern Music Publishing, Sydney, c1957
Hill	Mirrie	1892	God Be in My Head	Voice, piano		NLA	Chappell, London, c1950

Australian Chamber Music with Piano

Last name	First name	Birth year	Title	Ensemble	Date	Location	Publisher
Hill	Mirrie	1892	And Everyone will Love Me	Voice, piano	[195-?]	NLA	
Hill	Mirrie	1892	I Heard a Sound of Singing	Voice, piano		NLA	Chappell, London & Sydney, c1936
Hill	Mirrie	1892	She Walks Alone	Voice, piano		NLA	Chappell & Co., Sydney, c1946
Hill	Mirrie	1892	Caprice	Voice, piano		NLA	Chappell, London, c1950
Hill	Mirrie	1892	Home-coming	Voice, piano		NLA	Chappell, London & Sydney, c1937
Hill	Mirrie	1892	My Little Dove	Voice, piano		NLA	AMC, 1999
Hill	Mirrie	1892	Beloved Tree	Voice, piano		NLA	A Kynoch & Co., Melbourne, c1941
Hill	Mirrie	1892	Pierrette! Pierrot!	Voice, piano		NLA	Chappell, London & Sydney, c1957
Hill	Mirrie	1892	An Autumn Day	Voice, piano		NLA	Allan & Co., Melbourne, c1935
Hill	Mirrie	1892	At Dawn	Voice, piano		NLA	
Hill	Mirrie	1892	Civilised	Voice, piano		NLA	
Hill	Mirrie	1892	In the Night	Voice, piano		NLA	
Hill	Mirrie	1892	We are the Hunters	Voice, piano		NLA	
Hill	Mirrie	1892	Boastful One	Voice, piano		NLA	
Hill	Mirrie	1892	Three Songs for Voice and Piano	Voice, piano		NLA	J. Albert & Sons, Sydney, c1970
Hiscocks	Wendy	1963	Bush Christmas	Soprano and piano	1994	NLA	AMC
Hiscocks	Wendy	1963	Coral Fantasy	Piano, violin, violoncello	1993	NLA	AMC
Hiscocks	Wendy	1963	Day of the Singing Birds	Soprano and piano	1991	NLA	AMC
Hiscocks	Wendy	1963	Elegy	Soprano and piano	1993	NLA	AMC
Hiscocks	Wendy	1963	The Flame	Violin, piano	1999	NLA	AMC
Hiscocks	Wendy	1963	I Look Out and See: Four songs	Bass and piano	1999?	NLA	AMC

Appendix

Last name	First name	Birth year	Title	Ensemble	Date	Location	Publisher
Hiscocks	Wendy	1963	Libretto of the Eight Year Old	Mezzo, piano	1998	NLA	AMC
Hiscocks	Wendy	1963	Mother and Child	Clarinet, voice & piano	2000	NLA	AMC
Hiscocks	Wendy	1963	Poem	Cello & piano	1994	NLA	AMC
Hiscocks	Wendy	1963	The Twenty-Ninth Bather	Soprano and piano	1995	NLA	AMC
Hiscocks	Wendy	1963	Two Shakespeare Songs	Soprano and piano	1998	NLA	AMC
Hiscocks	Wendy	1963	Winter	Voice and piano	1994	AMC	AMC
Holford	Franz	1909	Arabesque	Oboe, piano	c1999	NLA	AMC
Holford	Franz	1909	Minuet	Clarinet, piano		NLA	Albert & Son, Sydney, 1976
Holford	Franz	1909	Nocturne	Clarinet, piano		NLA	Albert & Son, Sydney, 1975
Holford	Franz	1909	Oboe Sonata No. 4	Oboe, piano		NLA	J. Albert, Sydney, c1971
Holford	Franz	1909	Autumn Oaks	Cello & piano		NLA	Albert & Son, Sydney, 1969
Holford	Franz	1909	Dreamland	Oboe, piano		NLA	Albert & Son, Sydney, 1969
Holford	Franz	1909	Summer Madrigal	Oboe, piano		NLA	Albert & Son, Sydney, 1974
Holford	Franz	1909	Slumber Song	Oboe, piano		NLA	Albert & Son, Sydney, 1969
Holford	Franz	1909	Dance for a Gnome	Oboe, piano		NLA	J. & W. Chester, 1957
Holford	Franz	1909	Giga	Oboe, piano		NLA	Albert & Son, Sydney, 1974
Holford	Franz	1909	Saraband	Oboe, piano		NLA	Albert & Son, Sydney, 1974
Holford	Franz	1909	Pastorale; Goblin	Oboe, piano		NLA	Chester, London, c1959
Holford	Franz	1909	Three Lyric Songs	Voice, piano		NLA	Albert & Son, Sydney, 1965
Holford	Franz	1909	Given the Time	Voice, piano		NLA	Wirripang, 2007
Holford	Franz	1909	Felicity	Voice, piano	c1946	NLA	
Holford	Franz	1909	Expectancy	Voice, piano		NLA	Albert & Son, Sydney, 1977
Holford	Franz	1909	The Girl in Green	Voice, piano		Online	<http://catalogue.nla.gov.au/Record/2894946?lookfor=holford%20girl&offset=1&max=2>

Australian Chamber Music with Piano

Last name	First name	Birth year	Title	Ensemble	Date	Location	Publisher
Holford	Franz	1909	The Whitethroat and the Holly	Voice, piano		NLA	Albert & Son, Sydney, 1974
Holford	Franz	1909	Mangers	Voice, piano		NLA	Albert & Son, Sydney, 1970
Holford	Franz	1909	Chain of Memories	Voice, piano	[195-?]	NLA	<http://catalogue.nla.gov.au/Record/176816?lookfor=holford%20chain&offset=1&max=1>
Holford	Franz	1909	Three Songs	Voice, piano			Chappell, London & Sydney, c1950
Holford	Franz	1909	Come Away Death	Voice, piano		NLA	Albert & Son, Sydney, 1970
Holford	Franz	1909	The Fair Elizabeth: A carol	Voice, piano		NLA	Chappell & Co., Sydney, c1954
Holford	Franz	1909	June Midnight	Voice, piano		NLA	J. Albert, Sydney, c1976
Holford	Franz	1909	Love's Philosophy	Voice, piano		NLA	J. Albert, Sydney, c1975
Holford	Franz	1909	The Toll Gate	Voice, piano		NLA	Albert & Son, Sydney, 1974
Holford	Franz	1909	The Coming of Spring	Voice, piano		NLA	Albert & Son, Sydney, 1970
Holford	Franz	1909	Moonlit Apples	Voice, piano		NLA	J. Albert, Sydney, c1974
Holford	Franz	1909	Wily Cupid	Voice, piano		NLA	J. Albert, Sydney, c1973
Holland	Dulcie	1913	Alla Marcia	Clarinet, piano		NLA	Allans Music, Melbourne, c1970
Holland	Dulcie	1913	Ballad	Clarinet, piano		NLA	Bossey & Hawkes, Sydney, c1954
Hollier	Donald	1934	Five Songs to Poems of Christopher Brennan	Voice, piano	1970	NLA	AMC, 1999
Hollier	Donald	1934	Four Songs of John Dryden	Voice, piano	1966	NLA	AMC, 1999
Hollier	Donald	1934	Six Songs to Poems of Christopher Brennan	Baritone solo (or mezzo-soprano), piano	1998	NLA	AMC, 1999
Hollier	Donald	1934	Sonata for Trombone and Piano	Trombone, piano	1953	NLA	AMC, 1998

Last name	First name	Birth year	Title	Ensemble	Date	Location	Publisher
Hollier	Donald	1934	Sonnets Book 4: A little blue music	High voice, piano, alto saxophone, string quartet, percussion	1961	NLA	AMC, 1999
Hollier	Donald	1934	Variations on a Theme of Sitsky	Violin, piano	1970	ANU	AMC
Howlett	May	1931	Exhibits: Suite for flute and piano	Flute, piano	1992	NLA	Grevillea Editions, Ben Lomond, NSW, 1995, 1992c; Keys Press, 2003
Howlett	May	1931	Lahara's Stream	Clarinet, piano	1996?	NLA	Grevillea Editions, 1996
Howlett	May	1931	Nocturne	French horn, piano	2006	NLA	Wirripang, Wollongong, NSW, 2007, 2006c; Keys Press, 2006
Howlett	May	1931	Rosie, the Unruffled	Viola, piano	1996?	NLA	Grevillea Editions, 1996; Keys Press, 2000
Howlett	May	1931	Sacred Grove	Bassoon, marimba or piano	1998	NLA	Keys Press, 2000
Howlett	May	1931	Secrets	Voice with mixed quartet	1991	NLA	AMC
Howlett	May	1931	Songs of a Watchful Man	Baritone, piano	1989	NLA	AMC
Howlett	May	1931	To Beauty	High voice, piano		NLA	Keys Press, 2003
Howlett	May	1931	Wings of the Wind	Flute, piano	2007	NLA	Wirripang, 2007
Humble	Keith	1927	A Book of Songs of Love & Death	Soprano, piano	1966 (AMC) / 1961 (NLA)	NLA	AMC
Humble	Keith	1927	Five Pieces in Two Parts: For cello and piano	Cello, piano	1982	NLA	AMC
Humble	Keith	1927	Five Short Pieces for Violin & Piano	Violin, piano	1967	NLA	In Contemporary Australian Violin: Thirteen compositions for solo violin and piano, edited by Lawrence Whiffin, La Trobe University Press, Melbourne, c1991 (Out of print)

Last name	First name	Birth year	Title	Ensemble	Date	Location	Publisher
Humble	Keith	1927	Sonata for Flute and Piano	Flute, piano	1990	AW	AMC
Humble	Keith	1927	Sonata in C Minor for Violin & Piano	Violin, piano	1951	NLA	NLA MS
Humble	Keith	1927	Songs of Depression for Soprano Voice with Piano	Soprano, piano	1955	NLA	AMC
Humble	Keith	1927	Trio No. 2	Violin, clarinet, piano	1980	NLA	AMC
Humble	Keith	1927	Trio #III	Flute, percussion, piano	1985	NLA	AMC
Humble	Keith	1927	Trois Poemes d'Amour text Pierre Albert-Birot	Songs (medium voice), piano	1969	NLA	AMC
Humble	Keith	1927	Trombone Sonata	Trombone, piano	1992	AW	NLA MS
Hutchens	Frank	1892	Elegy	Violin, piano		NLA-n/a	
Hutchens	Frank	1892	Always Afternoon	Violin, piano		NLA	
Hutchens	Frank	1893	A Summer Evening	Violin, piano		NLA	AMC, 1999
Hutcheson	Ernest	1871	NIL			n/a	
Hyde	Miriam	1913	Before the Spring	Voice and piano	c1943	NLA	Wirripang, 2006
Hyde	Miriam	1913	Camellia	Voice and piano	1970	NLA	AMC, 1999
Hyde	Miriam	1913	Canon and Rhapsody	Clarinet, piano	c1950	NLA	Keys Press, 2002
Hyde	Miriam	1913	Cradle Song	Oboe and piano	1963	NLA	Wirripang, 2007
Hyde	Miriam	1913	Elfin Fantasy	Voice and piano	1958	NLA	AMC, 1999
Hyde	Miriam	1913	Dawn Service	Voice and piano	1961	NLA	AMC, 1999
Hyde	Miriam	1913	Dreamland	Voice and piano	1933	NLA	AMC, 1999
Hyde	Miriam	1913	Dryad's Dance	Violin or flute and piano	1989	NLA	AMC, 1999
Hyde	Miriam	1913	Evening Under the Hill	Flute and piano	1936	ANU	Allans, Melbourne?
Hyde	Miriam	1913	Beside the Stream	Flute and piano	1962	NLA	Allans, c1968

Last name	First name	Birth year	Title	Ensemble	Date	Location	Publisher
Hyde	Miriam	1913	Fantasia on Waltzing Matilda	Violin, viola and piano	1936	NLA	AMC, 1999
Hyde	Miriam	1913	Canzonetta	Viola and piano	1988	NLA	Keys Press, 2008
Hyde	Miriam	1913	Fireside Images	Flute and piano	1965	NLA	Wirripang, 2008
Hyde	Miriam	1913	Legend, Clarinet and Piano	Clarinet and piano	1986	NLA	EMI, c2002
Hyde	Miriam	1913	Nocturne	Flute and piano	1994	NLA	Keys Press, 2001
Hyde	Miriam	1913	The Constant Pool	Voice and piano	c1946	NLA	Wirripang, 2006
Hyde	Miriam	1913	Rhyme After Rain	Voice and piano	c1987	NLA	Wirripang, 2006
Hyde	Miriam	1913	The Wind in the Sedges	Voice and piano	c1987	NLA	Wirripang, 2006
Hyde	Miriam	1913	Lullaby	Voice and piano	1943	NLA	AMC, 1999
Hyde	Miriam	1913	Music	Voice and piano	c1942	NLA	Wirripang, 2006
Hyde	Miriam	1913	The Lotus Pool	Voice and piano	c1939	NLA	Wirripang, 2006
Hyde	Miriam	1914	Gay Comes the Singers	Voice, piano	c1948	NLA	Wirripang, 2006
Hyde	Miriam	1913	Sailing Boats	Flute, oboe, clarinet and piano	1969	NLA	Wirripang, 2007
Hyde	Miriam	1913	Prayer for Rain	Dramatic soprano and piano	1970	NLA	AMC, 1999
Hyde	Miriam	1913	Nightfall by the River	Voice and piano	1955	NLA	Wirripang, 2008
Hyde	Miriam	1913	Three Songs from Mediaeval Latin Lyrics [music]: For voice and piano	Voice and piano	c1944	NLA	Wirripang, 2006
Hyde	Miriam	1913	Sea Shell Fantasy	Flute and piano	1975	NLA	Castle Music, Sydney, c1986
Hyde	Miriam	1913	Sonata for cl and pf	Clarinet, piano	1949	NLA	Keys Press, 2000
Hyde	Miriam	1913	Marsh Birds	Flute and piano	1949	NLA	Allans, 1968
Hyde	Miriam	1913	Serenade	Violin solo with piano accompaniment	1955	NLA	Chappell & Co., c1955

Australian Chamber Music with Piano

Last name	First name	Birth year	Title	Ensemble	Date	Location	Publisher
Hyde	Miriam	1913	Sonata in B Minor for Viola and Piano	Viola and piano	1937	NLA	Keys Press, 1999
Hyde	Miriam	1913	Trio for Flute, Clarinet and Piano	Flute, clarinet and piano	1948	ANU	Keys Press, 2002
Hyde	Miriam	1913	Trio in B-flat for Flute, Oboe Pnd piano	Flute, oboe and piano	1952	NLA	Keys Press, 2002
Hyde	Miriam	1913	Two Pieces	Viola and piano	1946	NLA	Keys Press, 1998
Hyde	Miriam	1913	Wedding Morn	Flute and piano	1957	NLA	Allans, 1968
Isaacs	Mark	1958	Cantilena	Bass clarinet and piano	1987	ANU	AMC
Isaacs	Mark	1958	Elegy	Cello and piano	1987	NLA	AMC
Isaacs	Mark	1958	Memoirs	Vibraphone, percussion, piano and bass marimba	1986	NLA	AMC
Isaacs	Mark	1958	Mirage	Flute and pianoforte	2002?	NLA	AMC
Isaacs	Mark	1958	Night Songs	Viola and piano	2004	NLA	AMC
Isaacs	Mark	1958	Songs of the Universal	Clarinet in A, viola, violoncello, piano	1995	NLA	AMC
Joseph	David	1954	Fanciful Fancies	Clarinet, viola, violoncello and piano	1991	NLA	AMC
Joseph	David	1954	Piano Trio	Piano, violin & 'cello	1989	NLA	AMC
Kats-Chernin	Elena	1957	After Dinner Music—Album with some of below	Violin and piano	2003?	NLA	AMC
Kats-Chernin	Elena	1957	Augusta's Garden Waltz	Bassoon and piano	2004	NLA	AMC

Last name	First name	Birth year	Title	Ensemble	Date	Location	Publisher
Kats-Chernin	Elena	1957	Russian Rag	Flute, violoncello and piano	2004	NLA	AMC
Kats-Chernin	Elena	1957	Russian Rag	Clarinet in B-flat and piano	1997	NLA	AMC
Kats-Chernin	Elena	1957	Bucharian Melody	Violin and piano	1997	NLA	AMC
Kats-Chernin	Elena	1957	Charmer's Apprentice	Oboe and piano	2002	NLA	AMC
Kats-Chernin	Elena	1957	Colours of the Sea	Alto flute, violoncello and piano	2004	NLA	AMC
Kats-Chernin	Elena	1957	Music from Bombshells	Voice and piano	2004	NLA	AMC
Kats-Chernin	Elena	1957	Pink Breasted Robin in Silvery Light	Clarinet in A, cello and piano	2006	NLA	AMC
Kats-Chernin	Elena	1957	Slicked Back Tango	Bassoon and piano	2002	NLA	AMC
Kay	Don	1933	Coolness	Voice, clarinet, piano	1974, arr. 1994	NLA	AMC, 1999
Kay	Don	1933	Evocations	Violin, clarinet, piano	1985	NLA	AMC, 1999
Kay	Don	1933	Hastings Triptych	Flute, piano	1986	NLA	AMC, 2002
Kay	Don	1933	Piano Trio	Violin, cello, piano	1996	NLA	AMC, 1999
Keats	Horace	1895	Long, Long Ago	Violin/violincello, piano		NLA	Arrangement Allan & Co., Melbourne, c1935
Keats	Horace	1895	Ballad of the Convict's Daughter*	Voice, piano		NLA	W. H. Paling & Co., Sydney, c1945
Keats	Horace	1895	Blessed are They (The Beautitudes)	Voice, piano			W. H. Paling & Co., Sydney, c1945
Keats	Horace	1895	Four Songs by Horace Keats from John's Scrap Book	Voice, piano		NLA	Chappell & Co., Sydney, c1938
Keats	Horace	1895	The Constant Lover	Voice, piano		NLA	Chappell & Co., London & Sydney, c1946

Australian Chamber Music with Piano

Last name	First name	Birth year	Title	Ensemble	Date	Location	Publisher
Keats	Horace	1895	The Cry of the Fighting Forces	Voice, piano		NLA	Chappell & Co., London & Sydney, c1944
Keats	Horace	1895	The Devon Maid	Voice, piano		NLA	Chappell & Co., London & Sydney, [194-]
Keats	Horace	1895	The Truth about Jack and Jill	Voice, piano		NLA	W. H. Paling & Co., Sydney, c1945
Keats	Horace	1895	Why Did it Have to be You	Voice, piano		NLA	Arrangement L. Waddell, Leichhardt, NSW, [between 1940 and 1959?]
Keats	Horace	1895	Deep and Dewey Hour	Voice, piano		ANU	Wirripang, c1995
Keats	Horace	1895	Hymn to the God of Fate	Voice, piano		ANU	
Keats	Horace	1895	The Emperor's Palace	Voice, piano		ANU	Wirripang, 2008
Keats	Horace	1895	Long list of songs—see web site for more				<http://www.australiancomposers.com.au/>
Kelly	Frederick Septimus	1881	Trio in B Minor	Violin, viola and violoncello	1911	NLA MS	
Kelly	Frederick Septimus	1881	Trio in B Flat	Piano, violin and violoncello		NLA MS	
Kelly	Frederick Septimus	1881	Sonata for Violin and Pianoforte	Piano, violin	1905–19	NLA MS	
Kelly	Frederick Septimus	1881	Serenade for Flute, Op. 7	Flute, piano	1914	NLA MS	
Kelly	Frederick Septimus	1881	Violin and Pianoforte Sonata in D Minor	Violin, piano	1901	NLA MS	
Kelly	Frederick Septimus	1881	Mirrors	Voice, piano	c1910	Online	<http://catalogue.nla.gov.au/Record/3600009?lookfor=kelly%20mirrors&offset=1&max=14>
Kelly	Frederick Septimus	1881	Fulfillment	Voice, piano	1910	Online	<http://catalogue.nla.gov.au/Record/3600033?lookfor=kelly%20fulfillment&offset=1&max=13>

Last name	First name	Birth year	Title	Ensemble	Date	Location	Publisher
Kelly	Federick Septimus	1881	*Harvest Eve*	Voice, piano	1910	Online	<http://catalogue.nla.gov.au/Record/3600037?lookfor=kelly%20harvest&offset=1&max=9>
Kelly	Federick Septimus	1881	*March*	Voice, piano	1910	Online	<http://catalogue.nla.gov.au/Record/3600007?lookfor=kelly%20march&offset=1&max=176>
Kelly	Federick Septimus	1881	*The Sages Dance*	Voice, piano	1910	Online	<http://catalogue.nla.gov.au/Record/3600039?lookfor=kelly%20sages&offset=1&max=21>
Kelly	Federick Septimus	1881	*Two Songs, Op. 1*	Voice, piano	1912	Online	<http://catalogue.nla.gov.au/Record/3084303?lookfor=kelly%20two%20songs&offset=1&max=30>
Kelly	Federick Septimus	1881	*The Pride of Youth*	Voice, piano	1915	Online	<http://catalogue.nla.gov.au/Record/3599977?lookfor=kelly%20pride&offset=1&max=12>
Kelly	Federick Septimus	1881	*Six Songs, Op. 6*	Voice, piano	1910-13	Online	March', 'The Sages Dance', 'Weep You No More, Sad Fountains', 'Music, When Soft Voices Die', 'To the Daisy', 'The Daffodils', 'The Cherry Tree', 'When the Lamp is Shattered'
Kelly	Federick Septimus	1881	*Songs*	Voice, piano	1909	Online	<http://catalogue.nla.gov.au/Record/3564330?lookfor=septimus%20kelly%20songs&offset=1&max=18>
Kelly	Federick Septimus	1881	*Daffodils*	Voice, piano	1910	Online	<http://catalogue.nla.gov.au/Record/3600095?lookfor=septimus%20kelly%20daffodils&offset=1&max=5>
Kelly	Federick Septimus	1881	*Away! The moor is dark beneath the moon*	Voice, piano	1910	Online	<http://catalogue.nla.gov.au/Record/3600050?lookfor=septimus%20kelly%20away&offset=1&max=4>
Kerry	Gordon	1961	*A Colder Music*	Piano trio	2001	NLA	AMC
Kerry	Gordon	1961	*Dream*	Violin and piano	1987	NLA	Grevillea Editions, 1995
Kerry	Gordon	1961	*Im Winde*	Piano trio	2000	NLA	AMC

Australian Chamber Music with Piano

Last name	First name	Birth year	Title	Ensemble	Date	Location	Publisher
Kerry	Gordon	1961	Moonrise	Soprano and piano	1983	NLA	AMC
Kerry	Gordon	1961	Night after Bushfire, from Through the Fire	Soprano, piano	2003	NLA	AMC
Kerry	Gordon	1961	No Abiding City	Violin, horn and piano	2001	NLA	AMC
Kerry	Gordon	1961	No Orphean Lute: Trio in three movements	Violin, cello and piano	1994	NLA	AMC
Kerry	Gordon	1961	On the Summer Map of Stars	Bassoon and piano	2000	NLA	AMC
Kerry	Gordon	1961	Paradi	Viola and piano	1988	NLA	Grevillea Editions, 1996
Kerry	Gordon	1961	Rasa	Piano quartet	2000	NLA	AMC
Kerry	Gordon	1961	Sonata	Flute, percussion, piano and cello	1990	NLA	AMC
Knehans	Douglas	1957	Image—Shift	Flute, violin, violoncello, piano	1988	NLA	AMC
Knehans	Douglas	1957	Soar	Violoncello, piano	2004	NLA	AMC
Koehne	Graeme	1956	Three Poems of Byron — On camera	Voice and piano	1991	NLA	AMC
Krips	Henry	1912	Southern Intermezzo	Eb saxophone, piano	1956	NLA	APRA, Sydney
Krips	Henry	1912	The Beehive Inn	Voice, piano		NLA	Chappell & Co., London & Sydney, 1955
Krips	Henry	1912	Hush-a-Bye Lullaby	Polular voice piano		NLA	Boosey & Hawkes, Sydney, c1950
Krips	Henry	1912	Barossa March	German folk voice piano	196-?	NLA	
Krips	Henry	1912	A Waltz Refrain (Brings Back Again Vienna)	Polular voice piano		NLA	Boosey & Hawkes, Sydney, 1945
Krips	Henry	1912	Gone to the Dogs	Polular voice piano		NLA	D. Davis & Co., Sydney, c1939

292

Last name	First name	Birth year	Title	Ensemble	Date	Location	Publisher
Lacaze	Sophie	1963	Histoire sans Paroles	Violin, violoncello, piano	2002	NLA	AMC
Lacaze	Sophie	1963	Sons-jeux: Pour clarinette si b et piano	Clarinet, piano	2003	amc	Editions Notissimo
Lalor	Stephen	1962	Apropos Flying	Tenor saxophone or trumpet or clarinet, bass guitar, piano	1997	NLA	AMC
Lalor	Stephen	1962	Autostrada Waltz	Clarinet and piano	1988	NLA	AMC
Lalor	Stephen	1962	Bright Gulfs in the Distance	Mezzo-soprano and piano	1992	NLA	AMC
Lalor	Stephen	1962	Childhood Friend	Voice & piano	1990	NLA	AMC
Lalor	Stephen	1962	Prelude and Dance	Violin and piano	1988	NLA	AMC
Lalor	Stephen	1962	Six Angels: Song cycle	Baritone/tenor, piano	1988	NLA	AMC
Lalor	Stephen	1962	The Blue Dress	Female voice, piano	1990	NLA	AMC
Lalor	Stephen	1962	Stories Grandmothers Tell—Maroubra song cycle	Female voice, piano	1990	NLA	AMC
Lavater	Louis	1867	Numerous available Online			NLA	Check catalogue for availability
Le Gallienne	Dorian	1915	Four Nursery Rhymes: Peta White; Grey Goose and Gander; I Had a Little Nut-tree; Here was a King	Voice & piano		NLA	Keys Press, 2007
Le Gallienne	Dorian	1916	Beloved, Let us Love One Another	Voice & piano	1954	NLA	
Le Gallienne	Dorian	1915	Farwell!	Voice & piano	1954	NLA	

Australian Chamber Music with Piano

Last name	First name	Birth year	Title	Ensemble	Date	Location	Publisher
Le Gallienne	Dorian	1915	Four Divine Poems of John Donne	Voice & piano		NLA	Allans Music, Melbourne, c1967
Le Gallienne	Dorian	1916	Solveig's Cradle Song	Voice & piano		NLA	
Le Gallienne	Dorian	1915	Solveig's Song	Voice & piano		ANU	
Le Gallienne	Dorian	1915	Sonata	Flute, piano		NLA	Currency Press, Sydney, c1997
Le Gallienne	Dorian	1915	Sonata	Violin and piano		ANU	Australian Music Fund, Melbourne, c1969
Le Gallienne	Dorian	1915	Songs (1915–1963)	Voice & piano		ANU	
Leek	Stephen	1959	Colourwheel	Flute, clarinet and piano	1989	NLA	AMC
Leek	Stephen	1959	Goombungee	Violin (or viola or violoncello) and piano	1989	NLA	AMC
Leek	Stephen	1959	Plateau	Cello and piano	1988	NLA	AMC
Leek	Stephen	1959	Promotion	Clarinet, percussion and piano	1989	NLA	AMC
Leek	Stephen	1959	Rookery	Clarinet and piano	2000	NLA	Stephen Leek Music, 2000
Leek	Stephen	1959	Ross Roy	Clarinet and piano	2000	NLA	Stephen Leek Music, 2000
Leek	Stephen	1959	Ruined	Flute, clarinet, cello, percussion and piano	1989	NLA	AMC
Lehmann	Wilfred	1929	Forest Evening	Piano, violin	1987	NLA	
Lehmann	Wilfred	1929	Polish Variations: For violin and piano	Piano, violin	1986	NLA	
Lehmann	Wilfred	1929	Sonata d'estate	Violin, piano	1999	NLA	
Lehmann	Wilfred	1929	Sonata Seriosa	Violin, piano	1998	NLA	
Lloyd	Robert	1929	Starting from Zero	Vibraphone, 2 pianos	2002?	NLA	AMC
Loam	Arthur	1896	This Faithful Heart	Voice, piano		NLA	Chappell & Co., Sydney, c1950

Last name	First name	Birth year	Title	Ensemble	Date	Location	Publisher
Loam	Arthur	1896	A Bird's Prayer	Voice, piano		NLA	Allan, Melbourne, c1942
Loam	Arthur	1896	West Winds	Voice, piano		NLA	Allan & Co., Melbourne, c1961
Loam	Arthur	1896	Irish Fairies in June	Voice, piano		NLA	Allan & Co., Melbourne, c1940
Lumsdaine	David	1931	A Little Cantata	Treble recorder, soprano and piano	1996	NLA	University of York Music Press, [2003] c1996
Lumsdaine	David	1931	Bagatelles	Flute doubling piccolo, clarinet, piano, violin, viola, cello	1985	NLA	Music Press, [2003] c1996
Lumsdaine	David	1931	Caliban Impromptu	Piano, violin, violoncello, pre-recorded tape	1972	NLA	University of York Music Press, [2003] c1997
Lumsdaine	David	1931	Easter Fresco	Soprano voice, flute, horn, harp, piano	1966	ANU	Universal Edition, c1975
Lumsdaine	David	1931	Kangaroo Hunt	Piano and percussion	1971	ANU	Universal Edition, c1975
Lumsdaine	David	1931	Mandala 3	Flute, clarinet, cello, Chinese temple bell and piano	1978	NLA	University of York Music Press, [2003] c1996
Maddox	Richard Peter	1936	Clarinet Sonata, Op. 94: For clarinet in B-flat and piano	Clarinet in B flat, piano	2004	NLA	AMC
Maddox	Richard Peter	1936	Oboe Sonata No. 2	Oboe, piano	1997	NLA	Keys Press, Perth, 1998
Maddox	Richard Peter	1936	Oboe Sonata No. 3	Oboe, piano	2000	NLA	Keys Press, Perth, 2004
Maddox	Richard Peter	1936	Rondo: For oboe and piano	Oboe, piano	2001	NLA	AMC
Maddox	Richard Peter	1936	Sweet Barocky: For oboe and piano	Oboe, piano	2000	NLA	AMC
Maddox	Richard Peter	1936	Five Australian Songs	Piano, voice	1995	NLA	Keys Press, Perth, c2002

Australian Chamber Music with Piano

Last name	First name	Birth year	Title	Ensemble	Date	Location	Publisher
Maddox	Richard Peter	1936	Four Songs from the Far Side	Piano, voice	1973	NLA	Sumptibus, Swansea, NSW, 1992; Keys Press, 1998
Maddox	Richard Peter	1936	Two Songs for Teenagers, Op. 105	Soprano ('Drama Queen') or baritone ('A Sailor's Complaint'), piano	2006	NLA	AMC
Maddox	Richard Peter	1936	The Marriage of True Minds, Op. 103: Shakespeare on love, duet song cycle for soprano and bass	Soprano, bass, piano	2005	NLA	AMC
Maddox	Richard Peter	1936	Beauty Herself is Black: A song cycle for tenor voice and piano	Tenor voice, piano	1992	NLA	Keys Press, Perth, 1998
Maddox	Richard Peter	1936	Wayne's Farewell: For trumpet and piano	Trumpet in B flat, piano	2002	NLA	AMC
Maddox	Richard Peter	1936	Viola Sonata: For viola and piano	Viola, piano	2002	NLA	AMC
Maddox	Richard Peter	1936	Variations on a Nursery Song: For cello and piano	Violoncello, piano	1984	NLA	AMC
Maddox	Richard Peter	1936	The Song of the Cicadas: For voice, clarinet, cello, percussion and piano	Voice, clarinet, violoncello, percussion, piano	2002	NLA	AMC
Maddox	Richard Peter	1936	The Stranger in My Skin: Song cycle for voice, oboe and piano	Voice, oboe, piano	1995	NLA	Keys Press, Perth, 2004
Maddox	Richard Peter	1936	Letters from Armidale: For voice and piano	Voice, piano	1994	NLA	Keys Press, Perth, 1996

Last name	First name	Birth year	Title	Ensemble	Date	Location	Publisher
Maddox	Richard Peter	1936	The Kitchen: For voice and piano	Voice, piano	1998	NLA	AMC
Maddox	Richard Peter	1936	Izzy's Song, Op. 109: For voice, cello and piano	Voice, violoncello, piano	2006	NLA	AMC
Mageau	Mary	1934	Calls from the Heartland	Violin, piano	1995	NLA	AMC
Mageau	Mary	1934	Concert Pieces	Violin, cello, piano	1984	NLA	AMC
Mageau	Mary	1934	Dialogues	Clarinet, viola, cello, piano	1977	NLA	AMC
Mageau	Mary	1934	Ragtime Remembered	Oboe, clarinet, horn, bassoon, piano	1977	NLA	AMC
Mageau	Mary	1934	She is a Cat	Soprano, piano	2000	NLA	AMC
Mageau	Mary	1934	Son of Mine	Soprano, piano	1992	NLA	AMC
Mageau	Mary	1934	Suite with a Beat	Piano and 4 recorders	1986	NLA	AMC
Mahler	Hellgart	1933	Isochasm	Violin, cello and piano	1991	NLA	AMC, 1999
Mahler	Hellgart	1933	Skyscapes for Five Players	Horn, piano, percussion (3 players)	1989	NLA	AMC, 1999
Marcellino	Raffaele	1964	Amortality	Violoncello, guitar, marimba, piano	1999	NLA	AMC
Marcellino	Raffaele	1964	Credo in Them	Piano, flute, trombone, horn	1984	NLA	AMC
Marcellino	Raffaele	1964	Lottery in Babylon	Piano, flute, trombone, horn	1995	NLA	AMC
Marcellino	Raffaele	1964	Mangia: Alimentary aria with continuo	2 voices, keyboard	1998	NLA	AMC

Australian Chamber Music with Piano

Last name	First name	Birth year	Title	Ensemble	Date	Location	Publisher
Marcellino	Raffaele	1964	Songs from A Strange Kind of Paradise	Voice, piano		NLA	AMC
Marshall-Hall	George	1862	Popular Online			Online	
McKimm	Barry	1941	Concert Piece	Viola, piano	1983	NLA	Kookaburra Music, 2009
McKimm	Barry	1941	Rhapsody for Tenor Trombone and Piano	Piano, tenor trombone	1981	ANU	Kookaburra Music, 2009?, 1981?
McKimm	Barry	1941	Andante Tranquillo for Solo Tuba and Piano	Piano, tuba	1997	ANU	Kookaburra Music, 2009?, 1997?
Meale	Richard	1932	Divertimento	Violin, cello and piano	1959	AMC	AMC
Meale	Richard	1932	Las Alboradas	Flute, violin, horn and piano	1963	ANU	Boosey & Hawkes, c1966, 1970
Meale	Richard	1932	Rhapsody for Violin and piano	Violin, piano	1950	NLA	AMC, 2003
Meale	Richard	1932	Sonata for Flute and Piano	Flute, piano	1960	ANU	AMC
Middenway	Ralph	1932	Songs of Poverty	Baritone voice and piano	1995	NLA	AMC
Middenway	Ralph	1932	The Letters of Amalie Dietrich: Opera in one act	Vocal soloists and piano	1986	NLA	AMC
Middenway	Ralph	1932	The Stream of Time: Songs of Okura	Soprano, bass clarinet and piano	1984	NLA	AMC
Middenway	Ralph	1932	Stone River: New setting of Nine Songs of Hitomaro	Soprano, piano	1964 (NLA) / 1984 (AMC)	NLA	AMC
Mills	Richard	1949	Twelve Bagatelles for Flute and Piano	Flute, piano	1980	NLA	AMC
Mills	Richard	1949	Three Pieces for French Horn & Piano	French horn, piano	2004	NLA	AMC

Last name	First name	Birth year	Title	Ensemble	Date	Location	Publisher
Morgan	David	1932	Quartet for Piano and Strings	Strings and piano	1999	NLA	AMC
Morgan	David	1932	Quintet for Piano and Strings	Strings and piano	2000	NLA	AMC
Morgan	David	1932	Sonata No. 4 [musicl: For violin and piano	Violin, piano	2005	NLA	AMC
Morgan	David	1932	Suite for Horn and Piano	Horn, piano	1998	NLA	AMC
Morgan	David	1932	Three Cabaret Songs	Voice (S) with clarinet or bass clarinet, violoncello, piano and percussion	1999	NLA	AMC
Morgan	David	1932	Trio for Violin, Clarinet and Piano	Violin, clarinet, piano	2005	NLA	AMC
Morgan	David	1932	Trio No. 1	Violin, cello, piano	1952	NLA	AMC
Morgan	David	1932	Trio No. 2	Violin, cello, piano	1998	NLA	AMC
Morgan	David	1932	Trio No. 3	Violin, cello, piano	2005	NLA	AMC
Morgan	David	1932	Trio No. 4	Violin, cello, piano	2005	NLA	AMC
Morgan	Rees		Romance for Clarinet (B-flat) and Piano	Clarinet, piano		NLA	c1994
Oosterbaan	Andre	1947	3 Haiku	Flute and piano	1981	NLA	Grevillea Editions, 1997
Oosterbaan	Andre	1947	Sonata for Flute and Piano	Flute and piano	2002?	NLA	AMC
Orchard	Arundel	1867	Serenade	Voice, piano		NLA	Oxford University Press, c1929
Orchard	Arundel	1867	Two Elizabethan Lyrics	Songs, piano		NLA	Chappell & Co., Sydney, c1939
Orchard	Arundel	1867	Two Songs	Songs, piano		NLA	John Sands,Sydney, [1906?]
Orchard	Arundel	1867	Fantasie—Ballade for violin & piano	Violin, piano		Online	Auener, London, c1938
Orchard	Arundel	1867	Winter Words Twelfth Century	Songs, piano		Online	Oxford University Press, c1929

Australian Chamber Music with Piano

Last name	First name	Birth year	Title	Ensemble	Date	Location	Publisher
Orchard	Arundel	1867	Three Troubadour Songs Set to Music	Voice, piano		Online	Oxford University Press, c1929
Orchard	Arundel	1867	Return of Summer	Songs, piano		Online	Oxford University Press, c1929
Orchard	Arundel	1867	Monarch of Wine!	Voice, piano		Online	John Sands, Sydney, [1900?]
Orchard	Arundel	1868	Sweet and Low	2 women's voices, piano		Online	W. H. Paling & Co., Sydney, c1934
Penberthy	James	1917	Bedlam Hills	Chorus, piano	1962	NLA	AMC, 1998
Penberthy	James	1917	Closing Song BEAC Games	Chorus, piano	1962	NLA	Holograph
Penberthy	James	1917	Love Wine and Flowers	Soprano, piano	1992	NLA	AMC, 1999
Penberthy	James	1917	Oboe Sonatina	Oboe, piano	1993	NLA (Penberthy Papers)	Keys Press
Penberthy	James	1917	Odyssey 71	Voice, piano	1971–72	NLA (Penberthy Papers)	Keys Press
Penberthy	James	1917	Quartet–Perihelion	Clarinet, viola, cello, piano		NLA (Penberthy Papers)	NLA MS – Papers of Penberthy (Series 13, Packet 36). Unpublished? *Note: Edited title entry in database 5/2/10
Penberthy	James	1917	Six Violin Pieces	Violin, piano	1971	NLA	Keys Press, 2006
Penberthy	James	1917	Six Zen Songs	Voice, piano	1981	NLA	Keys Press, 2009
Penberthy	James	1917	Sonata for Violin and Piano	Violin, piano	1971		Keys Press, c2010
Penberthy	James	1917	Trio—Lament for a Kangaroo	Oboe, flute, piano	1983		Keys Press, c2009
Penberthy	James	1917	Zen Epigrams	Voice, piano	1990	NLA MS	
Perkins	Horace	1901	The Prelude (1. The River, 2. The Vale, 3. The Lake, 4. The Cottage)	Tenor, piano	196?	NLA	
Perkins	Horace	1901	Young and Old	Songs, piano	196?	NLA	Hymn, Young and Old, Farwell

Last name	First name	Birth year	Title	Ensemble	Date	Location	Publisher
Phillips	Linda	1899	*Exaltation*	Oboe, violin, cello and piano		Sitsky	Keys Press, 2009
Phillips	Linda	1899	*Joyce Songs Vol. 1*	Voice, piano		Sitsky	Keys Press, 2009
Phillips	Linda	1899	*Joyce Songs Vol. 2*	Voice, piano		Sitsky	Keys Press, 2009
Phillips	Linda	1899	*Purim*	Cello, piano		Sitsky	Keys Press, 2009
Phillips	Linda	1899	*Serenade*	Violin, piano		Sitsky	Keys Press, 2009
Phillips	Linda	1899	*Two Hebrew Songs: Ash Trees, The Golden Bird*	Voice, piano		Sitsky	Keys Press, 2009
Phillips	Linda	1899	*Winds of May*	Voice, piano		NLA	AMC, [2000]
Phillips	Linda	1899	*A Ship, An Isle, A Sickle Moon*	Voice, piano		NLA	AMC, [2000]
Phillips	Linda	1899	*Bright Cap and Streamers*	Voice, piano		NLA	Allan & Co., Melbourne, c1931
Phillips	Linda	1899	*Bush Evening*	Violin, piano		NLA	AMC, [2000]
Phillips	Linda	1899	*Bush Lyrics: Four Australian songs*	High voice, piano		NLA	Allan & Co., Melbourne, c1931
Phillips	Linda	1899	*Cherry Blossom*	Voice, piano		NLA	AMC, [2000]
Phillips	Linda	1899	*Collection of Songs*	Voice, piano	1949	NLA	
Phillips	Linda	1899	*Music from Lamentations*	Violin, cello and piano		NLA	AMC, [2000]
Phillips	Linda	1899	*Orchard Zephyr*	Voice, piano		NLA	Chappell & Co., London, c1949
Phillips	Linda	1899	*Rhapsody in G*	Violin and piano		NLA	Keys Press, 2009
Phillips	Linda	1899	*Songs of the Outback: Three Australian songs*	Voice, piano		NLA	Allan & Co., Melbourne, c1931
Phillips	Linda	1899	*Tell Me, Thou Soul of Her I love*	Voice, violoncello, piano	1950?	NLA	
Phillips	Linda	1899	*Two Moods*	Clarinet, piano		NLA	AMC, [2000]
Phillips	Linda	1899	*Two Songs*	High voice, piano		NLA	The Lady Northcote Permanent Orchestra Trest Fund, Melbourne, 1954

Australian Chamber Music with Piano

Last name	First name	Birth year	Title	Ensemble	Date	Location	Publisher
Phillips	Linda	1899	Who Goes Amid the Greenwood	Voice, piano		NLA	See Collection of Songs above
Phillips	Linda	1899	Yigdal: New year melody	Violin, piano		NLA	AMC, [2000]
Polglase	John	1959	Bring Me Rain	Bb clarinet, violin, viola, 'cello and piano	1999	NLA	AMC
Polglase	John	1959	Falling Years	Violin and piano	1999?	NLA	AMC
Polglase	John	1959	Six Miniatures	Viola and piano	1992	NLA	AMC
Polglase	John	1959	Three Songs	Violin, voice and piano	1999?	NLA	AMC
Pollard	Mark	1957	Portrait of Elsie May	Voice, oboe, clarinet, trumpet, trombone, pianoforte	1997	NLA	AMC
Pollard	Mark	1957	Spirits of Innocence	Flute doubling alto flute, piccolo clarinet doubling bass clarinet in Bb, violin, piano, percussion (one player) (vibraphone, glockenspiel, marimba—low A)	1990	NLA	AMC
Pollard	Mark	1957	Thrice Removed	Alto flute, violoncello and piano	1985	NLA	AMC
Pollard	Mark	1957	To Cast a Shadow	Tenor trombone, keyboards (1 player: piano, harpsichord, celeste)	1986	NLA	AMC

Last name	First name	Birth year	Title	Ensemble	Date	Location	Publisher
Pompili	Claudio	1949	*Wandrers Nachtlied I & II*	Soprano, piano	1991	NLA	AMC
Reeder	Haydn	1944	*About Brett*	Baritone voice, piano duet	1999	NLA	AMC
Reeder	Haydn	1944	*Chants at Play, with Solid Background: For flute, bass clarinet and piano*	Flute, bass clarinet, piano	1990	NLA	AMC
Reeder	Haydn	1944	*Encephalograph*	Clarinet, trombone, violoncello, piano, percussion (played by pianist)	1974	NLA	AMC
Reeder	Haydn	1944	*Interact*	Piano, flute, bassoon, horn, viola	1979	NLA	AMC
Reeder	Haydn	1944	*Siren's Echo*	Flute, marimba, percussion, piano, synthesiser	1985	NLA	AMC
Reeder	Haydn	1944	*Sonage 2*	2 pianos	1978	NLA	AMC
Reeder	Haydn	1944	*Stradevarie: For violoncello and piano*	Violoncello, piano	1983	NLA	AMC
Reeder	Haydn	1944	*The Obstinate Flute*	Flute, piano	1999	NLA	AMC
Reiner	Thomas	1959	*Encounter: For voice, piano, flute, alto saxophone, MIDI wind controller, percussion, live electronics*	Voice, piano, flute, alto saxophone, percussion	1991	NLA	AMC
Reiner	Thomas	1959	*Highett Pointillism, Version 2: For flute, bass clarinet and piano*	Flute, bass clarinet, piano	2002	NLA	AMC

Australian Chamber Music with Piano

Last name	First name	Birth year	Title	Ensemble	Date	Location	Publisher
Reiner	Thomas	1959	*Two Children, Threatened by a Nightingale: Chamber quartet after a painting by Max Ernst*	Alto flute in G, violin, viola, piano	1985	NLA	AMC
Rofe	Esther	1904	*Dinah's Song*	Voice, piano		NLA/ANU	In Australian Composers in Song, Allans, Melbourne, c1996 [Preface by Kay Dreyfus]
Rofe	Esther	1904	*Esther Rofe Songbook*			ANU	AMC, [2000]
Rofe	Esther	1904	*Two Pieces for Flute and Piano—Lament*	Flute, piano	1924	NLA	AMC
Rofe	Esther	1904	*Two Pieces for Flute and Piano—Scherzo*	Flute, piano	1929	NLA	AMC
Sabin	Nigel	1960	*Inner-City Counterpoints*	Clarinet, viola, violoncello, piano	1989	NLA	AMC
Sabin	Nigel	1960	*Points of Departure*	Clarinet/bass clarinet, violin, viola, piano	1991	NLA	AMC
Sabin	Nigel	1960	*Resting Point*	Viola and piano	1990	NLA	AMC
Schultz	Andrew	1960	*Barren Grounds 2*	Clarinet in B flat, violin, violoncello, piano	1988	NLA	AMC
Schultz	Andrew	1960	*Dead Songs*	Soprano voice, clarinet in B flat and piano	1993	NLA	AMC
Schultz	Andrew	1960	*I Am Black*	Female voice and piano	2001	NLA	AMC
Schultz	Andrew	1960	*Night Flight: From 'Mephisto'*	Violin and piano	2003	NLA	AMC
Schultz	Andrew	1960	*Respiro/Simple Ground*	Flute and piano	1993	NLA	AMC

Last name	First name	Birth year	Title	Ensemble	Date	Location	Publisher
Schultz	Andrew	1960	Stick Dance 2	Viola, B-flat clarinet and piano	1989 (rev. 2005)	NLA	AMC
Schultz	Andrew	1960	Stick Dance 3	Violin, B-flat clarinet and piano	1993	NLA	AMC
Schultz	Andrew	1960	Tonic Continent	Violin, cello and piano	2000	NLA	AMC
Schultz	Andrew	1960	After Nina	Clarinet in A, cello and piano	2007	NLA	AMC
Schultz	Andrew	1960	As	Bass clarinet and piano	2006	NLA	AMC
Schultz	Andrew	1960	Barren Grounds	B-flat clarinet, viola, violoncello, piano	1988	NLA	AMC
Schultz	Andrew	1960	Christmas Song	Horn in F and piano	2006	NLA	Publications by Wirripang, 2007
Schultz	Andrew	1960	Duo Variations	Viola and piano	1990	NLA	AMC
Schultz	Andrew	1960	Everlasting Arms	Clarinet and piano	1991	NLA	AMC
Schultz	Andrew	1960	L'Oiseau Fantastique	Clarinet, violin, violoncello, piano, organ	1984	NLA	AMC
Schultz	Andrew	1960	L'Oiseau Fantastique II	2 violins, viola, violoncello, piano	1984	NLA	AMC
Schultz	Andrew	1960	Master Mariner, Lost at Sea	Oboe and piano	2006	NLA	Publications by Wirripang, 2007
Schultz	Andrew	1960	Stick Dance	Clarinet, marimba, piano	1987	NLA	AMC
Schultz	Andrew	1960	Suspended Preludes	Double bass and piano	1993	NLA	AMC
Schultz	Andrew	1960	With a View to Infinity	Flute/piccolo, percussion, piano	1982	NLA	AMC
Sculthorpe	Peter	1929	Boat Rise	High voice, piano	1980	NLA	Faber, London, c1980

Australian Chamber Music with Piano

Last name	First name	Birth year	Title	Ensemble	Date	Location	Publisher
Sculthorpe	Peter	1929	*Darwin Calypso*	Flute, clarinet, 2 violins, viola, violoncello, piano	2002	NLA	AMC, 2006
Sculthorpe	Peter	1929	*Djilile*	Cello, piano	c1986	NLA	Faber, London, 1986
Sculthorpe	Peter	1929	*Eliza Fraser Sings*	Soprano, flute, piano	1978	NLA	Faber, London, 1978
Sculthorpe	Peter	1929	*From Nourlangie*	Piano quartet	1993, rev. 1994	NLA	Faber, London, 1997
Sculthorpe	Peter	1929	*From Saibai*	Violin, Piano	c1991 (AMC list 1992)	nla	Faber, London, 1991
Sculthorpe	Peter	1929	*From the River*	Piano quintet (db)	1999 (part of My country childhood); arr. 2000?	NLA	BMC, London, 2000
Sculthorpe	Peter	1929	*Landscape II*	Piano quartet	1978	NLA	Faber, London, 1979
Sculthorpe	Peter	1929	*Night Song*	Violin, cello, piano	1995	NLA	AMC
Sculthorpe	Peter	1929	*Parting*	Cello, piano	1947	NLA	Faber, London, 1997
Sculthorpe	Peter	1929	*Parting*	Voice, piano	1947	NLA	Faber, London, 1997
Sculthorpe	Peter	1929	*Piano Trio*	Violin, cello & piano	1961	NLA	AMC, 1999
Sculthorpe	Peter	1929	*Sea Chant*	Voices, piano, optional high instruments and percussion	1968	ANU	Faber, London, 1968
Sculthorpe	Peter	1929	*Song of Tailitnama*	Soprano, piano	1984	ANU	Faber, London, 1984
Sculthorpe	Peter	1929	*Songs of Sea and Sky*	Clarinet, piano	1987	ANU	Faber, London, 1991 [Note: Updated title in database (5/2/10)]
Sculthorpe	Peter	1929	*Stars Turn*	Voice, clarinet, piano	1970	NLA	Faber, London, 1995
Sculthorpe	Peter	1929	*Sydney Singing*	Oboe, piano	2002	NLA	AMC, 2004

Appendix

Last name	First name	Birth year	Title	Ensemble	Date	Location	Publisher
Sculthorpe	Peter	1929	Three Shakespeare Songs	Medium voice, piano	1980 (AMC) / 1988 (NLA)	NLA	Faber, London, 2001
Shanahan	Ian	1962	153 Infinities	For solo (concert grand) piano and optional percussion (6 players)	1996	NLA	AMC
Shanahan	Ian	1962	Harmonia [in PPJ: A 'lamentatio' for tenor recorder and (concert grand) piano	Tenor recorder, (concert grand) piano	2001	NLA	AMC
Shlomowitz	Matthew	1975	Deidre's Threat: For violin and piano	Violin, piano	2000	NLA	AMC
Shlomowitz	Matthew	1975	Remembering Beginning: For flute/bass flute, piano & harp	Flute/bass flute, piano, harp	1998	NLA	AMC
Smalley	Roger	1943	Capricio No. 1	Violin & piano	1966	NLA	Faber Music, 1966?
Smalley	Roger	1943	Monody	Piano with live electronic modulator	1975	NLA	Faber Music, 1975?
Smalley	Roger	1943	Movement	Flute, piano	1980 (AMC) / 1988 (NLA)	ANU/NLA	Faber Music, 1988
Smalley	Roger	1943	Piano Quintet	Strings, piano	2003	NLA	AMC
Smalley	Roger	1943	Piano Trio	Violin, cello & piano	1991	NLA	AMC
Smalley	Roger	1943	Trio	Clarinet, viola and piano	1999	NLA	AMC
Smalley	Roger	1943	Trio	Horn, violin & piano	2002	NLA	AMC
Smetanin	Michael	1958	Kartenspiel	2 pianos, percussion	1999	NLA	AMC

307

Australian Chamber Music with Piano

Last name	First name	Birth year	Title	Ensemble	Date	Location	Publisher
Smetanin	Michael	1958	Piano Trio No. 1	Piano, violin and 'cello	1978	amc	AMC
Smetanin	Michael	1958	Sharp	Bass clarinet, piano, viola, violoncello	1992	NLA	AMC
Smetanin	Michael	1958	Spray	Alto flute, bass clarinet, piano	1990	NLA	AMC
Smetanin	Michael	1958	Three Songs	3 female voices & piano	1980	NLA	AMC
Smetanin	Michael	1958	Under-tones	Bass clarinet, percussion, piano	1981	NLA	AMC
Spiers	Colin	1957	Sonata	Cello and piano	1999	NLA	AMC
Spiers	Colin	1957	Day of Death and Dreams	Tenor, piano	1989	NLA	AMC
Spiers	Colin	1957	Eulogy	Tenor, 'cello & piano	1989	NLA	AMC
Spiers	Colin	1957	Elegy	Viola and piano	1989	NLA	AMC
Spiers	Colin	1957	Fantasy	Viola and piano	1984	NLA	AMC
Spiers	Colin	1957	Nsj	Clarinet, basset-horn & piano	1995	NLA	AMC
Spiers	Colin	1957	Uwj	Viola and piano	1991	NLA	AMC
Spiers	Colin	1957	Zyj	Trumpet and piano	1993	NLA	University of Newcastle, 1993?
Staggs	Barton		Hindenburg Mix III: For solo piano, strings and tape	Piano, strings, tape	2001	NLA	AMC
Staggs	Barton		Other Voices Other Rooms	Piano, tape	1998	NLA	AMC
Stanhope	Paul	1969	Phospheric Variations	Clarinet and piano	1998	NLA	Reed Music, 1998/2007
Stewart	Henry	1885	NIL			n/a	

Last name	First name	Birth year	Title	Ensemble	Date	Location	Publisher
Strahan	Derek	1935	*Atlantis*	Flute/alto flute and piano	1992	NLA	AMC
Strahan	Derek	1935	*China Spring*	Cello and piano	1989	NLA	AMC
Strahan	Derek	1935	*Eden in Atlantis*	Soprano, flute/alto flute & piano	1994	NLA	AMC
Strahan	Derek	1935	*Escorts*	Flute, alto saxophone & piano	1989	NLA	Revolve Pty Ltd?, 1989?
Strahan	Derek	1935	*Rose of the Bay*	Mezzo-soprano, piano, clarinet	1987	NLA	Derek Strahan Music, 1987
Strahan	Derek	1935	*Trespassers will be Prosecuted*	Clarinet and piano	c1963	NLA	AMC
Strahan	Derek	1935	*Voodoo Fire*	Clarinet, percussion and keyboard	1995	NLA	AMC
Sutherland	Margaret	1897	*4 Blake Songs*	Voice, piano	1957	ANU	Keys Press, 2006
Sutherland	Margaret	1897	*Adagio and Allegro Giocosso*	Two violins and pianoforte		ANU	AMC
Sutherland	Margaret	1897	*Adagio for Violin and Piano*	Violin, piano		ANU	AMC
Sutherland	Margaret	1897	*Australian Skies*	2 voices, piano		NLA	Allans & Co., Melbourne, c1955
Sutherland	Margaret	1897	*Break of Day*	Voice, piano		NLA	Editions de L'Oiseau Lyre, Paris, [1934]
Sutherland	Margaret	1897	*Five Songs*	Voice, piano		NLA	Oxford University Press, London, c1948
Sutherland	Margaret	1897	*Gentle Water Bird*	Voice, piano		NLA	Wirripang
Sutherland	Margaret	1897	*Land of Ours*	Voice, piano		NLA	Allans & Co., Melbourne
Sutherland	Margaret	1897	*Nocture, Violin and Piano*	Violin, piano	1944	ANU	Published in Australian Violin Music: Concert pieces, edited by Phillippa Paige and David Bollard, Currency Press, Sydney, 1998
Sutherland	Margaret	1897	*Old Australian Bush Ballads*	Voice, piano	1948	NLA	Allans & Co., Melbourne, c1950

Australian Chamber Music with Piano

Last name	First name	Birth year	Title	Ensemble	Date	Location	Publisher
Sutherland	Margaret	1897	Six Songs (poems Judith Wright)	Voice, piano	1967	NLA	Keys Press, 2007
Sutherland	Margaret	1897	Sonata for Cello or Saxophone and Piano	Cello/saxophone, piano		NLA	AMC, [1999]
Sutherland	Margaret	1897	Sonata for Clarinet or Viola and Piano	Clarinet, piano	1949	ANU	Currency Press, 1993
Sutherland	Margaret	1897	Sonata for Violin and Piano	Violin, piano	1925	ANU	Lyrebird Press, c1935
Sutherland	Margaret	1897	Sonatina for Oboe or Violin and Piano	Oboe/violin, piano	1957	NLA	Kurrajong
Sutherland	Margaret	1897	Song Be Delicate	Voice, piano		ANU	See Six Songs above
Sutherland	Margaret	1897	Songs: For voice and piano	Voice, piano		ANU	AMC, [1999]
Sutherland	Margaret	1897	Strange Requiem	Voice, piano		NLA	Wirripang
Sutherland	Margaret	1897	The Orange Tree for Voice	Voice, clarinet, piano		NLA but ANU missing	Lady Northcote Trust
Sutherland	Margaret	1897	The Meeting of Sighs	Voice, piano	1934	ANU	Editions de L'Oiseau Lyre, Paris, [1934]
Sutherland	Margaret	1897	They Call Her Fair	Voice, piano		ANU	Editions de L'Oiseau Lyre, Paris, [1935]
Sutherland	Margaret	1897	You Spotted Snakes	Voice, piano		ANU	
Sutherland	Margaret	1897	Homage to John Sebastion	Trumpet, piano		AMC	
Sutherland	Margaret	1897	Green Singer	Voice, paino		NLA-n/a	Dyer
Tahourdin	Peter	1928	Dialogue	Violin & piano	1971	NLA	AMC
Tahourdin	Peter	1928	Ern Malley Sequence	Tenor and piano	2007	NLA	AMC
Tahourdin	Peter	1928	Sonata	Violin and piano	2008	NLA	AMC
Tahourdin	Peter	1928	Songs of Love and Fortune	Baritone and piano	1992	NLA	AMC

Last name	First name	Birth year	Title	Ensemble	Date	Location	Publisher
Tate	Henry	1873	*Tone Sketch for Violin and Piano*	Violin, piano	c. 1923 - 1926	Online	<http://catalogue.nla.gov.au/Record/568254?lookfor=tate%20tone&offset=1&max=4>
Tate	Henry	1873	*Australian Spring*	Song, piano	c1913	Online	<http://catalogue.nla.gov.au/Record/2796783?lookfor=tate%20australian%20songs&offset=8&max=24>
Tate	Henry	1873	*Songs of Reverie*	Song, piano	[192-?]	Online	<http://catalogue.nla.gov.au/Record/1331461?lookfor=tate%20songs%20reverie&offset=1&max=1>
Thwaites	Penelope	1944	*A Lambeth Garland*	Soprano, alto, tenor, baritone, piano duet	1987	NLA	Bardic Edition, 1989
Thwaites	Penelope	1944	*Psalm 19*	Voice, piano or organ	1973	NLA	AMC
Thwaites	Penelope	1944	*Vijay's Fable*	Piano, violin & cello	1994	NLA	AMC
Travers	Cathie		*Obsession*	Percussion (2 players), piano, saxophones (soprano, alto, baritone), synthesisers	1990 (Full Orch-estral), 1995 (Ensem-ble)	NLA	AMC
Vella	Richard	1954	*Five Studies on a Trombone Melody*	Flute/alto, flute/piccolo, oboe/cor anglais, trombone, vibraphone/marimba/glockenspiel, piano, baritone voice (optional)	1988	NLA	AMC
Vella	Richard	1954	*Tales of Love Suite*	Piano, clarinet, violoncello	1990	NLA	AMC

Australian Chamber Music with Piano

Last name	First name	Birth year	Title	Ensemble	Date	Location	Publisher
Vella	Richard	1954	Memory Pieces	Piano, tape, 2 pianos (2nd piano optional) on 'You Must Remember This', piano, tape, speaker (Beethoven)	1985	NLA	AMC
Vella	Richard	1954	Duo No. 1 for Cello and Piano: Sonata	Violoncello, piano	1994	NLA	AMC
Vella	Richard	1954	3 Songs for Piano and Voice	Voice, piano	1977?-1983?	NLA	AMC
Vella	Richard	1954	Tango: From 'Tales of Love'	Clarinet, piano	1990	ANU	AMC
Vick	Lloyd	1915	Eggs to Sell	Soprano/(s) & piano	1995	NLA	AMC
Vick	Lloyd	1915	How Slowly Through the Lilac-Scented Air	Soprano & piano		NLA	AMC
Vick	Lloyd	1915	Miller's Daughter	Soprano and piano with shadow chorus		NLA	AMC
Vick	Lloyd	1915	Rebecca	Cello & piano	1986	NLA	AMC
Vick	Lloyd	1915	Tuesday	Soprano voice (or unison soprano voices), piano	1988	NLA	AMC
Walker	Allan	1955	Hexamiton	Clarinet, piano, percussion, violin, flute, cello	1992	AMC	AMC
Walker	Allan	1955	Six Scenes	Flute, piano	1992	ANU	AMC
Walker	Allan	1955	Songs and Dances	Violin & piano		AMC	AMC
Webb	Peter	1948	Sonata for Clarinet	Clarinet and piano	1981	NLA	AMC

Last name	First name	Birth year	Title	Ensemble	Date	Location	Publisher
Werder	Felix	1922	Aristophanes Peace, and the War Party	Soprano voice, violin, flute, clarinet, piano		NLA	AMC, 1999
Werder	Felix	1922	Basis	Trumpet, percussion, piano	1977	NLA	AMC, 2002
Werder	Felix	1922	Blake's Emanations	Soprano and violin, viola, cello, piano		NLA	AMC, 1999
Werder	Felix	1922	Conference	Cello, piano	1956	NLA	AMC, 1999
Werder	Felix	1922	Critchlow Paradox	Soprano, flute, oboe, clarinet, horn, pianoforte, percussion, Cb	1980	NLA	AMC, 2003
Werder	Felix	1923	Encore	Violin, piano	1979	NLA	Centraton Musikverlag
Werder	Felix	1922	Flute Recital	Flute, piano	1977	NLA	AMC, 2002
Werder	Felix	1922	Fractured Fancies	Viola, percussion and piano	1984	NLA	AMC, c2000
Werder	Felix	1922	Graphonia	Soprano voice, flutes (both doubling piccolo), clarinet in B, alto saxophone in E flat, piano, percussion (4 players)		NLA	AMC, 1999 – Updated ensemble
Werder	Felix	1922	Phantasia Judaica	Violin, piano & flute	1995	NLA	Archive of Australian Judaica, Sydney, 1996
Werder	Felix	1922	Sonata No.3	Violin, piano	1986	ANU	Autograph
Werder	Felix	1922	Tafelmusik	Piano, clarinet, violoncello	1991	NLA	AMC, 2003 – Updated ensemble
Werder	Felix	1922	Trio Sonata	Clarinet, violin and piano	1980	NLA	AMC, 1999

Australian Chamber Music with Piano

Last name	First name	Birth year	Title	Ensemble	Date	Location	Publisher
Werder	Felix	1922	*Vier Lieder nach gedichten von Walther v/d Wogelweide*	Baritone and piano	c.1989	NLA	Centraton Musikverlag
Wesley-Smith	Martin	1945	*I'm a Caterpillar of Society (Not a Social Butterfly)*	Voice & piano	1979	NLA	AMC
Wesley-Smith	Martin	1945	*Oom Pah Pah*	Flute/alto flute & piano	1996	NLA	AMC
Wesley-Smith	Martin	1945	*Recollections of a Foreign Minister*	Voice, piano	2006	NLA	AMC
Wesley-Smith	Martin	1945	*Second-Hand Sale*	Voice, piano	2006	NLA	AMC
Wesley-Smith	Martin	1945	*Snark-Hunting*	Flute, keyboards, percussion, 'cello & tape	1984	NLA	AMC
Wesley-Smith	Martin	1945	*Tommy Tanna*	Voice & piano	1988	AMC	AMC
Wesley-Smith	Martin	1945	*Our Andy's Gone with Cattle*	Voice & piano	1997?	NLA	Contained in Ten Songs (AMC)
Whiffin	Lawrence	1930	*Mot d'heures-gousses, rames*	Mezzo, piano	1994	AMC	AMC
Whiffin	Lawrence	1930	*Red Letter Days*	Baritone voice, flute/piccolo, oboe/cor anglais, trombone, vibraphone/percussion (1 player), marimba, piano/synthesiser or ondes martinot, conductor (sings during one section of the work)	1988	NLA	AMC – Updated ensemble

Last name	First name	Birth year	Title	Ensemble	Date	Location	Publisher
Whitehead	Gillian	1941	Haiku	Voice, viola, piano	1995	NLA	AMC
Whitehead	Gillian	1941	Ahotu (O matenga)	Harpsi-celeste, flute, trombone, percussion, violoncello, piano	1983	NLA	AMC
Whitehead	Gillian	1941	Angels Born at the Speed of Light	Dancer, improv trio of flute/ saxophones, percussion, piano, narrator	1992	NLA	AMC
Whitehead	Gillian	1941	Ava Herea = Braided Rivers	Soprano, piano	1993	NLA	AMC
Whiticker	Michael	1954	Min-ame	flute, bass clarinet and piano	1988	NLA	AMC
Whiticker	Michael	1954	Korokon	violin and piano	1983	NLA	AMC
Whiticker	Michael	1955	Love's Blazing Fire	mezzosoprano, baritone and piano	1991	ANU	AMC
Wilcher	Phillip	1958	Ave Maria: For voice and piano	Voice, piano	1995	NLA	AMC
Wilcher	Phillip	1958	Blue Glaze: Flute and piano	Flute, piano	1999	NLA	AMC
Wilcher	Phillip	1958	Brouhaha: 'Cello and piano	Violoncello, piano	2000	NLA	AMC
Wilcher	Phillip	1958	Down by the Salley Gardens: Voice and piano	Voice, piano	1998	NLA	AMC
Wilcher	Phillip	1958	Elegy: For bassoon or cello and piano	Bassoon (or violoncello), piano	2007	NLA	Keys Press, 2007
Wilcher	Phillip	1958	Incantation: For violin and piano	Violin, piano	1998	NLA	AMC

Australian Chamber Music with Piano

Last name	First name	Birth year	Title	Ensemble	Date	Location	Publisher
Wilcher	Phillip	1958	Pavane: For flute, violoncello and piano	Flute, violoncello, piano	2004	NLA	Keys Press, 2004
Williamson	Malcolm	1931	Celebration of Divine Love: For high voice and piano	High voice, piano	1963	NLA	Novello, London, c1967
Williamson	Malcolm	1931	From a Child's Garden	High voice, piano	1968	NLA	Josef Weinberger, London, c1968
Williamson	Malcolm	1931	Hasselbacher's Scena: From the opera Our Man in Havana	Bass voice, piano	1963	NLA	Josef Weinberger, London, c1963
Williamson	Malcolm	1931	North Country Songs: For low voice and piano	Low voice, piano	1965	NLA	Josef Weinberger, London, c1966
Williamson	Malcolm	1931	Piano Trio	Violin, cello, piano	1976	NLA	Josef Weinberger, London, c1976
Williamson	Malcolm	1931	Pas de Deux: For clarinet (Bb) and piano	Clarinet, piano	1972	NLA	Josef Weinberger, London, c1967
Williamson	Malcolm	1931	Pas de Quatre: For flute, oboe, clarinet, bassoon and piano	Flute, oboe, clarinet, bassoon, piano	1967	ANU	Josef Weinberger, London, c1967
Williamson	Malcolm	1931	Quintet: For piano and strings	Piano quintet	1968	ANU	Josef Weinberger, London, c1968
Williamson	Malcolm	1931	Serenade: For flute, piano and string trio	Flute, violin, viola, violoncello, piano	1967	ANU	Josef Weinberger, London, c1969
Williamson	Malcolm	1931	Variations: For violoncello and piano	Violoncello, piano	1964	NLA	Josef Weinberger, London, c1966
Wunderlich	Ernest	1859	The Minstrel's Curse	Baritone or bass voice, piano		NLA	W. H. Paling & Co., Sydney, c1936
Wunderlich	Ernest	1859	Song Album: 20 songs	Voice, piano		NLA	Breitkopf & Hartel, London, c1913
Yu	Julian	1957	Four Haiku	Soprano and piano	1992	NLA	Universal Edition, 1996?
Yu	Julian	1957	Night Piece	Baritone and piano left hand	2007	amc	AMC
Yu	Julian	1957	Prelude and Not-a-Fugue	Piano trio	1999	NLA	AMC

Appendix

Last name	First name	Birth year	Title	Ensemble	Date	Location	Publisher
Yu	Julian	1957	*Quartet*	Piano, violin, viola & cello	1992	NLA	AMC
Yu	Julian	1957	*Scintillation II*	Piano, two vibraphones and glockenspiel	1987	NLA	Unversal Edition, 1989?
Yu	Julian	1957	*Scintillation III*	Flute and piano	1987	NLA	Unversal Edition, 1990?
Yu	Julian	1957	*Sonata: For flute and piano*	Flute and piano	2004	ANU	AMC
Yu	Julian	1957	*Song of the Tajiks*	Trombone and piano	1978	NLA	AMC
Yu	Julian	1957	*Trio, Opus 26a*	Piano, violin and 'cello	1994	NLA	AMC
Yu	Julian	1957	*Uygur Dance*	Bassoon and piano	1976	NLA	AMC

www.ingramcontent.com/pod-product-compliance
Lightning Source LLC
Chambersburg PA
CBHW060928170426
43192CB00031B/2862